Paul Rand

Steven Heller

Paul Rand

Foreword by Armin Hofmann
Introduction by George Lois
Essay by Jessica Helfand

Research
Elinor Pettit
Georgette Ballance

Phaidon Press Limited
Regent's Wharf
All Saints Street
London N1 9PA

First published 1999
Reprinted in
paperback 2000
© 1999 Phaidon Press
Limited

ISBN 0 7148 3994 9

A CIP catalogue record for
this book is available from
the British Library.

Printed in Hong Kong

Frontispiece
Paul Rand, 1995
(photographer:
Simpson Kalisher)

Contents

Foreword *by Armin Hofmann* 7

Introduction *by George Lois* 8

1   **Routes:** The boy art director 10

2   **Advertising:** Modernism comes to Madison 32

3   **Publishing:** The play instinct at work 84

4   **Corporate Identity:** Good design is good business 144

5   **Paul Rand:** Author 214

     Paul Rand: The modern professor *by Jessica Helfand* 224

Chronology *by Georgette Ballance* 242

Notes 244

Bibliography 247

Index 250

Acknowledgements 254

Foreword *by Armin Hofmann*

My friendly relationship with Paul Rand lasted for more than forty years, up to the time of his death. Our close cooperation was not so much concerned with practical tasks as with ideas. It centred mainly on questions of the social and cultural situation of an originally artistic profession within our increasingly technical and scientific civilization. We were both concerned above all with the ceaseless development of the mass media and the resulting aims of the entertainment and consumer industries. Likewise, and in a particularly significant way, the teaching profession in which we both took part was affected by the upheavals specific to the media. Design education, which had clearly obtained its guidelines from an understanding of artistic and art-historical instruction (as experienced by both Paul Rand and myself during our student years), seemed to be gradually losing its role. Other forms of instruction and other kinds of talent suddenly came into demand. The schools of art and design, which used to be largely orientated towards craft work, unexpectedly became obliged to grapple with the basics of another and quite different world: that of technical equipment. This concern with the growing complexity of technical systems no longer had much to do with a 'Journey into the Interior' as was appropriate to a teaching philosophy committed to humanism. Planned procedures, realistic thinking and adaptation to highly developed equipment were the new educational guidelines. In the end, they came to apply to almost all sectors of social life.

I believe that these historical observations are necessary for a true appreciation of Paul Rand's work and teaching career. He repeatedly drew attention to the fact that the creation of a new visual culture had to be seen in the whole context of inherited values. As someone with a sense of history, he found that an unclouded, forward-looking view was not enough. He was one of those personalities who succeeded, on account of their enquiring spirit, representational talents and art-historical education, in creating a link between European-based design culture and a new formal language. As a teacher he endeavoured to reinvigorate the model of individual instruction rather in the spirit of the medieval masters. His own way of working formed the basis of a teaching method in which philosophical thinking, committed to semiotics, takes precedence over instrumental reason. Paul Rand worked tirelessly with his students on the renovation and invigoration of our sign-world. At the same time he recognized the fact that there is now hardly any basic research within the field of visual communications. At Yale University, and later on the summer course in Brissago, Switzerland, he developed forms of exercises where several teaching processes interweave: the representational process, art-historical thinking and the search for new visual forms.

I consider myself fortunate to have spent decades in the company of Paul Rand and other like-minded people, at Yale University and in Brissago, teaching a philosophy of responsibility.

Introduction *by George Lois*

'Every art director and graphic designer in the world should kiss (as they say in Paul Rand's native Brooklyn) his ass.'

That was the last line of a speech I made honouring Paul Rand while he was still alive. In the audience, Paul sat at the front and centre, his fair Marion by his side. At the close of the festivities, Paul came up to me, held me close and rasped, 'Ah, Georgie … you're always too kind … too generous …' Then he leaned even closer to my ear and said '… And every goddam word is *true!*'

Well, since Paul's untimely death at the age of eighty-two … yes, untimely – and even at ninety-two or a *hundred*-and-two this great man's death would have been untimely – I've seen no reason to rewrite that punchline.

The world's community of art directors does not bring forth truly famous men – in the sense that da Vinci or Demosthenes or DiMaggio have earned eternal fame. None-theless, among the greatest heroes of my life, I include, devoutly, a handful of art directors. 'A hero,' said the Spanish philosopher, Ortega y Gasset, 'is one who wants to be himself.'

During my learning years, the heroes I held in the highest esteem were those who wanted to be nothing but themselves – designers like Cassandre and Bill Golden and Herb Lubalin and Lou Dorfsman and Bob Gage were, to me, the great pioneers and innovators of our beloved craft. Their art thrilled me even as their ideas inspired me. Their work had an awesome visibility, and – to the astonishment of their contemporaries – their work evoked a powerful response from a diverse audience.

These inspired forefathers of our craft drew their inspiration from the boldest artists of the past – artists who were great because they were gutsy enough to break with the traditions that preceded them, and independent enough to be themselves.

At the very pinnacle, stands the name of Paul Rand. Cantankerous, irascible, loving – bristling with talent, brimming over with taste, and endowed with invincible personal conviction – the original and badass Paul Rand showed the way. For those of us who knew how to see, his mind and instinct created an absolutely supreme standard for the rest of our lives.

I regard the body of his work as the reflect-ion of a marvellously honest sensibility that is true only to the artist's character. It is a unique sensibility that can revere values while rejoicing in change. But Paul's art has nothing to do with putting images on canvas. The constant concern of the scholarly and humanistic Paul Rand was to create images that snared people's eyes, penetrated their minds, warmed their hearts and made them act. And he did it, believe me, His Way. His major concern was to strive for cause and effect in the creation of his work, and with tireless and selfless effort, teach, write and inspire younger generations to march to his beat.

Here the pioneer Paul Rand is acknowledged and reinforced as the father of the expression of modern graphic ideas, of the exquisite blend of theme, image and typography that defied anything that came before him. But few know of the incredible happenstance of history, when a young copywriter by the name of Bill Bernbach (Brooklyn-born, just like Paul Rand) was assigned to help Rand tool the words in his Ohrbach's ads. Working under Paul Rand, Bill Bernbach learned, happily, to worship the art director's power in creating the visual image. Bernbach seemed to understand, as if it were an epiphany, what was now possible: great advertising could spring from great imagery, that the essence of powerful communication had to be the unforgettable image. Studying the work of Paul Rand, he was astonished to see a new kind of art direction whose goal was an imagery that was a marriage of the verbal and the visual, where one and one made three.

Bernbach arrived at the advertising scene at exactly the right moment. The First World War was over, America was changing and people, like Bernbach, were thirsting for a new grace and clarity in this brave new world. He met the one-man demolition crew named Paul Rand and he revelled in Rand's ability to conjure up images.

So, when Bill Bernbach started the world's first creative agency, he started with the art director. And, he started with the art director who Paul Rand told him to start with, young Bob Gage. Bernbach's powerful revelation brought taste to our business by summoning art directors to their rightful role – as creators in the advertising process, as makers of memorable images, as the vital other half of the creative mystery that is the heart of great advertising.

Bernbach went on to act as mentor for many 'Art Director Hall of Famers', and his special wisdom changed the role of the art director, of graphics and typography, and of the art of advertising, for the next hundred years.

To truly understand the historical significance of Paul Rand, we must more than understand his explosive contributions to our visual language. His legacy to us is never-ending. Because without the great Paul Rand, to learn from, to emulate, even to try to surpass, there would have been no Bill Golden, no Herb Lubalin, no Lou Dorfsman, no Bill Bernbach, no Bob Gage, no Creative Revolution, no you and no me.

It's sad. As today's art directors become more and more successful and move up the company ladder, they move away from conception and become critics, more akin to observers (and then they become known as Creative Directors!). Paul Rand, unlike the hot-shot art directors we know so well, stayed at his drawing board, doing his work, his way, using *his* head and *his* heart and *his* hands! (Not fingers on buttons – his *hands*.)

Study Paul Rand's work today; every job he ever put his mind to is incredibly and consistently up to snuff. His work – forty, fifty, even *sixty* years later – is still so fresh that the ink still looks wet on the page!

A media critic in *New York* magazine remarked recently that she was surprised to see that a giant ad agency had a surprisingly good reel of commercials. She was right. They do fine work for about thirty million dollars of their *two billion* dollar agency. But, great agencies and great art directors hit doubles and triples every time. Rand hit homers, one after the other, and he did it for well over half a century.

The work of the heroic Paul Rand is an extraordinary legacy for all who delight in talented, emotional and intellectually driven communications, and for all who followed him in our beloved profession.

Routes: The boy art director

1

A salesman from a graphic arts house was in the other day with nothing apparently on his mind. Queried, he said, 'My boss says the great Paul Rand works here, and I thought I might get a look at him.' Just then Rand swept through the room. Asked if he was impressed, the salesman said, 'But he's so young.'

'Paul Rand', *The Insider*, September 1939

When Paul Rand died on 26 November 1996 at eighty-two, his career had spanned six decades, three generations and numerous chapters of design history. In the late 1930s he began to transform commercial art from craft to profession. By the early 1940s he influenced the look of advertising, book and magazine cover design. By the late 1940s he proffered a graphic design vocabulary based on pure form where once only style and technique prevailed. By the mid-1950s he altered the ways in which major corporations used graphic identity. And by the mid-1960s he had created some of the world's most enduring corporate logos, including IBM, UPS, ABC and Westinghouse. He was the channel through which European modern art and design – Russian Constructivism, Dutch De Stijl and the German Bauhaus – was introduced to American commercial art. The first of his four books, *Thoughts on Design*, published in 1946 when he was thirty-two, was a bible of Modernism. In his later years he was a teacher, theorist and philosopher of design. Although intolerant of faddish trends, Rand ended his career with the same guiding belief as when he had begun: good design is good will.

Rand did not set out to reform graphic design, he just wanted to be the best at what he did. Reared in the commercial art production departments – or 'bullpens' – of New York's publishing and advertising industries, he understood the demands of the marketplace and accepted that design was a service not an end, or an art, in itself. Yet he was critical of the poor aesthetic standards that prevailed, maintaining that everyday life – especially commercial art – could be enriched by the artist's touch. He modelled himself on avant-garde artists, such as painter Paul Klee, designer El Lissitzky and architect Le Corbusier, each of whom advocated a timeless spirit in design. Adhering to Le Corbusier's dictum that 'to be modern is not a fashion, it is a state', Rand devoted his life to making what he modestly called 'good work', and what others called exceptional design.

When Rand was twenty-four, just barely into his career, *PM* (October/November 1938), America's leading graphic arts trade magazine, hailed him as the most promising young influence on American graphic design. He was singled out for editorial, advertising and promotional work that was so original in form and content that it caught the conservative graphics magazines so unawares that they subsequently ignored him. But *PM* demanded that Rand be taken seriously because neither dogma nor fashion dictated. 'Rand is unhampered by traditions,' the magazine declared. 'He has no stereotyped style because every task is something new and demands its own solution. Consequently, there is nothing labored or forced about his work.'[1]

Hard sell, copy-driven American advertising that spanned the turn-of-the-century through the 1930s was laboured and forced. The Great Depression of 1929 had brought America's phenomenal post-war economic growth to a standstill, yet the marketing strategy known as forced obsolescence, which when introduced during the 1920s ushered in an era of fervid consumerism, continued to demand aggressive advertising campaigns in order to capture what consumer dollars remained. A handful of inspired advertising campaigns were exceptions to an overall industry standard that favoured proven formulas and tired clichés. The credo was, if at first it did succeed, milk it for all it is worth. Clients demanded the squeezing of superfluous decoration on to layouts like icing on a wedding cake. And what passed for art was what Rand derisively called the 'Uncle Joe school of realistic illustration'.[2]

Left:
Frank Davis, maquette
for book jacket, 1929

Below:
Park & Tilford, maquette
for advertisement, *c.*1929
In his student days, Rand
taught himself drawing
and lettering but looked
to European design
magazines for inspiration.

Rand repudiated what passed for acceptable design. He argued that it was wrong just to make pictures of Uncle Joe. 'It doesn't solve any problems … it's run-of-the-mill thinking. It depends completely on the skill of the illustrator; and back then there weren't many good ones.'[3] Looking to the European Moderns for inspiration, he developed a fresh and individual approach to visual communications. His magazine and advertising layouts wedded functional simplicity to abstract complexity. They did not cater to the common denominator. Devoid of ornament, they were conceptually sharp and visually smart. Every detail was strategically planned to attract the eye and convey a message. Yet nothing was formulaic. The page was a stage on which Rand performed feats of artistic virtuosity. 'He is an artist's artist, yet he delights the man in the street with his wit, inventiveness, and showmanship,' hailed Percy Seitlin in *American Artist* (1942); 'It is quite an accomplishment to make art and entertainment out of advertising.'[4] Rand's work was so distinct from both his traditional and faddish contemporaries – so radically counter to the accepted norms yet progressive in ways that acutely tested the limits of the print design – that his admirers called him the Picasso of Graphic Design.

Paul Rand was born Peretz Rosenbaum on 15 August 1914 and was raised in the Brownsville section of Brooklyn, New York, in a strict Orthodox Jewish home, along with his twin brother Fishel (Philip) and an older sister Ruth. His father, Itzhak Yehuda, an immigrant from Galicia, Poland, and mother, Leah, from Brooklyn, worked long hours running a neighbourhood grocery store. Rand remembered that his father's clientele included mobsters from the 'Jewish mafia', the notorious Murder Incorporated, 'who were always polite and paid in cash'.[5] Besides working in the store, as youngsters Rand and his brother attended a Brooklyn state school by day and studied the Talmud at the local Yeshiva (religious school) in the afternoons. Their grandfather, who was later brutally bludgeoned to death by a robber while taking a ritual bath at a Mikvah, referred to the boys as the 'two goyim' because they occasionally cut religious school for sojourns outside the neighbourhood. But the first sign of Rand's rebellion had emerged much earlier.

At three he began copying pictures of the attractive Palmolive models shown on advertising displays hanging in his father's store. 'I used a tiny stool as my table and I drew without stopping,' Rand recalled; adding, 'But you realize, in the Orthodox religion you don't draw the human figure. It's against the rules.' Showing his independence, however, he violated the religious strictures and drawing became his emotional and creative release. While the neighbourhood children played outside, he remained inside the dark back room of the grocery store devoted to his precious scraps of paper. His artistic interests were later piqued by the comic strip 'Krazy Kat' by George Herriman, Frederick Opper's 'Happy Hooligan', and the comic women by Mel Brinkley in *The New York World*. And as his secular interests broadened, Rand recalled that on numerous occasions he was scolded for reading comic books: 'We will lose you because you live in a secular world,' chided his father. 'Your language is Yiddish, and your faith is Hebrew. Reading this will spoil you; it will destroy you as a Jew.'[6]

The two brothers were torn between observing their parents' religious traditions and aspiring to live in the outside world where basic urges were not arrested by ancient ritual. Together they took baby steps and then giant ones further from the fold. One chose art and the other became a musician (Philip played in dance bands in his twenties until he was killed in an automobile accident on his way to a job in the Catskill Mountains). Rand's friend and former colleague, Morris Wyszogrod, explained that 'they both somehow ventured out because they wanted to see how the weather looked outside – and they managed to do so. Ultimately Paul realized you can live in the world and believe in your faith.'[7]

At Public School 109 in East New York, Rand created signs for school events and painted a large mural with a picture of a stone bridge that hung behind the faculty sign-in desk. These extra-curricular duties, he explained, got him excused from 'not-so-interesting classes, like gym, math, social studies, and English.'[8] He earned the title 'chief class artist' and drew in the realistic styles of American illustrators J.C. Lyendecker and Norman Rockwell. 'As a matter of fact,' he confessed, 'I went Lyendecker and Rockwell one better.'[9] While they used models or photographs, Rand did not. 'I thought [an artist] had to sit down and do something without any reference. And I never did.'[10] Later on, in high school he knew people who used to produce what he called designs – 'abstract things without reference which I could do too'.[11] And once in elementary school, he recalled making wallpaper: 'I think it was trees, very simplified forms, and I didn't have any great difficulty doing it. But I thought that that was only for decorators. It was something less than being able to draw soldiers dying on the battlefield which is what I used to do – Civil War, World War I, soldiers in the trenches – childish notions of what art should be.'[12]

When Rand entered high school, other students prepared themselves for jobs or professions that guaranteed liveable wages in a Depression-ravaged city, but he was intent on making artwork. Putting his religious convictions aside, Rand's father frequently warned that art was no way to make a living. Nevertheless, his father agreed to advance the $25 entrance fee that enabled Rand to enrol in night school art classes at Pratt Institute in Brooklyn on the condition that he attend Harren High School in Manhattan during the day. While riding the Canarsie subway back and forth across the East River left little opportunity for recreation, Rand was most content to pursue his passion. In 1932 he successfully earned two high school diplomas – a general one after four years at Harren High and an art certificate after three years at Pratt. Though proud of his accomplishments, these documents were ultimately empty symbols.

Neither school had offered Rand enough stimulation to satisfy his needs. Harren High barely had an art department and Pratt Institute was mired in convention. In later years he severely criticized his teachers at Pratt who, he insisted in retrospect, went out of their way to ignore Matisse, Gris and Picasso. 'I literally learned nothing at Pratt; or whatever little I learned, I learned by doing myself.'[13] He remembered a painting teacher who did beautiful work but he used to walk around talking about Raphael. 'Not that you could learn anything from him; he would just say things like "Raphael was a great painter," and other meaningless historical statements.'[14] He also recalled another teacher whose entire pedagogy was 'how to indicate the three-dimensional by having a highlight on one side, and the darkest near the lightest spot'.[15] Indeed if Rand wanted knowledge, he knew he had to acquire it on his own.

Perhaps school soured him, or his father's pragmatism swayed him, or simply growing up poor was enough motivation, but Rand decided early on that 'I was too practical to want to be a painter.'[16] Making money, at least earning more than his parents earned, was an important determinant in how he saw his future unfolding. He therefore focused on the commercial side of art as a career. One of the keys to economic solvency was learning to letter. But even this practical skill was not well taught in art school. 'You'd be given a book, and you'd copy the alphabet,' he reported. 'There wasn't any explanation of basic principles, like the verticals should be the heaviest optically, the horizontals are the lightest, diagonals are in between, the round letters are bigger than the others – you never had any of that. I just did it myself.'[17] The reason for this paucity of such useful information was that most of the art teachers were illustrators. They were not concerned with layout and lettering *per se*, but with exactly how models looked and what kind of clothing they wore. Rand summed up his years in art school as 'all fact, no fancy'. But in truth, there was not even enough fact.

Rand's genuine education had already begun in 1929 at Macy's department store in Manhattan. 'My mother and I used to buy cigarettes to sell in our store at Macy's because they were cheaper there than from wholesalers,'[18] he related. While his mother filled up her shopping bag, he used to look around Macy's bookshop and there he found a bound volume of *Commercial Art*, the leading British graphics trade magazine. 'I'd never heard of Picasso or Modernism until reading about it here.'[19] Coincidentally, that same year, at a small bookstore adjacent to the Brooklyn Paramount theatre, he stumbled upon his first copy of *Gebrauchsgrafik*, Germany's premier advertising arts journal, which routinely showcased an international array of leading practitioners. 'The cover was a sort of imitation of Léger – not very good,' he recalled. 'But I never forgot it.'[20] And from that moment on he collected all the bilingual issues, which later became the cornerstone of an expansive design library. In that single issue, he discovered such notables as the Bauhaus master László Moholy-Nagy;

Paul and Philip Rand,
*c.*1917
In a scene captured by a
street photographer, Rand
(on the right) and his twin
brother are seen in a
horse-drawn cart in
Brownsville, Brooklyn,
New York.

the painter Richard Lindner, who had originally designed posters in Germany; and a virtuoso German trademark designer, Valentin Ziatara. But *Gebrauchsgrafik* offered more than an introduction to contemporary graphic art masters; it opened his eyes to the formal issues inherent in all art, especially commercial art.

One memorable issue contained the reproduction of a cigarette poster that used classical forms as props rendered in a contemporary, modernistic style. A figure shown smoking a cigarette was wearing a laurel wreath of victory, in which the overlapping leaves were pointed ovals. Rand was intrigued that the tip of the cigarette shown in the poster was also an oval marked by points along its curves: 'I asked my teacher "How is it possible to draw an oval with points?" He replied that "the [poster artist] just didn't know how to draw." But I said to myself that this couldn't be … Everything else was so beautifully done … Then I realized that the interesting thing about [this poster], which my teacher failed to see, was that the artist was repeating the oval shapes everywhere else. It was not only a beautiful drawing, it was brilliant design.'[21]

It was also Rand's first epiphany that art and design were unified – a notion that forever changed his attitude and set him on the course that would lead him to reject forever pure illustration in favour of graphic design.

Still, Rand complained that the teachers at Pratt encouraged students to identify themselves only with the great artists Michelangelo and Rembrandt, because they represented the highest level of human endeavour. 'Graphic design was rarely mentioned,' he opined. Despite the revolutionary modern design being practised in Europe, Rand regretted that such things were ignored, and that discussions of the avant-garde never surfaced in his classes. 'Being at Pratt Institute, you didn't know about [Jan] Tschichold [the codifier of the New Typography in the mid-1920s],' adding sarcastically, 'or for that matter, you didn't know about him if you were in Brooklyn, or Brownsville or East New York. What you knew about were gangsters and icepick murderers.'[22]

Discouraged by the dearth of practical information about design and a surfeit of what he called 'misinformation', Rand consoled himself behind the large oak doors of Room 313 at the main branch of the New York Public Library on Fifth Avenue. In this grand old reading room, he consumed the library's rich collection of art books, European design annuals, and printing and type journals. It was here that he learned about the work of Cubist-inspired advertising poster artists in France and England, A. M. Cassandre and E. McKnight Kauffer. Through their abstract and symbolic compositions for department stores, shipping lines and railway companies, he could see the intersection of functionality and imagination. He began to understand that in Europe art was not hidden away from view, entombed in exalted institutions, but rather was part of ordinary life. Commercial art was one means of disseminating art to the masses. And this total experience, he learned, was the mission of Europe's modern art movements and schools.

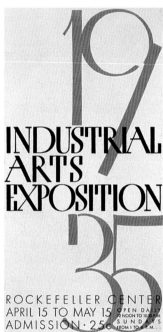

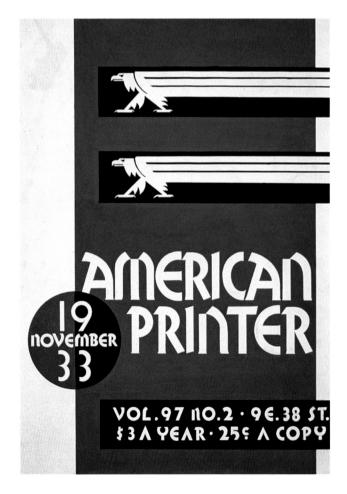

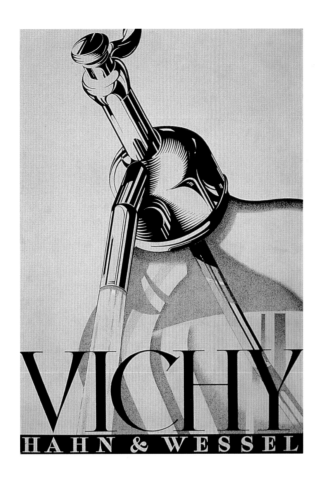

Far left:
American Printer,
maquette for cover, 1933

Left:
Industrial Arts Exposition,
poster, 1935

Right:
Vichy, maquette for
advertisement, 1932
Rand noted that whatever
he learned during his
art school years he learned
by doing himself. Giving
himself practical assign-
ments, he discovered the
basic principles of lettering.
These three examples are
precisely rendered and
hand-lettered with pen and
ink and gouache.

One day, during a lengthy stay in Room 313, he found an article in *Commercial Art* that introduced him to the progressive design pedagogy of the Bauhaus. For over a decade this state-sponsored school of arts and crafts had fought the Weimar, Dessau and Berlin authorities to supplant bourgeois standards with a universal design language in order to democratize the common objects of everyday life. Bauhaus theory blurred the line between high and low artistic endeavour and made art into an unfettered commodity. Upon returning home that evening, an excited young Rand asked his mother if he could attend school in Germany. 'Her are-you-kidding-look was enough to let me know that I shouldn't pursue the matter any further,' he recalled.[23] Yet from that moment on he became a vicarious adherent of the Bauhaus.

Years later he mused that, 'coming from Brooklyn is a very good reason to get out of Brooklyn'.[24] However, Manhattan was as far as he got on the few dollars he had squirreled away since graduating from high school. In 1933, the same year that the Nazis closed the Bauhaus, he enrolled in classes at the Art Students' League on 57th Street, a distinguished institution of classical art training known for its open drawing and painting studios. It was also in 1933 that George Grosz, the acerbic German political satirist and founder member of the Berlin Dada group, escaped the Nazis and took up residence in New York City where he taught a drawing class at the League which Rand attended. Grosz barely spoke English, yet Rand said that just being around the man had a cathartic effect on both his spirit and technique: 'I drew an arm, and he came over, made marks on my paper, and he said, "draw on top, draw on top." It took me I don't know how many weeks to figure out what he was talking about, but what he meant was to indicate volume.'[25] Although Grosz never fully articulated his ratio-nale, Rand referred to this as a seminal moment when he realized that possessing drawing profi-ciency was the key to even the most abstract art. In fact, he was so determined to perfect his rendering skills – and thus master the basic

language of art – that he obsessively drew from models in classes at the League, at Parsons School of Design, and at a studio loaned to him by a friend down the block from the League where he and a few cronies 'used to have a helluva time, because it was the atmosphere of the Viennese salons'.[26]

In 1934 Rand took his first professional part-time job as an illustrator for Metro Associated Services, a syndicate that supplied maps and stock advertising cuts to newspapers and magazines. Along with the art director and four much older men sitting elbow to elbow at a row of drawing boards, Rand made all kinds of graphic clichés – from cuts of Fourth of July festivities, butter-and-eggs, farm animals, snow scenes, children at play and men at work, to novelty headlines for going-out-of-business or fire-sale ads. Though he was not particularly proud of the 'junk' that they produced, he learned more about graphic techniques – the invaluable tricks of the trade – than he had in school. He was also earning money – less than $10 a week, but enough to make his own way in New York. Although he had no visual persona of his own, his professional self-confidence was growing.

Rand's professed goal was to earn $50 a week – a king's ransom during the Depression – and this prompted him in early 1935 to rent a 'closet-sized' studio at 331 East 38th Street with designer C. W. D. Stillwell (who later became the assistant to the industrial designer Norman Bel Geddes). In this space, on the periphery of Manhattan's advertising district, he launched his first freelance practice and landed a few minor accounts. After some months on retainer doing layouts and spot advertisements for his biggest client, *Glass Packer* magazine, he had a viable portfolio that he said 'was terrible stuff, but I managed'.[27]

Rand was never satisfied doing such menial work, so he sought advice, and perhaps even presumed he would get offers of better jobs, from designers he had read about in the trade magazines. First on his list was F. G. Cooper, a comic illustrator and letterer well known at that time for his witty 'Father Knickerbocker' trade character promoting the Consolidated Edison Company. Cooper, however, was abruptly dismissive of Rand's efforts, which mimicked the advertising posters of German *émigré* Lucian Bernhard. Undeterred, Rand's next stop was the upper East Side studio of Bernhard himself, one of Germany's maestros – inventor in 1906 of the *Sachplakat* (an object poster with a minimalist, though often colourful, design, and a graphic representation of the product) and proponent of graphic design that rejected superfluous decoration in favour of a stark prop or object. After emigrating from Berlin in 1922, Bernhard established a successful business in New York designing typefaces, logos and poster/billboard campaigns for major corporations. Rand greatly admired the austerity of Bernhard's 1906 poster for the Priester Match company. A masterpiece of graphic erudition, this poster (which showed two colourful matchsticks against a dark maroon background, topped with the word Priester in block letters) set the standard for twentieth-century simplicity and at the same time was an unmistakable signature for its maker. Rand aspired to work in this manner *and* with the master. Nevertheless, Bernhard was not the least bit interested in conversing with his uninvited acolyte. 'He was not welcoming at all,' Rand recalled, 'rather he played the big-shot.'[28]

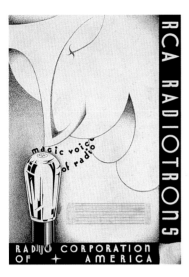

Far left:
The Glass Packer,
magazine cover,
January 1936
Rand produced layouts and
spot advertisements for the
Glass Packer, one of his
earliest freelance clients.
'It was terrible stuff,' he
recalled.

Below:
Hamburg American Line,
advertisement, 1936
This advertisement for
a West Indies pleasure
cruise emulates the
elegant drawing style of
Gustav Jensen, whom
Rand described as the
quintessential artist/
designer.

Left:
**Radio Corporation of
America,** maquette for
advertisement, *c.*1932/3
Not one of Rand's favourite
early pieces, this example
nevertheless shows his
mastery of hand lettering,
visual translation and
stippling techniques.

Disappointment never held Rand back. He regrouped quickly; he also began to emulate the Secessionist style of Gustav Jensen, 'designer for industry'. This former aspiring opera singer's elegant, classically inspired, moderne drawing style (inspired by the Exposition Internationale des Arts Décoratifs et Industriels Modernes in Paris, 1925) stood out among the *faux* romantic/heroic (Art Deco) mannerisms of the day. While more decorative than Bernhard, Jensen nevertheless used ornament purely as functional architecture – a foundation on which his selling messages were built. Known for his streamlined packages (notably the Golden Blossom Honey jar and label), advertising campaigns for Charles of the Ritz perfumes, and sleek designs for cutlery and hand-basins, Rand saw in Jensen the quintessence of the integrated artist/designer and a model on which to base his own practice. 'I desperately wanted to work for him,' he recalled; 'I would have done it for free.'[29] Jensen, however, declined Rand's offer but in an agreeable way, explaining that he always worked alone.

At Switzer's, Rand was finally on the right trajectory. No longer doing tawdry piecework, but rather designing handsome packages for Hormell meats and daily newspaper advertisements for Squibb, the pharmaceutical company, he was able to put the dictum 'less is more' into practice in layouts that were functionally elegant and conceptually astute. He accumulated a very impressive portfolio for someone of his age. The work was not radical – he had not yet created a design idiom out of whole cloth – but it was skilful, imaginative and clean enough (a real virtue amid the clutter of the times) to prove that he had special abilities.

Rand was, nevertheless, convinced that the quality of his work was not enough to guarantee his success. During the 1930s the sons of immigrants filled many of the bullpens and art departments in advertising agencies and industrial design firms, while the majority of the account executives, vice presidents and presidents were drawn from America's dominant Protestant class. Executives belonged to an exclusive club that hobnobbed with clients who belonged to the same club; there was a gentleman's agreement that Jews need not apply. This was not, of course, unique to the advertising or design industries, and it was common for many different professionals to change or shorten ethnic surnames in order to fit in – or at least not stand out. Convinced by friends that an overtly Jewish name might be an impediment to getting meaningful work, Rand reluctantly changed his name. Morris Wyszogrod explained it thus:

Below:
Paul Rand, *c.*1937
(photographer unknown)
This portrait was taken
when Rand was working as
an art director for *Esquire.*

Right:
Esquire, brochure, 1940
Rand combined his
editorial and advertising
skills to produce special
issues and promotional
pieces for the Chicago
based Esquire/Coronet
publishing company. In
this 'going back to school'
promotion he used the
Eskie trademark in pho-
tomontages and typewriter
type for the text copy.

Rand's tenacity kept him knocking on more and more doors in search of work until he met Ervin Metzl, a successful typographer, poster and book cover designer known for his sinuous calligraphic lettering and modernistic illustrations for *Fortune* and other magazines. Metzl immediately acknowledged Rand's innate talent and helped him land freelance rendering jobs from Young and Rubicam, the agency handling the Nabisco and Camel accounts, and R. H. Macy's art department doing ads for Saybrook fabrics. But Metzl's most enduring contribution to Rand's career was an introduction to George Switzer, which resulted in an apprenticeship with the successful package and industrial designer, whom Rand noted was influenced by progressive French and German designers. At the time of this introduction, a new breed of self-proclaimed 'industrial designer' had already succeeded in convincing major American businesses that they were the white knights of commerce. 'Styling the goods', which is how they described the transformation of old products into new ones by changing their outer skin and packages, was how these designers injected themselves as experts. Switzer ranked just below the acknowledged leaders, Norman Bel Geddes, Raymond Loewy, Henry Dreyfuss and Walter Dorwin Teague, in terms of national notoriety, but in his own right was a respected, award-winning exponent of modern practice with highly visible clients.

'… he started looking for jobs, going from studio to studio, and they said, "What's your name?" And he would say, "Rosenbaum." And then they would ask, "What's your first name?" And he was afraid to say Peretz, so he said, "Paul." He remembered that an uncle in the family was named Rand. So he figured that "Paul Rand," four letters here, four letters there, would create a nice symbol. So he became Paul Rand.'[30]

On the strength of his Switzer work, in 1936 Rand was hired as a freelancer to help produce additional layouts for an anniversary issue of *Apparel Arts*, a popular men's fashion magazine owned by the Chicago based Esquire/Coronet company, with offices in New York. Here Rand proved he had an extraordinary talent for transforming otherwise mundane still-life photographs into dynamic compositions, which did not merely decorate but gave editorial weight to the page. This feat earned him a full-time position in the *Esquire* bullpen, and, although he wasn't particularly interested in fashion, he was stimulated by the formal challenges of organizing and juxtaposing such diverse material into a unified whole. He designed many of the special fashion and gift features with a flair that was exceptional for this magazine, where undistinguished layouts were the norm. On his merits, after less than a year, he was plucked

right out of the bullpen and offered the job of art director of special features. To the management's dismay, Rand refused the job, saying, 'I'm not ready to be an art director.'[31]

Rand was not so much intimidated as cautious. He was about five foot, seven inches tall, he had an impish baby face with a pug nose, and was at least a generation younger than everyone else in the art department. Although he was a more talented designer, he still had a lot to learn about both design and *Esquire* before he could command the others' respect. 'I just preferred to do the work,' he explained about this decision to continue his education. 'When they asked me to do airbrushing. I wouldn't admit that I'd never used it. So we had a tiny little room in the back, and if you closed the door you would be asphyxiated in there with the airbrush! All day long I practised. But it was a terrific experience, and you learned everything on your own.'[32]

What really made *Esquire*'s managers intent on promoting Rand was the meticulous attention to detail that gave him design fluency and total command over the material. His will to succeed forced Rand to master as much technical skill as possible. 'I went to the photographer and I'd lay out all the merchandise,' he said, describing a routine day. 'Sometimes there were as many

as 150 items on one page. Instead of taking individual shots of 150 items, I laid them all out on the camera so that only four shots were necessary.'[33] He would then put a tissue on the ground plane of the camera, and divide the layout into four units. All the big things, such as baggage and suits, were in the back, and in the front was all the jewellery. Each piece was carefully laid out to accommodate the camera's depth of field. Often he worked well into the morning, adding: 'I left work at five o'clock, went to the photographer, worked all night long, and then went home in the morning, or went back to the office. I remember going back once, and sat down outside the boss' office, waiting for him to come in at 7 o'clock. Boy, was he was amazed to see me.'[34] He was proud of his stamina, and his devotion to work remained with him throughout his life.

Rand's hybrid blend of editorial and advertising – or what one admiring critic referred to as a display window layout – was what distinguished his work from other fashion magazine layouts, which usually showed either drawn or photographed models. Even *Esquire*'s editorial features, which were designed by other designers at the main office located in the Palmolive Building in Chicago, were much more ordinary, without the hint of creative forethought. 'Paul's editorial spreads were glorified ads,' explains Frank Zachary, the former editor of *Portfolio* in the late 1940s and art director of *Holiday* magazine during the 1950s and 1960s. 'Rather than present the material without any spin on it, Paul would always give it an inflection.'[35] He often designed double-page spreads as if they were surrealistic paintings. After a year of producing impressive fashion pages, Rand finally accepted the job as art director of *Esquire*'s New York office, where he also designed *Esquire*'s seasonal promotional features and *Ken*, a short-lived political magazine. There was not yet a distinctive Paul Rand look, but a particular formal vocabulary was evidenced in the *Esquire* layouts as well as the covers designed for *Apparel Arts*.

Rand's *Apparel Arts* covers bore no
resemblance to other mass-market magazines,
including *Esquire* itself, which was illustrated
with clay models of Eskie (the magazine's
haughty mascot) engaged in mildly lascivious
acts. With *Apparel Arts* what began for Rand as
'chalk salads', loose (but realistic) drawings of
men in Homburgs and raincoats, evolved into
witty collages, montages, and dramatically
cropped photographs, unburdened by cover
lines. During this period nearly all mass-market
magazine covers relied on comic or romantic
representational paintings laden with hard-sell
cover lines. Photography was rarely used, with
the notable exception of *Life* with its strong
single, tightly cropped photograph. Rand's
designs, however, relied more on the surprising
juxtaposition of cut-and-paste images than overt
narratives. Each cover conveyed a rebus-like
message, either about the particular season of
the year or the special theme of the issue. It was
up to the viewer to decipher the visual elements.
Although this method was unconventional, for
it relied on the intelligence of the viewer, it was
never so extreme that Rand's editors were afraid
of being too different. He earned their trust and
they gave him a long leash.

For Rand's part, he was not irresponsible
but rather stubbornly opposed to following
ephemeral trends. A few years earlier he had
read an article in the July 1930 *Commercial Art*,
a translation of Jan Tschichold's introduction to
The New Typography, retitled 'New Life in Print',
which introduced him to modern designers
whose work he would continue to celebrate
throughout his life: Piet Zwart, Kurt Schwitters,
El Lissitzky, Max Burchartz, Ladislav Sutnar,
Walter Dexel, Wilhelm Defke and Moholy-Nagy.
Afterwards, he fell totally under the spell of *The
New Typography*, which continued to inspire
him to venture into more sophisticated realms
of modern graphic design. Rand embraced
Tschichold's dogma concerning modern typography – including the preference for machine-
made over hand-made processes, functionality
over ornament, asymmetry over symmetry, and
so on. Taking these commandments literally,
he argued: 'How else do you learn? You have to
take it literally. You can't just be lackadaisical
about learning. You either learn it or you don't
learn it.'[36] And throughout his career he put his
lessons into practice, not as it is done today in
an academic hothouse or through a marginal
cultural group, but while working for
mainstream clients.

APPAREL ARTS

Clockwise from top left:
Apparel Arts, cover,
December 1939
Hats and gloves were
important accessories for
the well-dressed man and
were thus used in various
compositions.

Apparel Arts, cover,
October/November 1938
Summer offered an endless
supply of visual symbols
and quirky juxtapositions.

Summer, interior page for
Apparel Arts, 1939
In this illustration,
Rand used montage and
painting to entice viewers
to enjoy the pleasures of
outdoor summer sports.

Christmas, interior page
for *Apparel Arts,*
December 1940
The techniques of painting
and three-dimensional
construction were cleverly
combined for this festive
feature.

Americana, interior page
for *Apparel Arts,* 1939
Collage played a large role
in the evolution of Rand's
signature method. Here he
composed sewing props in
a feature page on the
American fashion industry.

Right:
N.S., interior page for
Apparel Arts, 1939
Using photomontage,
'illustration by association,
by juxtaposition', Rand
pulled together the sports
of snow- and water-skiing
for this full-page image.

Below:
Apparel Arts, cover,
April/May 1940
Rand juxtaposed a ball/
globe, net and hand and
transformed ordinary
images into a unique
whole in this summer
issue.

Below right:
Apparel Arts, cover,
January/February 1941
Rand's characteristic wit is
evident in this golfing pun
– a montage and drawing
of a golf ball and a 'birdie'.

His earliest breakthroughs evolved out of
the design problems he was given at work. And
while he refused to impose his will where it
wasn't appropriate, he took every opportunity to
redefine the brief so that the solution could be
solved according to his vision. When once asked
why he adhered so strictly to his own icono-
clastic ideas, Rand suggested that American
designers were too fond of clichés, and he
continued by saying that the difference between
him and most other designers at the time was
that: 'I was not in sync with convention because
I was aware of what was going on in Europe at
the time. I was familiar with the Germans and
the kind of work they were doing – and it was
the best work that anybody had done. And it
was not done in this country at all ... Can you
think of anybody before 1920 who did anything
that was remotely abstract in this country in
terms of graphic design?'[37]

In truth, Rand was not the only American
who borrowed from across the Atlantic. By
1930, Jan Tschichold's classic handbook *Die
Neue Typographie* was interpreted in a variety
of mainstream American design handbooks,
including *Modern Typography and Layout*
(1929) by Douglas McMurtrie and *Technique of
Advertising Layout* (1930) by Frank Young,
which authorized designers to reject archaic
methods and come aboard the modernistic
juggernaut. When combined with contemporary
American design mannerisms, the New
Typography was a cross between progressive and
moderne – or Modernism with dulled edges.
And it was this that Rand at first emulated and
then rebelled against.

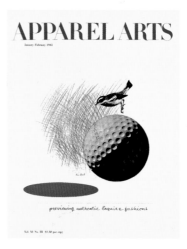

Designer T. M. Cleland declared in a talk before the American Institute of Graphic Arts, which was later published as a pamphlet entitled *Harsh Words* (Carteret Book Club, 1940) that 'the embarrassing ineptitude of current efforts toward a "new typography" is even more distressing than similar contortions in other fields'.[38] He referred to modernistic fashion, yet by the late 1930s emigrants fleeing the Nazis were bringing with them real examples of Dada, Constructivism and the Bauhaus to the United States, and a few Americans were also beginning to engage seriously with European influences. Most notably, Lester Beall proffered a Modern approach that fused both Cubist and Dada aesthetics by combining photographic fragments and discordant typefaces on posters and advertisements. By the early 1940s Alvin Lustig further imbued such notions of form and space found in Surrealism and Dada in his book jacket designs. The aim of knocking the eye off centre was found in progressive culture and arts magazines, such as *Broom*, *The Little Review* and *View*, where Modern aesthetics were showcased. But between 1937 and 1938 Rand was putting into practice, and therefore setting a standard for, a variant of Modernism that was not merely a sampling of foreign influences, but rather a synthesis of European formalism and design philosophy fused with American vernacular – function and wit – which ultimately became Rand's signature.

In addition to his long hours spent on the *Esquire* job, Rand also freelanced for a variety of clients, usually accepting meagre fees in order to get his thoughts on design seen and accepted. Rand believed that his design ideas were meaningless if they went unfulfilled. 'In a country that was used to decorative work, I realized that as a matter of common sense one way to have my approach accepted was to do it for free.'[39] In 1938 he accepted what was to be his most important commission to date from Marguerite Tjader Harris, the daughter of a wealthy munitions manufacturer and publisher of *Direction*, a cultural magazine with a left-wing slant and anti-fascist bias. After seeing the article in *PM* she asked Rand to design some covers. The fee was negligible, but the offer of creative freedom (and eventually a few original Le Corbusier drawings) was too enticing to refuse. The *Direction* covers that Rand produced from 1938 to 1945 expanded upon the vocabulary that he began with the *Apparel Arts* covers, only now he was dealing with more substantive content.

His first *Direction* cover, symbolizing Nazi Germany's vivisection of Czechoslovakia, was a cut-out of a map of the imperilled nation photographed on a copy camera against a white background. It is lit so that a slight shadow gives the illusion of three dimensions, while two intersecting bars carve the map apart, suggesting the lines of German annexation. Rand once explained that this cover 'pinpoints the distinction between abstract design without content and abstract design with content. You can be a great manipulator of form, but if the solution is not apt, it's for the birds.'[40] Likewise, the 1940 Christmas cover shows pieces of barbed wire criss-crossing the image area like gift ribbon, with little red circles symbolizing drops of blood randomly placed. This cover was an acerbic commentary on the conflagration that was just about to engulf the world. Another politically charged cover, dated Winter 1942, showed that Rand had not given up drawing altogether. A simple pen-and-ink sketch of a rat with Hitler's iconic moustache proved that minimal lines could evoke maximum emotion. 'The *Direction* cover, the one with the rat-face of Hitler, was a pretty nice drawing,' he admitted; 'I hated to do it because I hate rats and I hated Hitler. But this *was* a rat with a Hitler moustache.'[41]

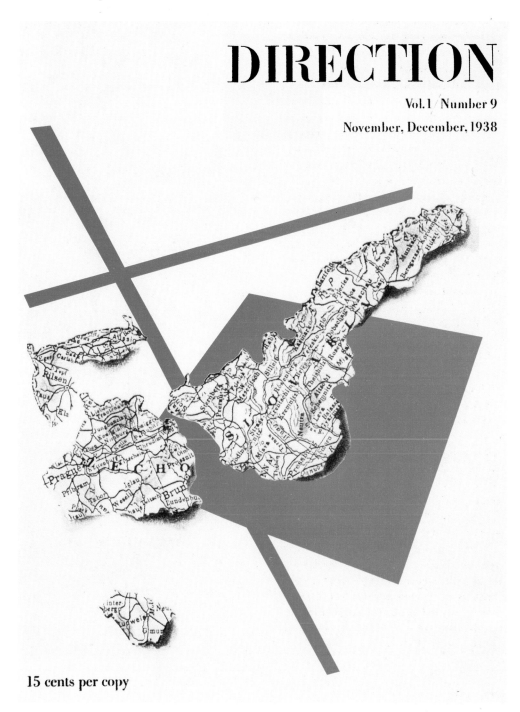

DIRECTION

Vol. 1 / Number 9

November, December, 1938

15 cents per copy

Far left:
Direction, cover,
December 1940
The covers created for this
small anti-fascist, left-
leaning magazine of art and
culture represent Rand's
most experimental period.
In the spirit of the
European avant-garde,
Rand played with drawing,
collage and lettering,
transcending the conven-
tions of mass magazine
cover design. In this issue,
what appears to be a
Christmas package is tied
with a barbed-wire ribbon.
According to Rand, 'the
form is intensified by
dramatic narrative association. The literal meaning
changes according to
context: the formal quality
remains unchanged.'

Left:
Direction, cover,
November/December
1938
Rand noted that the
somewhat abstracted cross
on this, his first *Direction*
cover, was designed 'to
suggest a pair of shears
cutting up the map of
Czechoslovakia'.

Below:
Direction, cover,
Winter 1942
Rand made a trenchant
anti-Nazi statement in
this freehand drawing
of a rat with Hitler's
iconic moustache.

Clockwise from top left:
Direction,
cover, March 1939
cover, January 1941
cover, January/
February 1939
cover, April 1940

Opposite,
clockwise from top left:
Direction,
cover, December 1941
cover, Summer
Fiction Number 1941
cover, April/May 1942
cover, March 1941
cover, February/
March 1942

Direction covers were
designed by Rand between
1938 and 1945, resulting in
a good showing of diverse
methods and concerns.
Although many were tied to
cultural themes, critical
references to world events
were common. The 1941
'Summer Fiction Number'
cover, with a sinister death's
head sun, evoked the sense
of wartime foreboding as
America entered the
conflict.

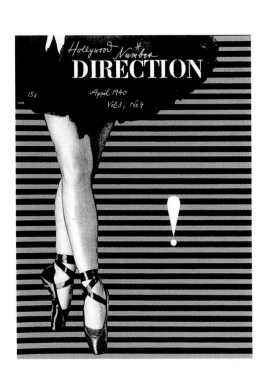

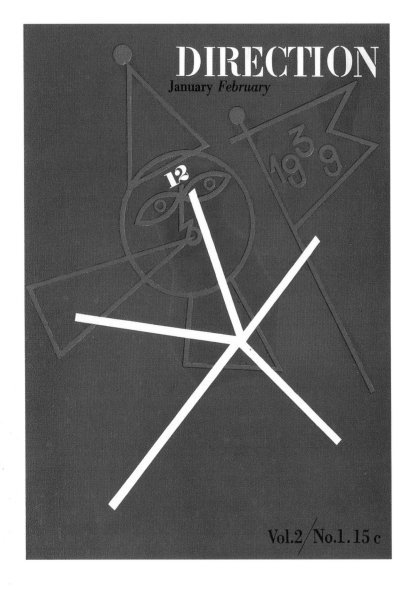

The 1941 cover with a swastika, shattered by the 'v' (for victory), expressed Rand's own wish for a speedy and devastating blow to the Nazi machine. *Direction* allowed Rand to experiment with a wide range of themes and formal solutions influenced by De Stijl, Constructivism and Dada, using collage, montage, drawing, and hand-lettering to test the limits of visual communication and aesthetic presentation.

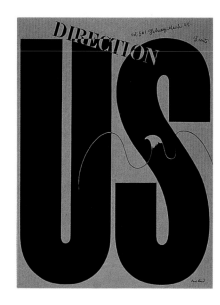

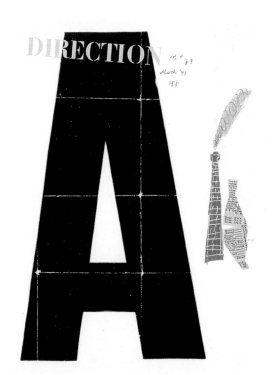

Clockwise from top left:
Direction, cover,
Summer Fiction
Number 1942
For the 'Summer Fiction Number', Rand makes a subtle political statement, as the ghoulish faces of these fish are those of the Axis leaders. This deceivingly perceptive image is reproduced in black, white and greys (not summer colours at all) to add a further level of drama.

Direction, cover,
Summer Fiction
Number 1944
The large capital 'D' with a cross and helmet in the centre represents D-Day and the death of the Nazi occupation of Europe. This poster-like image is not typical of conventional propaganda imagery but, without resorting to cliché, Rand suggests the monumental effect of the D-Day invasion.

Direction, cover,
November 1943
Rand illustrated the idea that 'French culture lives on', by affixing a heart containing the Eiffel Tower to the Louvre's Victory of Samothrace.

Direction, cover,
Christmas 1943
As a testament to the horrors in war-torn Europe, Rand created a montage of three starving children and a sculpture of a fallen angel.

Right:
Direction, cover, Fall 1945
'Less is more' is operative with this line drawing, contrasting light and dark, on the theme of 'one race'.

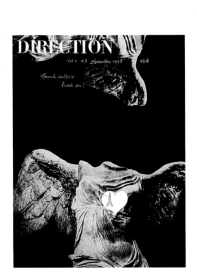

Economy was the mother of Rand's inventions in more ways than one. Since his fees for *Direction* covers were low and his allowed expenses nil, he did his own photography on a copy camera at the engraver's plant and used a handwritten scrawl to eliminate the need for costly typesetting. This seemingly *ad hoc* execution of Rand's ideas is why his *Direction* covers are as fresh today as when they were published over sixty years ago. There was no comparison at that time even between other artists' *Direction* covers in terms of formal or conceptual invention. Yet Rand played down their originality, saying that they were influenced by Picasso and Surrealism, and were homages to the avant-garde arts magazines *Verve* and *Minotaure*. 'When I was doing the covers of *Direction* I was trying to compete with the Bauhaus, not with Norman Rockwell,' he added; 'I was trying to compete with Van Doesberg and Léger and Picasso. "Compete" is not the right word. I was trying to do it in the spirit.'[42] Homage or not, the *Direction* covers marked the beginning of Rand's mature visual persona.

Two years after the first *PM* article, the February/March 1941 issue of *AD* (the name *PM* was relinquished for use by a new, adless daily newspaper) featured an unprecedented second cover story on Rand's recent work accompanied by illustrations of his *Apparel Arts*, *Esquire* and *Direction* work, and photographs of furniture and fabrics that he designed for use in his modest apartment on East 50th Street. By the time he was twenty-seven he had so thoroughly synthesized the European avant-garde vocabulary that there was barely a hint of derivation. His work was so strikingly unique that in the introduction to *AD*, László Moholy-Nagy, who had left Nazi Germany to found the New Bauhaus in Chicago, celebrated Rand's graphic design as the essence of Modernism in America. This serves as a fitting coda to the first phase of his career:

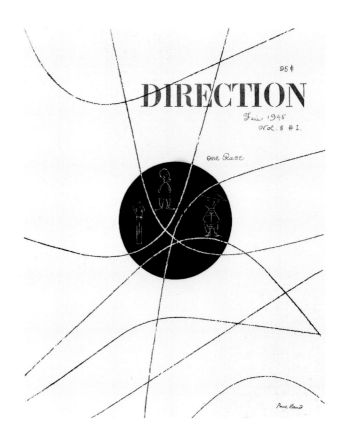

'When I came to this country I was greatly surprised to find that we Europeans were, to a certain extent, more American than the Americans. I found that our imagination went too far. It is true all this technological progress was developed on the highest level in this country but the Americans did not care too much for it. They created their high civilization by instinct, introducing invention after invention into their daily routine. However, they did not attach any philosophy to it as we did in Europe. For them the nostalgia remained for the "good old" traditional art.

'This was a strange experience for me, as I felt that our efforts in Europe to live up to the contemporary status of the Americans proved to be without a real background. It took me a long time to understand the Victorian dwellings, the imitations of colonial architecture or the old-fashioned advertising. Fortunately I soon saw that a new generation was rising with the potentiality and discipline of that America imagined by us in Europe.

'Among these young Americans it seems to me that Paul Rand is one of the best and most capable ... He is a painter, lecturer, industrial designer, [and] advertising artist who draws his knowledge and creativeness from the resources of this country. He is an idealist and a realist, using the language of the poet and business man. He thinks in terms of need and function. He is able to analyse his problems but his fantasy is boundless.'

Advertising: Modernism comes to Madison

2

Wanted: Art Director with a modern, creative touch. Need not be a Rand but must be able to inspire an art department.

Classified ad in the *New York Times* and
New York Herald Tribune, 1953

The advertising work that would skyrocket Rand to the top of his profession began to take shape while he was in the *Esquire* bullpen. As a loss leader used to snare advertisers, *Esquire's* management offered the services of its designers to prospective clients who were not tied to any agencies – and Rand often drew the short straw. One of these jobs was for Abe Spinnell, the eccentric owner of Playtex and inventor of its latex products. Rand designed ads using Futura type instead of the so-called 'perfume scripts' that were common to lingerie advertising at the time. This minor deviation from the norm thrilled Spinnell because it immediately set his message apart from the others by symbolizing the product's newness. He gave Rand additional freelance work and routinely summoned him to his thirty-fifth floor office in the Empire State Building for meetings. 'He gave me a chair in front of his desk and had me sketch ideas right on the spot,' Rand recalled about the advertisements that earned him $5 to $10 a piece and a sandwich from Longchamps restaurant. But he was also given a freedom that most advertising designers never knew. 'For those prices,' he added flippantly, 'Spinnell had no choice.'[1]

Although Rand's design solutions departed from time-worn verities, he was careful not to compromise the image of the product. He stayed within the bounds of what Raymond Loewy once described, referring to his own work, as MAYA: 'Most Advanced Yet Acceptable'. The ads sold Playtex effectively and efficiently – but they were also simpler looking, and in turn more eye-catching, than typical advertisements. 'I knew that other guys [in the agencies] weren't doing this,' Rand admitted with ingenuous modesty, 'but I never thought it was any great achievement, because I was just doing what they were doing in Europe.'[2]

By the end of the 1930s, when Rand started to produce advertising in earnest, the ad industry was building a renewed head of steam after the sluggish days of the Depression. Shortly before the United States' entry into the Second World War American companies were spending larger sums to advertise their products. And by the opening day of the 1939 New York World's Fair, dubbed the 'World of Tomorrow', which symbolically marked the end of the Great Depression, American industry was celebrating itself as a force for progress. The huge fairground in Flushing Meadow, Queens, with its modernistic and futuristic pavilions exhibiting the latest wares of General Motors, Ford, Chrysler, Dupont Chemical, Bell Telephone and Westinghouse Electric, among other corporate giants, was the showplace of the industrial design revolution – the industrial makeover of America. Indeed, the great industrial designers – Loewy, Bel Geddes, Dreyfuss and Teague – were all responsible for monumental exhibition designs. The Fair's centrepiece and logo, the Trylon and Perisphere, a gigantic needle and sphere inspired by Russian and German modern architecture, symbolized a new age in which consumerism and commodification were wedded. Selling modernity became the job of advertising agencies, which not only produced ads but developed brands and created the packages that contained commercial bounty.

It was owing to this promise of an expansive economy that advertising projected itself as a growth profession, scientifically based, with creative aspirations. Nevertheless, although a few agencies (such as Calkins and Holden in New York and N. W. Ayer in Philadelphia) attempted to transcend the ordinary, the industry was largely mired in hucksterism and hampered by antiquated notions of what constituted good advertising.

Cashing in on this advertising boom, William H. Weintraub, a senior partner at *Esquire/ Coronet,* sold his shares in the company to publisher David Smart, and in mid-1941 opened his own advertising firm in a spacious office at 30 Rockefeller Center. The goal of William H. Weintraub & Co. was to compete with the leading New York firms for the plethora of national accounts then flooding the market. Weintraub was the consummate salesman, with a genius for persuasion and an eye for hiring talent that would support claims that his firm was a world-class outfit. Within a very short time, the Weintraub agency became the first so-called 'Jewish agency' in a field of WASP hegemony to acquire an impressive and lucrative client list, including Dubonnet, Schenley Liquors, Lee Hats, Disney Hats, Revlon, Hilbros Watches, United Cigar Company, Stafford Fabrics, Emerson

Radios, the Kaiser-Frazer Corporation and Autocar Corporation. Weintraub often acknowledged that a major reason for his success was that his chief art director had almost single-handedly modernized, and thus raised the level of standards, of advertising design. Even more important, he made advertising that sold the goods.

Three years at *Esquire* was just about enough for the restless twenty-seven-year-old Rand, so when Weintraub offered him the job of chief art director of the fledgling agency, he accepted without a moment's deliberation. The only prerequisite was that he be given the mandate to run the art department and direct the design of the campaigns without interference. Weintraub appreciated Rand's artistic temperament and sought the unique virtues he demonstrated at Esquire/Coronet, so he agreed to these terms.

Within a year Rand had made a mark. 'Paul was the creative revolution,' explains Onofrio Paccione, who in the early 1950s was an art director at Weintraub working on the Revlon account and afterwards founded his own agencies. 'He was the guy who started this whole thing, and people forget that! It was like Cézanne; and after Cézanne came Braque and Picasso and they went on to [invent] Cubism. But it all originated with Cézanne. We [art directors in the 1950s] took a lot of the things that Rand did, because he brought ideas and intelligence to advertising where before him there was no semblance of thought.'³

At the outset, Rand hired a comparatively small staff of art assistants, some direct from the *Esquire* bullpen. Later on he named a few of these as associate art directors on particular accounts. But he rarely delegated any of the conceptual work, preferring to conceive virtually everything himself (unless it was an account that he had absolutely no interest in handling). This was uncommon in ad agencies, where assembly-line delegation was the rule and quality was the first casualty. Yet Rand claimed that his orientation had nothing to do with advertising, 'except an awareness that you're not doing museum stuff, and whatever you're doing should communicate, so the guy in the street should know what the heck you're trying to sell.'⁴ He, therefore, ran Weintraub's art department according to his own vision – which was an anomaly in the industry.

Prior to the early 1940s very few American advertisements were specifically designed *per se*, but were composed by a boardman, who followed templates, formats and styles that made one ad look more or less like the next. Copywriters reigned supreme, and layouts were dictated by the length of the copy. In many cases the copywriters imposed rough sketches on the layout artists, who simply finessed them. This convention was total anathema to Rand. He asserted that advertising composition was a design problem; the message was best conveyed through a marriage of text and image articulated through the layout, and only the designer was responsible for that function. Helen Federico, who worked in the Weintraub art department from 1943 to 1951, recalls: 'Paul's inner need for quality was always present. And the copywriters and the account executives were the arch-enemy, because the account executives wanted to please the client at all costs, and the copywriters were committed to wordy headlines, sub-headlines, sub-sub-headlines, and then a whole bunch of garbage down at the bottom. Paul was always having arguments with them, and rightly so. There was a lot of shouting. But he pretty much won, because Weintraub realized what a treasure he had.'⁵

To the consternation of many of the advertising veterans who were also hired by Weintraub, Rand took pleasure in tearing up their layouts and otherwise flexing his muscle. He exhibited little patience and was often dismissive, even rude, to those who attempted to impose their own will. He explained his philosophy simply: 'I was not going to let myself be treated like a job printer on Pitkin Avenue.'⁶

Left:
**William H. Weintraub &
Co.,** c.1942
In this typical 'men only'
dinner portrait, Rand
stands behind and to the
right of the seated William
H. Weintraub, at the centre.

Below:
Isaac Goldmann Printers,
calendar cover, January
1942
This calendar is an early
example of collage,
influenced by European
methods.

Right:
Emerson Electronic Radio,
maquette for
advertisement, 1947
Rand borrowed certain
conceits from European
Modernism, such as the
relationship of large and
small elements on a page as
achieved through collage.
This piece is typical of
the modern aesthetic
of the time.

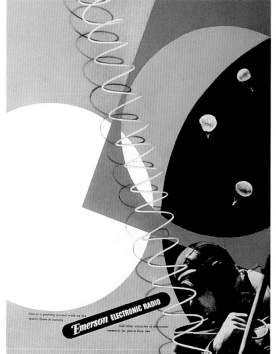

Had Rand complied, mediocrity would certainly have prevailed. The Weintraub Agency specialized in mass-market product advertising, not the corporate genre that N. W. Ayer was known for (i.e. the Container Corporation), which conveyed a more institutional message about a corporate philosophy and was, therefore, easier to design in an abstract or sophisticated manner. On the contrary, these were hard-selling pitches that appeared in weekly magazines and daily newspapers aimed at moving products off the shelves. Rand noted that most good designers did trademarks or posters, 'and not posters for cornflakes, either,' but he believed that design was design, regardless of purpose, and he possessed a keen ability to create smart-looking advertising for the most run-of-the-mill commodities. 'I'm not saying that it was great,' he would argue, 'but I did a lot of mass-market stuff, which very few good designers did. They just never got a chance. What agency guy, in fact what client, would let you do it well?'[7]

What Rand accomplished in pages for Disney Hats or Schenley Liquors or Air-Wick air freshener, compared to other agencies' more mundane product advertisements for clothing, beverages or household products, exhibited the same contrast between his *Direction* and other mainstream magazine covers. He redefined the problem and customized a solution that forced alternative perceptions not only on the client but on the audience. He realized, for example, that a newspaper ad had to compete with a large number of other graphic elements – headlines, pictures, rules, borders, and so on – on the same and/or opposite pages, and that consequently there were two ways of addressing the problem. Either design an ad that screamed much louder, or situate an ad within a frame of empty space and considerably turn down the typographic volume. He reasoned that the latter – a more elegant approach – would compete more effectively in the presence of the conformity that prevailed. The audience may indeed feel more comfortable with the tried and true, but it is more likely to be aroused by the new and different. Moreover, as an artist he preferred the creative options of working with modern sans serif typefaces (even typewriter type) and abstract forms in asymmetrical configurations, rather than central axis layouts with strained novelty faces. In addition, by using montage rather than detailed renderings he found ways to create (and control) serendipitous imagery. Even Rand's own childlike drawings were more unexpected than the typical advertising fare.

Left:

Various packages, 1947–53
At William H. Weintraub &
Co., Rand was responsible
for – what is now called –
branding and packaging for
Nutri Bottling Co., Robeson
Cutlery Co., Seeman
Brothers (Air-Wick), B. T.
Babbitt (Bab-O), Stafford
Fabrics, Country Club Ice
Cream Co., and Brandy
Distillers, Inc.

Below and right:
Schenley,
bottle labels, 1942
Rand used collage elements
– vintage paper design and
script typefaces – to give a
'modernist' pedigree to this
hard liquor.

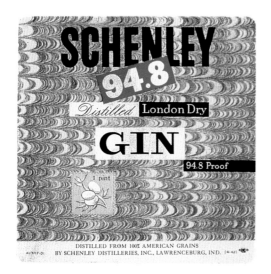

Left:
Coronet Brandy,
trademark, 1941
For one of his earliest
advertising clients, Rand
developed the Coronet
Brandy Man whose head
was fashioned out of a
snifter. The background
dot pattern (signifying
carbonated bubbles) was a
key element in the entire
advertising campaign.

Right:
Coronet Brandy,
gift bottle, *c.*1942
Rand was not just a two-
dimensional designer;
he designed numerous
packages and containers,
including this elegant
and decidedly modern
special edition decanter.

Rand held the title of 'art director', but he rarely operated as one in the traditional sense. In most agencies the art director was a handmaiden to the account executive. He would manage the artists who sketched out the visual ideas and would then commission other artists, illustrators, photographers or typographers to finish them. Sometimes Rand hired illustrators such as Ludwig Bemelmans or William Steig. But from his modest office adjacent to the larger bullpen, with Mozart's *Eine Kleine Nachtmusik* playing in the background, he developed all the ideas and conceived most of the basic artwork himself, while the mechanicals and technical renderings were given to an assistant to finish. Bob Blend, who worked as Rand's 'direct assistant' from the early 1940s to 1955, recalls that 'Paul used to scribble them out, and then I would carry them out. He did a lot of work that required technical expertise. The [characters] that you see in some of the ads, like the Snifter Man for Coronet Brandy, were painted or airbrushed by me.'[8] Rand insisted that the reason for wanting this degree of control was purely pragmatic: 'I was doing all the dirty work – coming up with the idea – why *should* I give it to somebody else to finish?'[9]

In fact, on the rare occasions when Rand did commission an artist to do something that he could not do himself, he issued such detailed instructions that nothing was left to chance. A case in point was the first time he worked with the German artist Richard Lindner, who after emigrating from Germany, and before becoming a successful figurative painter, was an accomplished commercial illustrator. 'I took him off the boat, he worked in my studio and I gave him a job in the agency,' Rand explained by way of introduction. 'We were trying to get the United Airlines account and I had an idea for a booklet that would be presented during the pitch. I did the sketch, then I showed it to Richard, and said, "We'd like you to do comps for this." He said, "What do you mean, you'd like *me* to do it? *You* already did it."'[10]

Rand rarely sought input from others. He had an uncanny ability to internalize a problem and quickly seize on a solution himself. He constantly scribbled ideas on scraps of paper, cocktail napkins and the insides of matchbooks, a practice he maintained throughout his life. The drafting skills he perfected at the Art Students' League came in handy, because these simple notations were so well articulated that even an account executive or brand manager could understand them. 'Paul would come in early in the morning, around 9.30,' recalled Morris Wyszogrod. 'By that time he would have his designs all lined up, because his mind worked twenty-four hours a day. He would place his ideas on the table, would walk around the art department, and [his direct assistant, either Allen Hurlburt or Bob Blend] would distribute the work to everybody who was familiar with the accounts.'[11]

Coronet Brandy,
advertisements, 1945–8
Rand developed scores of
different versions of the
Coronet advertisement,
which appeared in
magazines, newspapers and
as point-of-purchase counter
displays. Routinely he would
spend a day or two making
sketches which his assistants,
including Bob Blend, would
then render. Blend recalls
that his desk was always full
of sheets of the ubiquitous
halftone dots.

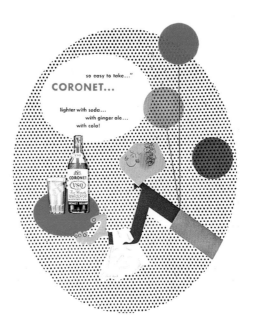

Rand presented the associates and bullpen artists with his own rough sketches and directed them both to mock-up layouts and to work with certain colours. Upon completion they presented him with layouts based on the original idea, which he then evaluated and reduced down to one crystalline idea. 'Paul did not like to present any client with more than one or maximum one-and-a-half ideas,' continued Wyszogrod. '"If you show them more than two ideas," he repeated over again, "then you weaken your position." "You don't write two letters," he would say, "you make one statement, and this is it."'[12]

Anything Rand said around the agency was law. 'Weintraub danced around him like a carousel,' recalls Wyszogrod, 'making nice-nice because he was draining Paul for his benefit.'[13] Weintraub also went through a ritual of pre-paring clients for Rand's unorthodox methods. Bob Blend remembered that, 'when the clients came to the agency, they had already been honed in by Bill Weintraub as to what this art director could do, and so consequently a lot of the ads were art-wise oriented'.[14] By the early 1940s Rand was well acknowledged throughout the industry as what Helen Federico calls 'the Kid Wonder'. She remembers the period, saying,

'When I left Paul [after being interviewed for the job of assistant] I was in such a state I couldn't stop talking about this incredible man.'[15]

As a designer he was incomparable. But as a manager he was painfully uncomfortable, and his uneasiness was physically manifest in a chronic eye twitch that developed early in his tenure at Weintraub and remained with him throughout his life. Although Rand exercised authority, he never relished disciplining others. His Brooklyn vocal cadence, gruff exterior, and arrogant demeanour, born of insecurity in the managerial position, betrayed a rather warm heart. The Weintraub art department, however, was nothing less than his personal domain and existed solely to serve his creative needs according to his strict requirements. 'The staff was afraid of him,' Wyszogrod declared. When Rand was unsatisfied with someone's perfor-mance, 'he would say "your work is no good." "You don't understand me." "You didn't come through." "You didn't hear what I said." But at the same time he deserves credit for being very just. He would explain what was wrong. He wouldn't just dismiss it out of hand. He would reason with you … and you had to agree most of the time – if you liked it or not.'[16]

Helen Federico also acknowledged that his

intolerance of the employees' imperfections was balanced by the even tougher demands he placed upon himself. Wyszogrod concurs that he was harshly critical of his own achievements: 'Sometimes he would be helpless and he'd say to me, "I made three designs and I'm still not satisfied." So he would do it again. When once I brought him a sketch of something that I designed personally, he said, "How many sketches did you make?" I said, "Three or four." He said, "I made fifty before I showed one." Then he said, "If you think it comes easily, it's not easy. I can solve any problem in the world, but it does not always come instantly."'[17]

Rand invested a huge amount of himself in his work and demanded the two 'Rs' in return: recompense and recognition. Despite his claim that he was a chronically poor businessman, by 1945 the trade press reported that he was earning a whopping $75,000 a year and paying a five-figure income tax. In 1950 Frank Zachary noted in an article in *Portfolio* magazine that he earned $100,000 a year – no small sum in a field in which an art director's annual salary averaged between $20,000 and $30,000. The other 'R', recognition, came in large part as a result of the signature that adorned every piece of printed matter that he touched. Even if one of his assistants did the final layout, since Rand had conceived the overall idea, he took the credit. He began signing his work at the outset of his career as a way to publicize himself. He never took out a promotional advertisement in the trade press nor produced a promotional mailing piece; the signature was his only public notice. Although signing ads was common in Europe, it was rare in America because designers were subordinate to the overall identity of the agency.

On one occasion he remembered being called into Weintraub's office to discuss this issue: 'On his desk there was the first Dubonnet ad I signed, and he wanted me to take my name off so that the glow would not be on me – it would be on the agency. I said, "Bill, this is your agency; you take my name off, and you can take it off your register, too – I'm getting out." And he didn't take it off. Now, if a client had wanted it off, that's something else.'[18] But no client ever made such a demand.

Allowing Rand to use his signature was a small price for Weintraub to pay for his continued employment. After all, the campaigns that bore his name would not have existed had he not created them. But signing those Dubonnet ads was a test of Rand's strength because it was complicated by the fact that A. M. Cassandre had created the original French campaign a decade earlier with the emblematic Dubonnet Man (a comic figure whose stiff outstretched arm held a glass of the aperitif). When it was agreed that the trade character would continue to be featured in the American ads, Rand hired the Italian caricaturist Paolo Garretto (who was working in New York before being deported to Italy as an enemy alien) to render the figure in seasonal and thematic costumes. Since the figure was invented by Cassandre and re-rendered by another artist, how original was the campaign? And therefore what right did Rand have in signing it? The answer was clear in Rand's mind: he didn't simply usurp someone else's idea, he transformed it into an American idiom while maintaining the very characteristics that gave the product its identity. 'Joseph Binder had the account before me, and he tried to be original but it was just terrible,' Rand argued: 'He changed the position of the guy, and I said to myself, "This guy should never be in any position other than the way Cassandre did it." I met Cassandre many years later, and he really appreciated the fact that I didn't screw up his work, that I understood that this is the symbol, and all I did was change his outfits or the situation around him. I never tried to improve on Cassandre, which would have been stupid. It's like Coca-Cola. You recognize the configuration – the *gestalt*. And the moment you change that position, it's something else.'[19]

Dubonnet,
advertisements, 1943–54
Advertisements for alcoholic drinks in magazines and newspapers were not the easiest to design. Clients routinely demanded that the bottle and label be prominent, leaving little room for humour (which was Rand's stock and trade). Rand overcame the obstacles with a virtually limitless array of witty vignettes for the Dubonnet campaign for over half a decade.

Dubonnet

made to order for summer !

Dubonnet PARTY PUNCH
Pour I bottle Dubonnet
into pitcher. Add I pint gin. Add
juice of 6 limes and shells,
large bottle of soda. Stir. Serve
with ice in tall glasses.

For your summer parties, remember this...no drink turns off the heat like a frosty

Dubonnet cooler. Dubonnet is so mild, it always treats you like the gentleman you are!

It's the nicest way known to make an occasion out of a meal. Try Dubonnet tonight!

For free recipe book (in states where legal) write Dept. B, Dubonnet Corp., Phila., Pa.
Dubonnet Aperitif Wine, Product of U.S.A. © 1954 Dubonnet Corp., Phila., Pa.

MERRY WIDOW
One-half Dubonnet.
One-half dry vermouth.
Stir with ice. Strain.
Add twist of lemon peel.

Dubonnet LIME RICKEY
1½ jiggers of Dubonnet.
Juice of half a lime,
with shell. Add ice
cubes, soda and stir.

Dubonnet COCKTAIL
One-half Dubonnet.
One-half gin. Stir
with ice. Strain.
Add twist of lemon peel.

Dubonnet ON-THE-ROCKS
Pour over ice cubes.
Add twist of lemon peel.

Dubonnet and soda
jigger of Dubonnet
juice of ¼ lemon
add ice cubes
fill with soda and stir.

Dubonnet STRAIGHT
Serve well chilled,
no ice. Add twist of
lemon peel.

Rand shared the creative ownership of Dubonnet, but it was the only instance when he did not create a campaign from the whole cloth. Otherwise, he introduced a litany of unique approaches, including ragged typewriter type and old engravings for Air-Wick, inspired by Dada; abstract colour fields against engravings and silhouetted photographs for Disney Hats, inspired by Constructivism and De Stijl; and floating cars in white space for Kaiser-Frazer automobiles, inspired by Surrealism. He also earned one of his many Art Directors' Medals for the best design and the best complete ad with his campaign for Jacqueline Cochran. Instead of showing the usual pretty girl, Rand had a shapely feminine limb towering up from the base of the page and balancing a beach ball, atop which was poised a bottle of Cochran leg lotion. He divided designs into two component parts: a large mass that commands attention and a smaller mass that draws that attention closer.

Left:

Benzedrine,
advertisements, 1943
Today Benzedrine is looked
upon as an addictive,
prescription drug but in
1943 it was an approved
method of boosting one's
spirits. Rand's witty ad for
Smith, Kline & French
Laboratories is among his
most playful. The others
are exemplary pieces of
contemporary design that
use negative space and
sans serif type to evoke
a sense of calm.

Below and right:

Air-Wick, advertisements,
1944
Could there be a more
challenging problem than
to design ads for an
everyday room air
freshener? Although Rand
did not entirely avoid the
typical symbols for 'odour',
he developed a campaign
that was visually distinct
from the conventional
comic strip ads of the day.
He gave the ads cachet by
using old engravings of fish
(and other odiferous
examples), and for
immediacy he introduced
typewriter type.

when you've fish to fry…keep air-wick by !

proved 3 times as effective as imitations !*

air-wick kills unpleasant indoor odors like nothing else possibly can. It's the only
household deodorizer that contains chlorophyll. And when tested against imitations, air-wick
was scientifically proved to be 3 times as effective. Other products try to look like
air-wick, but none of them works like air-wick. That's why more women buy air-wick than all other
household deodorizers combined…not only in the United States but also in
Canada and 54 other countries around the world! So for greater economy and effectiveness,
use only genuine air-wick to kill disagreeable odors from cooking, stale tobacco
smoke and other sources…upstairs and down.

…remember ! 5 o'clock is cooking time…so 5 o'clock is time

*The findings of 2 authoritative research laboratories.

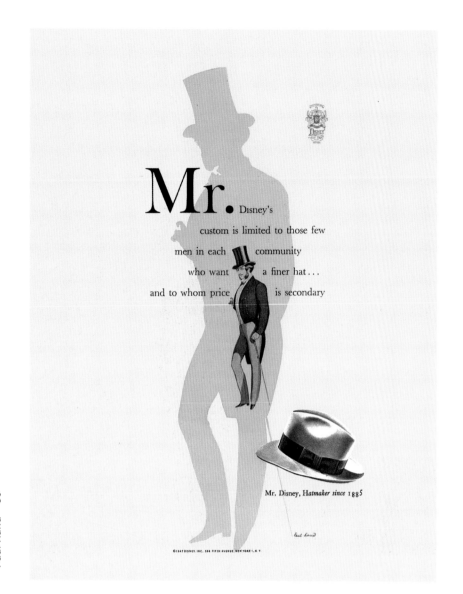

Mr. Disney's custom is limited to those few men in each community who want a finer hat... and to whom price is secondary

Mr. Disney, *Hatmaker since* 1885

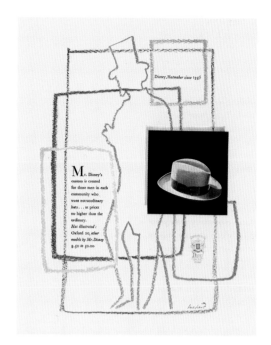

Disney Hats,

advertisements, 1947–9
Prior to Rand's involvement,
hat (like most clothing)
advertisements included
idealistic renderings of
smiling models. Rand's ads
bucked the trend. He
developed a mascot from a
nineteenth-century painting
of a sartorially splendid, top-
hatted gentleman who was
ever-present, but shared the
stage with the product. Over
the course of this campaign
Rand essentially manipulated
three elements: the mascot,
a hat (or hats) and squares
and rectangles that framed
the other elements and
evoked a sense of modernity.
Remarkably Rand main-
tained both consistency and
variation in a campaign that
prefigures his later corporate
identity work.

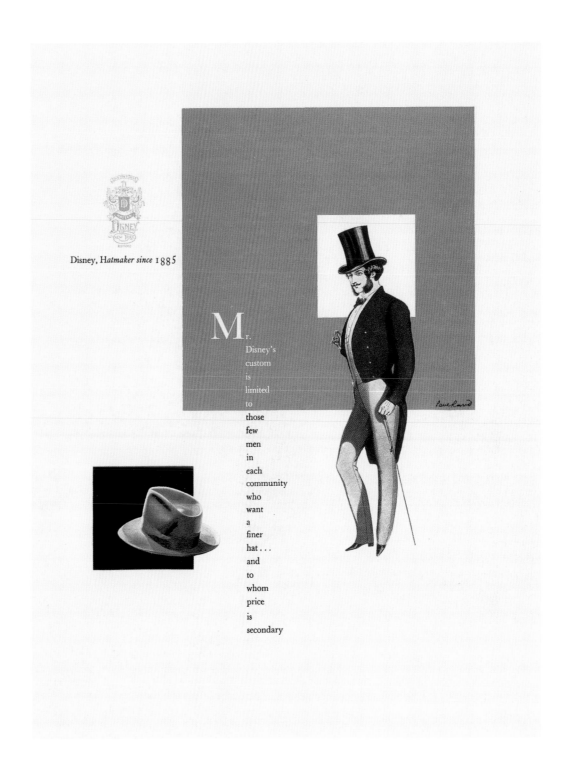

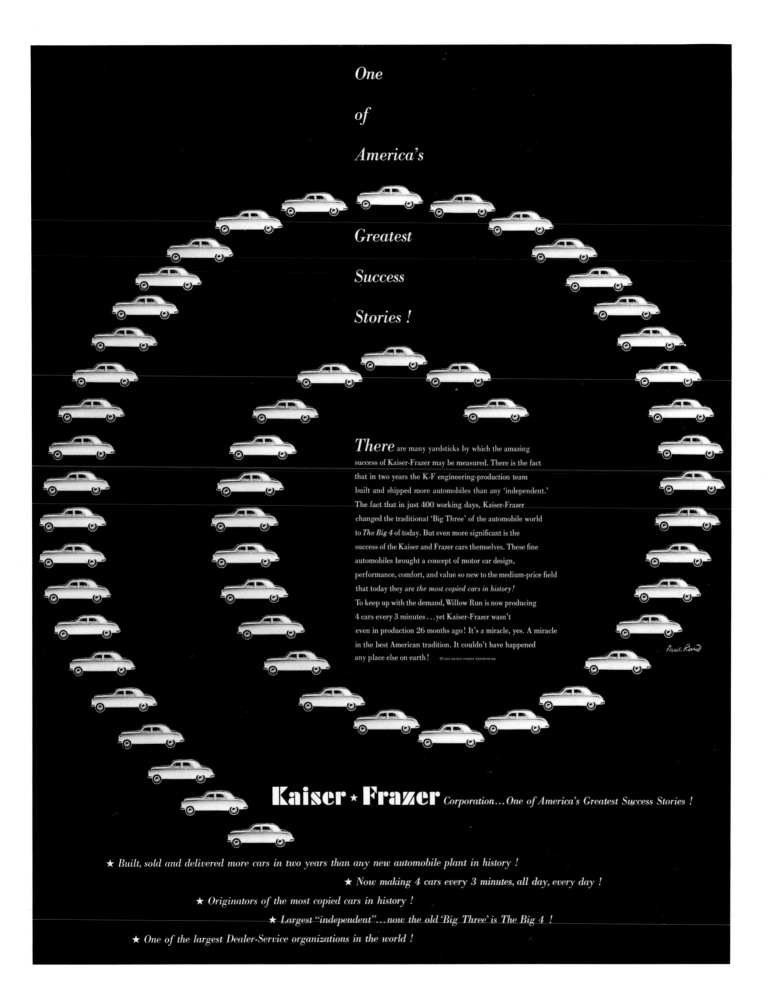

One

of

America's

Greatest

Success

Stories !

There are many yardsticks by which the amazing success of Kaiser-Frazer may be measured. There is the fact that in two years the K-F engineering-production team built and shipped more automobiles than any 'independent.' The fact that in just 400 working days, Kaiser-Frazer changed the traditional 'Big Three' of the automobile world to *The Big 4* of today. But even more significant is the success of the Kaiser and Frazer cars themselves. These fine automobiles brought a concept of motor car design, performance, comfort, and value so new to the medium-price field that today they are *the most copied cars in history!* To keep up with the demand, Willow Run is now producing 4 cars every 3 minutes...yet Kaiser-Frazer wasn't even in production 26 months ago! It's a miracle, yes. A miracle in the best American tradition. It couldn't have happened any place else on earth! ©1948 KAISER-FRAZER CORPORATION

Paul Rand

Kaiser ★ Frazer *Corporation...One of America's Greatest Success Stories !*

★ *Built, sold and delivered more cars in two years than any new automobile plant in history !*

★ *Now making 4 cars every 3 minutes, all day, every day !*

★ *Originators of the most copied cars in history !*

★ *Largest "independent"...now the old 'Big Three' is The Big 4 !*

★ *One of the largest Dealer-Service organizations in the world !*

beauty stops them...   at any age...

at three, the beauty of naturalness,
at thirty, the fresh, smooth skin that
proclaims careful grooming, and a deep sense of
the charm that is eternally feminine...achieved
by smart women the country over by the
habitual use of the superb skin softener...

JACQUELINE COCHRAN facial oil

Jacqueline Cochran,
advertisements, 1943–6
Historically, advertisements
for cosmetics were a little
better designed than other
product pitches, though not
greatly. Rand's campaign
for Jacqueline Cochran,
however, set a new
standard for conceptual
advertising. He used all the
sales weapons in his large
arsenal, with special
emphasis on collage and
montage. Typographically,
the ads were as minimal as
possible, with generous
amounts of negative space
used as a buffer between
them and the dense
editorial contexts in which
they ran.

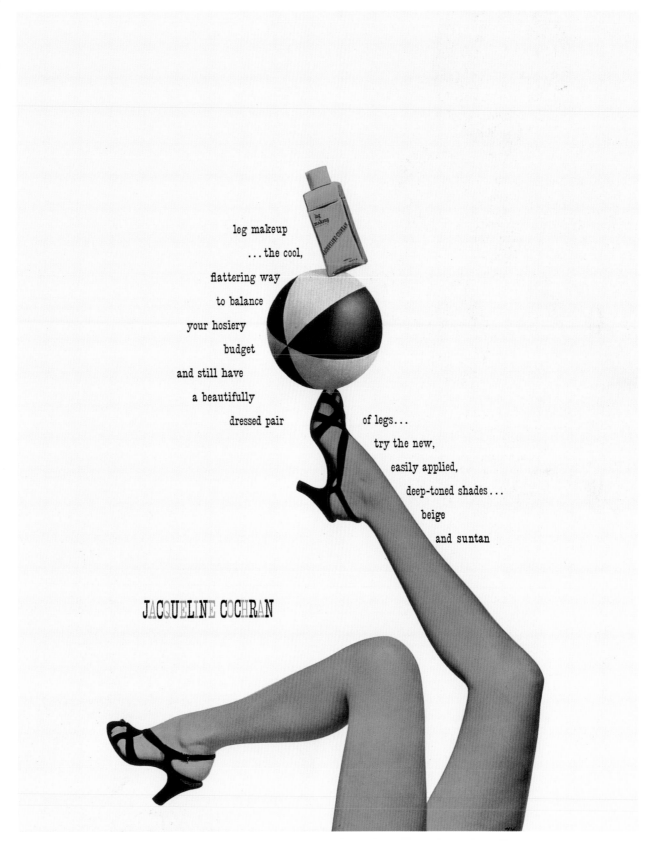

leg makeup
... the cool,
flattering way
to balance
your hosiery
budget
and still have
a beautifully
dressed pair   of legs...
                      try the new,
                      easily applied,
                      deep-toned shades...
                      beige
                      and suntan

JACQUELINE COCHRAN

Left:
El Producto,
trademark, *c.*1952
Rand was master of the
visual pun because his
ideas were not laboured or
contrived. For the GHP
Cigar Company he did not
create yet another Coronet
or Dubonnet Man; he
simply took a cigar, gave it
a hat and hands (no feet,
that would have been
too silly), and instantly a
mascot was born.

Right:
El Producto,
advertisements, 1953–7
For Rand, these 'comps'
for newspaper ads
came effortlessly, almost
subconsciously, and
usually at a rate of twenty
or thirty in one sitting.
He would do the drawings
on a few large sheets of
paper and then one of
his assistants made up
the finished piece.

Perhaps Rand's most emblematic advertising
campaign was for El Producto cigars. It was
the perfect synthesis of all the modernisms. To
animate El Producto, he used many of his own
comic line drawings to anthropomorphize the
otherwise lifeless cigar. And then on one of El
Producto's gift boxed 'albums' he took a radical
departure from the traditional chromolitho-
graphic cigar box label showing beautiful women
or historical vignettes, by designing the box top
with a photogram. 'There was nothing esoteric
about it; they were shapes of cigars,' he said,
illustrating that even his most audacious solution
was totally pragmatic. In fact, the trade publication *Packaging Parade* (February 1952) reported
that 'Sales, after adoption of new package,
were reported higher than ever before and the
company reported an unusually high percentage
of women customers. Jump in sales was attributed
by Mr Rand to "shock value" of a non-plain
cigar box. Mr Rand compared livening up of cigar
boxes to status of self selling packages with the
use of colour, art and display on phonograph
albums.' As for Rand, this solution was just one of
many salvos in his barrage against mediocrity.
'A cigar is almost as commonplace as an apple,'
he wrote in *Daedalus, Journal of the American
Academy of Arts and Sciences* (Winter 1960), 'but

if I fail to make ads for cigars that are lively and original, it will not be the cigar that is at fault.'

The El Producto campaign was typical of Rand's *modus operandi* and consistent with the agency's strategy. Rand developed a logo (or trademark) for virtually every new account prior to designing the advertisements themselves. The iconic device became the touchstone for everything that followed. It further triggered what Rand would later call the 'Play Principle', a stream of consciousness used to devise solutions that played off the mark. He quickly became very philosophical about these devices. 'A trademark is not merely a device to adorn a letterhead, to stamp on a product, or to insert at the base of an advertisement; nor one whose sole prerogative is to imprint itself by dint of constant repetition on the mind of the consumer public,' Rand wrote in *The Trademark as an Illustrative Device* (1952). 'The trademark is a potential illustrative feature of unappreciated vigor and efficacy; and when used as such escapes its customary fate of being a boring restatement of the identity of the product's maker. When fully exploited the trademark can actively stimulate interest in the product or brand.'

The El Producto logo was a stencilled typeface, which echoed the stencils found on bales of tobacco, and the letters were placed in alternating coloured squares for mnemonic effect. Once the logo was in place, the content of the advertisements was developed. With El Producto, line drawings were collaged to photographs of cigars, giving them human-style personalities. Every week a different cigar was featured as a player in a serial comic drama. While the practice of using contiguous narratives in advertising was not new, Rand's method – the serendipitous, sketchy quality – was at the time both unique and alluring. Rand once boasted that it took him less than a day to draw thirty gestural images for as many ads. After the campaign got going, it took viewers an instant to recognize the brand.

I always feel like traveling

with an **EL PRODUCTO**

I feel like a millionaire

with an **EL PRODUCTO**

I feel so bright with an El Producto

I feel like going places **with an EL PRODUCTO**

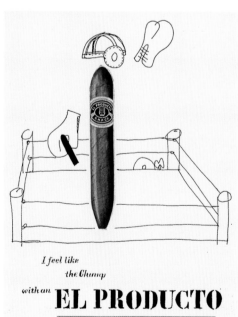

I feel like the Champ *with an* **EL PRODUCTO**

I feel like cheering with an **EL PRODUCTO**

El Producto, sketches for advertisements, 1953–7 Rand created well over a hundred of these serial advertisements and in the process gave El Producto a distinctive brand that appealed to the casual as well as the regular cigar smoker. He also attracted the non-smoker who simply wanted to see the vignettes develop from week to week.

El Producto,
counter cards and gift
boxes, 1953–7
Years before Rand made
his first children's book he
was applying what would
later become his 'kid's
style' to El Producto's
speciality lines.

El Producto,
gift box, 1952
Cigar box illustration
followed a formula:
embossed engraving of an
historical vignette or
figure. Rand changed all
that with this 'cigar
album', illustrated with a
photogram of different
cigar styles. 'What's the
big deal,' he said of the
radical concept, 'I was just
showing the cigars.'

Stafford Fabrics,
advertisements, 1942–4
Before Rand designed
an ad, he designed a logo
or trademark – one of
the bonuses that the
Weintraub agency offered
its clients. For Goodman &
Theise's Stafford Fabrics
the mark was a horse
composed of different
fabrics, which in large and
small versions appeared
on, and was seamlessly
integrated into, every ad.

His facility for designing logos and trademarks separated Rand from others in the advertising business who believed that the pitch – the
ad, billboard or sign – was more important than
developing a brand identity. Of course, the brand
concept wasn't new – emblematic trade characters had been used for various products since the
nineteenth century – but most of Rand's marks
were sophisticated visual puns rather than
character-driven cartoons. He relied on gesture
rather than slapstick. In *The Trademark as an
Illustrative Device* he wrote that, 'The trademark
becomes doubly meaningful when it is used both
as an identifying device and as an illustration,
each working hand in hand to enhance and
dramatize the effect of the whole.' Without the
logo or trademark as an anchor, every advertisement was more or less interchangeable with any
product. With a strong logo as focal point, showing the product was often unnecessary. He
accomplished wonders with the heraldic majesty
of the Stafford Stallion logo to convey the aura
of this fabric company, and the effervescent aura
of the Coronet Brandy Man, accomplished by
enlarging halftone dots to symbolize an explosion
of bubbles in the air. These representational
and other more abstract logos had a marked
influence on how products were promoted.

the
stafford stallion
has gone
to war

fabrics

by

stafford

fabrics with a pedigree

...hanging by a thread

Whether it's parachutes or the most distinctive patterns to be found in
men's neckwear...you'll find they're sired by the Stafford Stallion. This
is the symbol of Stafford Fabrics...those famous textiles woven in
Pennsylvania and printed in the little Connecticut town for which they are
named. Tomorrow you'll see new marvels produced by today's wartime
research...fabrics for both men and women...for shirts, sportswear, smart
costumes for town and country...all stamped with the spirit and stamina
of the Stafford Stallion, your assurance, now and always, of
fabrics with a pedigree.

GOODMAN & THEISE, INC., New York, Stafford Springs, Conn., Scranton, Pa.

Paul Rand 64

Stafford Fabrics,
advertisements, 1942–4
Rand enjoyed working
with a variety of shapes
and colours, which was
fortuitous when designing
for a fabric manufacturer
that offered a wide range
of motifs. Many of these
ads, employing found
art and amorphous
shapes, prefigured his
book jacket designs.

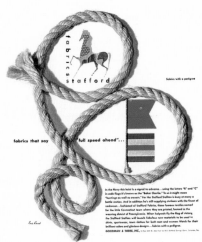

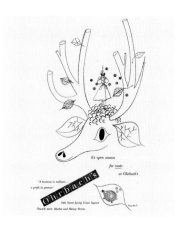

A trademark comprised of letters in blocks was the key component in another of Rand's successful campaigns, this one for Ohrbach's, a department store located on 14th Street in Manhattan. 'There are times when the trademark and the illustration are inseparable,' he wrote, 'as demonstrated by the advertisements for Ohrbach's. The use of the same element in diverse and unexpected visual situations … dramatizes the trademark (in this case the name of the store).' To Weintraub's dismay this was one of Rand's freelance projects that earned him much kudos, for example this rave review in *Fashion Trades* (November 1946): 'they went down to the store in droves, crowded the lingerie counters, snapped up the slip that was depicted in the corner page (sans description of price) … The ad was part of a series of 12 running from September to December, prepared by a 32-year old typographer-designer-painter Paul Rand.'[20] Like El Producto, Ohrbach's serial campaign piqued the audience's curiosity to see what image (idea) would appear next. In the New York daily *PM* Shana Anger wrote:

'Short of wearing our head in a bucket we cannot accept the spectacle of American advertising, so naturally we are grateful to any man who designs ads we actually like to look at. A recent survey showed that 63 per cent of men and 85 per cent of women newspaper readers read [Paul Rand's] Ohrbach's ads. Before he began illustrating actual merchandise, hundreds of people wrote in asking where to buy the clothes Rand had invented to decorate the page.'[21]

These full-page newspaper advertisements were not, however, just one of his most celebrated campaigns, they marked a significant moment in Rand's professional life – his collaboration with Bill Bernbach, the future architect of advertising's Creative Revolution of the late 1950s and 1960s, and co-founder of the trailblazing agency Doyle Dane Bernbach. Much has been made of the chemistry between the two men, and there is consensus among advertising scholars that their relationship triggered advertising's 'creative team'; the partnering of an art director and copywriter. This, of course, was rare in the 1940s, but was the key development sparking the Creative Revolution. How this fruitful relationship changed the course of advertising has been the subject of considerable debate. Some argue that through Rand, Bernbach was introduced to the virtue of having

a strong, conceptual art director. Others say that Bernbach helped hone Rand's raw talent into an effective tool of advertising. Frank Zachary, who worked briefly at the Weintraub agency in 1942, suggests that Rand taught Bernbach 'simplicity and focus. Nothing extraneous. Drip it down to its pith and drive it home. That's what Paul did on those Ohrbach ads.'[22] And this was certainly realized in Bernbach's renowned 'Think Small' Volkswagen and Levy's 'You Don't Have to be Jewish to Love Levy's Jewish Rye' campaigns of the early 1960s. 'As for what Rand learned from Bernbach,' continues Zachary, 'I think it was the value of good writing, good words, good titles. When I first met Paul he inveighed against bad copywriters. Then Bill came up with the right stuff.'[23]

Ohrbach's,
advertisements, 1946
Working directly with
William Bernbach, Rand
designed scores of weekly
ads for this downtown
New York department
store. Rand often wrote
dummy headlines that
Bernbach could fine-tune
or leave alone. Like El
Producto, each ad was
a part of a larger whole
and was anticipated by
the public who liked
them enough to frequent
the Ohrbach store in
record numbers.

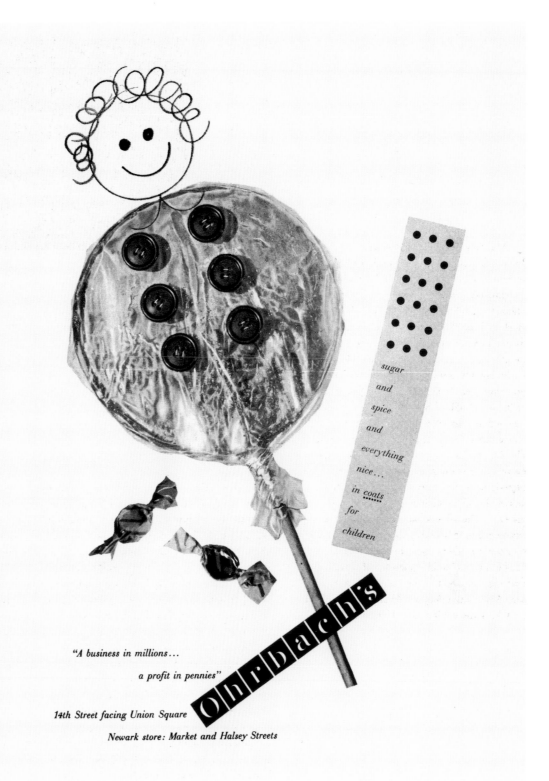

*sugar
and
spice
and
everything
nice…
in coats
for
children*

"A business in millions…

a profit in pennies"

14th Street facing Union Square

Newark store: Market and Halsey Streets

MECHANIZED MULES OF VICTORY

THE AUTOCAR COMPANY
ARDMORE, PENNSYLVANIA

With the Second World War at its height, the Autocar Corporation converted its manufacturing plant in Ardmore, Pennsylvania into an armoured military vehicle assembly line. This brochure, intended to promote the company's war efforts, became a showpiece of Rand's ingenuity. Using only two colours (black and yellow), he transformed mediocre photographs into dynamic page layouts. Splitting the pages in half, he allowed for a flow of collage and repeated images on top, while using an informal typewriter text face below. This project also marked the first time Rand and Bernbach collaborated.

In 1939 Bill Bernbach handled public relations (along with Frank Zachary) and ghostwrote speeches for the charismatic Grover Whelan, the chairman of the New York World's Fair and later President of Coty Cosmetic Company. Bernbach did not have any previous advertising experience, but in 1942 Weintraub realized his potential and hired him to write copy at the agency. His first job was a collaboration with Rand on a booklet for the Autocar Corporation, which was manufacturing armoured tank/personnel vehicles for the army. This would prove to be a fortuitous merging of talents. But originally, Rand hired Andreas Feininger to take photographs of the assembly line at the manufacturing plant in Ardmore, Pennsylvania. 'It was a terrible job,' said Rand about the junk-shop clutter in the hangar-like space. 'What the hell can you do with a place like that? Not much, unless you focus on *things*.'[24] So he directed Feininger to photograph parts coming off a conveyor belt, but the result was dull. To transform the project into something both creative and effective, Rand designed a series of contiguous pages that were divided in half along the same axis. The top was for images – silhouettes, montages and repetitions that suggested movement – the bottom was for

an unusually large amount of copy to explain Autocar's process and complement the images. The text was set in American Typewriter, an unorthodox face for such a project. 'I told Bill this is what I wanted. And he filled the space with copy. That's *all* he did. But it was great copy.'[25] In 1942 *American Printer* magazine praised the design of the spiral bound brochure as a 'successful variation on the Bauhaus theme, in yellow and black typewriter type.' Yet it was just as significant as an audition for Bernbach, who passed with flying colours and earned Rand's trust.

Bernbach did not, however, stay at the Weintraub agency for long. After serving a short stint in the army – discharged with a chronic stomach ailment – he accepted a better offer at Gray Advertising where he handled the Ohrbach's account. Rand agreed to design the ads on a freelance basis as a favour to his friend and colleague. Ohrbach's already had a history of good design: Erik Nitsche had directly preceded Rand as the designer, and Jerry Ohrbach, scion of the retailing family, was such a connoisseur of art that in the early 1940s he commissioned sixty paintings from such luminaries as Thomas Hart Benton, George Grosz and Peter Hurd, with the best given full-

page newspaper advertisements. This atmosphere enabled Rand to stretch his wings even further. Looking at the advertisements today it may be difficult to imagine that they had such a popular impact, but the marriage of Bernbach's clever copy and Rand's playful art and collage, which so seamlessly complemented each other, struck a chord with the consumer. At a certain point in their relationship, Rand was so in sync with Bernbach's writing style that he was in a position to second guess him. 'All I got was a list of merchandise,' recalled Rand about the routine of making the ads: 'It would say "kids clothing" or "ladies' shoes" or "underwear" or "pocketbooks". I would do usually about twelve ads at a time. Then I would go and see Bill, show him the ads, and he would sit there and nod. I would write the headlines, not with the idea that they would be final, but just to give Bill an idea so he could change it. I had no pride of authorship. But he very rarely changed it, or if he did, it would be either a comma or a noun or a verb. Basically, that was the way it was done.'[26]

The men who work on the vitals of these vehicles are unexcelled in their mechanical skill. Their hands move with the swiftness and sureness of a surgeon's, darting decisively from tool box to point of work. Armed with tremendous resources of skill and experience, the army of men at Autocar wages a relentless and victorious war against time. These men are in the front ranks in the battle of production. They are doing all in their power to supply America with an ever mounting number of military trucks.

What the artisans of Autocar production are doing now for America's military forces they have done countless times for American industry. They have built every kind of hauling vehicle from the light delivery truck to huge motorized transports for oil and gasoline. Now, for their Number 1 customer, Uncle Sam, they have increased their plant by 93,000 square feet and have added 1,500 employees to the staff, all within little more than a year's time. They permit nothing to stand in the way of production for victory.

Rand and Bernbach communicated extremely well. Each was sensitive to the other's ego. Conflicts never erupted, that is until they no longer worked together. Frank Zachary was friendly with both men and recalled that when Bernbach took the Ohrbach's account and started his own agency, he no longer used Rand's drawings: 'He used photographs and Paul wouldn't forgive Bill for that.'[27] Rand did not feel betrayed because he lost the account, but he was disturbed that Bernbach was turning his back on his method. Zachary says that Bernbach made the decision to achieve a more popular impact and shift the emphasis towards the product. I think no matter how charming, whimsical, elegant, beautiful, whatever the drawing is, it just did not have the impact of a photograph,' argues Zachary.[28] But from Rand's viewpoint, the shift to studio photography was a bad idea because of the artifice endemic to dramatically posed pictures. Rand favoured ideas, not moods. He did not have high regard for many of the up-and-coming advertising photographers (with the exception of Irving Penn). Conversely, Bernbach believed that photography, rather than the so-called 'designy' method that Rand practised, marked the new wave of advertising.

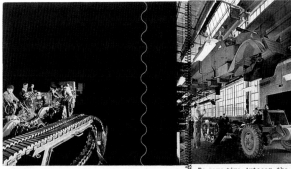

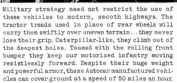

Military strategy need not restrict the use of these vehicles to modern, smooth highways. The tractor treads used in place of rear wheels will carry them swiftly over uneven terrain...they never lose their grip. Caterpillar-like, they climb out of the deepest holes. Teamed with the rolling front bumper they keep our motorized infantry moving resistlessly forward. Despite their huge weight and powerful armor, these Autocar manufactured vehicles can cover ground at a speed of 50 miles an hour.

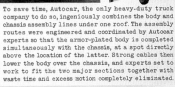

To save time, Autocar, the only heavy-duty truck company to do so, ingeniously combines the body and chassis assembly lines under one roof. The assembly routes were engineered and coordinated by Autocar experts so that the armor-plated body is completed simultaneously with the chassis, at a spot directly above the location of the latter. Strong cables then lower the body over the chassis, and experts set to work to fit the two major sections together with waste time and excess motion completely eliminated.

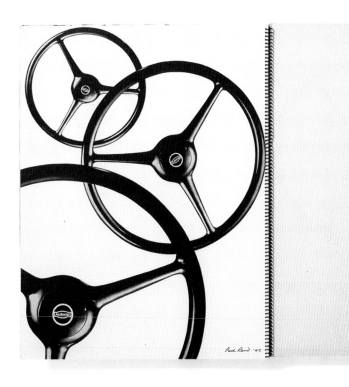

Dunhill Clothiers,
advertisement, 1947
This is an example of the
ad as logo and logo as ad.
Rand did not consider
himself a 'fashion' designer,
but many of his most
original designs were for
fashion clients.

DUNHILL

'I talked to Bill about it,' concluded Zachary, 'and he said "It's business!"' The inevitable outcome of losing Rand as a friend ultimately did not seem to matter as much to Bernbach as forging his own direction. Zachary observes, 'they were in business together and that was all. In fact, they did not see much of each other after the rift.'[29] Over the ensuing years, despite Bernbach's occasional references in books and interviews to Rand's influence on him, Rand was quietly angry that Bernbach never fully recognized his debt while taking full credit for the Creative Revolution. Shortly before his own death, after years of unspoken resentment, Rand confided that 'it is a myth that Bernbach taught me everything that I know'.[30]

By the late-1940s Rand was such a sought-after commodity in his own right that he demanded that Weintraub give him double the pay for half the time. 'He was in a state of shock for ten days,' Rand impishly recalled, 'but he finally agreed.'[31] Weintraub reasoned that it was better to give in on these conditions than to make Rand a partner, which would have compromised his own power base. So Rand came into the office on Tuesday, Wednesday and Thursday, splitting his seven-day work schedule between the agency and his apartment at 44 East 50th Street, in Manhattan, where he did a growing number of freelance advertising,

packaging and publishing projects. Although he was committed to doing the highest quality work for the agency, his professional loyalties never resided in one institution or with a single client. His first duty was to the work itself: 'For me, the quality of the work always preceded everything else … and … by quality, I mean is it correspondent to some image or some painter or some person that I was following or inspired by. If it didn't, to hell with it.'[32]

Rand insisted that during the early days at the agency he did not have a particular vision – or Rand style – but the term 'good work' was certainly his mantra. By 1946, when he wrote his first book, *Thoughts on Design*, he had defined his ideas in philosophical and theoretical terms, but during the early years at Weintraub, Rand viewed design more as black and white – good and bad. He totally embraced Modernism as the guiding principle for attaining good work, but his intuitive response to the rightness of form really guided him. Of course, he accepted certain rules of design codified by the European Moderns, but he adhered to an inner set of rules, which often included exceptions to Modern dogma. Rand once defined good work as having 'a practical basis' and returned to that simple pronouncement throughout his life. It did not matter what the precise elements of design were, so much as the spirit behind them. Of typography, for example, he said: 'Good typography, whether old or new, doesn't make a hell of a lot of difference. I respect people who can do traditional typography in a way more than I can some people who do so-called "modern" typography. It has to do with spacing, it has to do with the layout, it has to do with contrasts. But If you're looking for a catchword, *appropriateness* is an important word.'[33]

Below:
Big Families,
advertising flyer, 1947
Rand always tried to put
a happy (if not witty)
face on his drug client's
products – even on the
otherwise unfriendly
hypodermic syringe.

Below right:
Tomectin,
advertising flyer, 1948
Rand believed that art
could enhance everyday
life, and the abstract
painting for this digestive
drug certainly makes the
product more palatable.

Another important word was *function*. No matter what was being advertised, the overall design scheme had to function as art and persuasion, and style was a mere by-product. 'The implication that you do things willy-nilly just because you want to have a certain look, as far as I'm concerned, is nonsense,' he argued on countless occasions. 'I think that everything you [design] has to make sense, and has to have a practical aspect, because it's a practical problem. In this way it is distinguished from painting, but the formal problems are identical. You still have problems of colour, proportion, and scale.'[34] Rand said that his work was inspired by art, but he also wanted to make a clear distinction between fine and applied art: 'I think that unless the thing is practical, it's not art. Because that quality that makes art is the fact that it works. You can do abstract things and everything looks lovely, but it doesn't do a bloody thing.'[35] Further qualifying the difference between the fine art maker and the commercial art worker, he argued that 'art comes in the ingenuity of a designer who is able to, in a way, conceal art as a service to business.'[36] At times Rand expressed his ambivalence about wanting to be a painter himself. But Onofrio Paccione suggests that, 'deep down he knew that he wasn't really a painter. Because everything he did was very designy. To be a great painter you have to have a great sense of design. But the design should not be apparent.'[37]

Rand's work was resolutely modern. Nevertheless, his staff rarely heard him invoke the 'm' word. Helen Federico recalls that Rand would sometimes say that 'he thought pink and green was a marvellous combination; that he adored Mozart; and that Paul Klee was his master,'[38] but he did not expand on these thoughts. Morris Wyszogrod suggested that Rand's conversations were more pragmatic than theoretical, recalling that on many occasions 'Paul said that he could not understand how the American population accepts and makes peace with advertising which looks ridiculous.'[39] Wyszogrod also remembers that Rand would give short lectures to the bullpen on how to achieve visual impact, but preferred speaking to his staff individually: 'He was a good teacher, but not always a pleasant teacher … He did not have the patience to go into lengthy discussions. If you questioned his authority or if you had any doubt he adamantly refused to answer. He hated to confront criticism straightforward. He would put it into his memory bank, take it home, digest it, and come back with a bunch of answers and designs to explain what he meant.'[40]

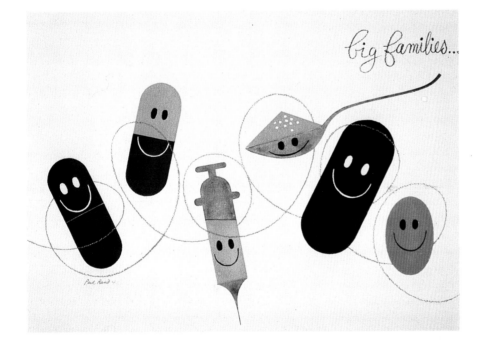

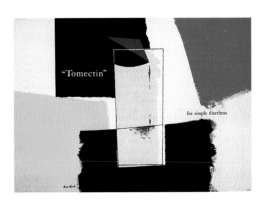

Kaufmann's,
advertisements, 1947–8
When he was chief art
director at William H.
Weintraub & Co., this
Pittsburgh department
store was one of Rand's
best freelance clients.
Although a consistent
Rand style emerges
throughout his work
at this time, each client
received customized
solutions. Kaufmann's got
a good dose of Rand's
characteristic wit and
dynamic scale changes.

Rand was more comfortable teaching by example. His example. Other than showing work by his European heroes, he rarely used another designer's work as representative of what he wanted his staff to learn. His textbook was his own portfolio, from which he tried to convey that an advertisement was successful if it was imbued with transformative powers that made the commonplace extraordinary. Yet even his own work did not always explain success in the market-place, which was something of a mystery to Rand.

'Who knows why a product sells?' he mused. 'There are millions of reasons why things sell that have nothing to do with art or design. If you gave the consumer a deal, like 50 per cent off, you'd sell like hell regardless of whether it was abstract or concrete or whatever.'[41]

He was keenly aware of the dichotomy between the kind of advertising that the public accepted and how far he would go to satisfy that acceptance: 'People think in very simple, literal ways. If you're talking about cereal, you show a mother and her little kid eating cereal. What's more appropriate? But is that the best way to sell cereal? Who knows? Maybe it is. Though, I doubt it very much. It's one way. But dramatizing a bowl of cereal, and dramatizing the luscious cornflakes or the content or the ingredient is a hell of a lot more convincing than just showing a mother-and-child eating cereal. So who knows? The ramifications of marketing are too complicated for a simple mind like mine to delve into. I think you have to deal with a psychologist or a sociologist, and even they would give you a lot of guesses.'[42]

It was axiomatic that advertising artists were required to compromise their principles in the service of selling. Art was something one dabbled in on Sunday not on the job, where the dictates of the client prevailed. But Rand did not accept this axiom, asserting that, 'you can't be an artist one day a week.'[43]

Through the workaday routine of addressing clients' capriciousness, he insisted that, although a designer may not be an actual artist, at least art must be the goal of all designers. Frank Zachary noted that for Rand this had deep-seated implications, 'his ego did not permit him to be lumped together with the guys who did signs on windows and billboards. That was the distinction that he *had* to make.'[44] Rand also took strong exception to the common view of the advertising man as huckster: 'As long as you have that idea, you're finished … I consider myself somebody who contributes something to the quality of life.'[45]

Around 1946 Rand found himself in the enviable position of being an expert in an industry which was about to become an even more potent force in the national economy. With the growing consumerism that flourished at the end of the Second World War, the advertising industry was poised for attack.

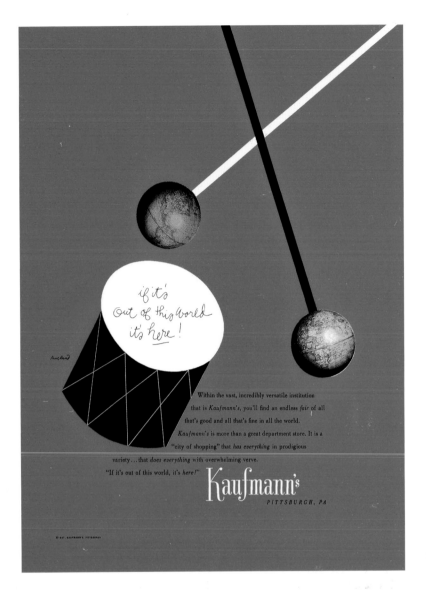

Despite the sporadic rants against modern design by disgruntled old-fashioned designers and the occasional criticisms from clients about too much wasted white space, Rand's ideas were largely accepted – and his signature was ubiquitous. Moreover, his position as a role model for many young designers was incontestable. Naiad Einsel, who worked in the bullpen at the Weintraub agency in the early 1940s, was typical: 'I wouldn't tell people that I worked for the Weintraub Agency … I would say that I worked for Paul Rand. I was just thrilled to be there.'[46] Rand was also routinely invited to lecture on design. As early as 1939 he was appointed to the faculty of the Laboratory School of Industrial Design in Manhattan, and in 1942 the American Advertising Guild announced 'A course in Advertising Design by dynamic young Paul Rand … [A] series of laboratory forums aimed at creating a new "graphic voice".' However, teaching such an excruciating test of his ability to overcome shyness that he frequently missed scheduled classes, sending surrogates in his place. Instead he tried his hand at writing.

Rand claims that his readings about art theory and history were triggered by a casual remark made by Moholy-Nagy when they first met in 1939: 'I remember, Moholy asked me, "Do you read criticism?" And I said, "No". His reply was, "Pity".'[47] So Rand began to consume books and essays, particularly on aesthetics. Inspired by Moholy-Nagy's *The New Vision* and John Dewey's *Art and Experience*, Rand developed ideas of his own, and after some cajoling by editors, he timidly started writing short articles for trade journals and magazines. 'I remember that I resisted that whole business,' he said about being asked by the George Wittenborn, publisher of Wittenborn & Co., to write a book on advertising design: 'I said I wasn't a writer, I didn't even know where to begin. So [George] had a friend who was a freelance writer, and he said, "Why don't you start with her?" She came up to the house one day and we sat down and talked; I was talking about all the concepts. And she said, 'You don't need me. Why don't you just do it yourself?' And I did.'[48]

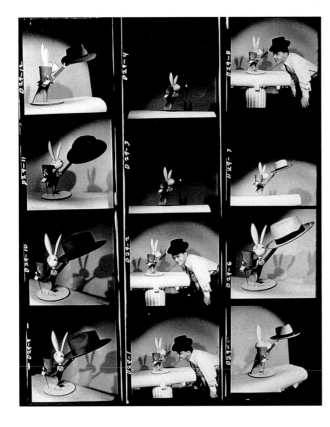

Rand eventually worked closely with a copy-editor, Betty Norgaard, who was also one of the few copywriters he countenanced at the Weintraub agency. About his first attempt at writing a book Norgaard recalls that, 'he was as certain about what he wanted to say in words, as he was about how he wanted to design. All I did was clean it up.'[49]

Thoughts on Design was a manifesto disguised as a monograph. A milestone of design literature, this was not, however, the first graphic design text published in the United States. Other author/ designers, including W. A. Dwiggins, Joseph Binder and Ervin Metzl, wrote how-to-do books and manuals, but Rand's was a why-I do book, using his own work to show how Modern principles functioned in advertising. The preface explained that, 'This book attempts to arrange in some logical order certain principles governing advertising contemporary design. The pictorial examples used to illustrate these principles are taken from work in which I was directly engaged. This choice was made deliberately, and with no intention to imply that it represents the best translation of those principles into visual terms. There are artists and designers of great talent whose work would be perhaps more suitable. But I do not feel justified in speaking for them, nor secure in attempting to explain their work without any possibility of misrepresentation.'[50]

Thoughts on Design was a well-written, precisely structured collection of concise commentaries, which combined Bauhaus analysis, Jungian psychology and homespun candour. Rand addressed such previously ignored issues as 'The Role of Humor', 'Reader Participation', and 'The Symbol in Advertising'. *Thoughts on Design*'s influence on American designers of the late 1940s and 1950s is often compared to the impact that Jan Tschichold's *The New Typography* had on European practice of the late 1920s and 1930s. Although Rand resisted the label of reformer (indeed he once said that he published *Thoughts on Design* because, 'God forbid, there would ever be a fire, at least I'd have all my samples in one place'), like the European Modern zealots he believed that his methods could have a decisive impact on other designers, and ultimately on the field as a whole.

Rand's public and print personalities were very different. He wrote with the brevity of a copywriter and the grace of a poet but he spoke in gruff Brooklynese, punctuated by expressive phrases that denoted approval or disapproval. When asked to comment on something that was below his standard, the word 'lousy' cut like a sabre. Another of his favourite expressions, 'for the birds', was phrased in such a way as to render the object of his criticism meritless. In print, however, he eschewed these Randisms for a clear prose style. The formality and permanency of writing demanded more rigorous and precise language. Although his later writing employed allusion, his earlier efforts were decidedly straightforward. In 'Too Many Cooks', a short essay published in the British magazine *Art & Industry* (1947), Rand both defined his design method and by extension underscored his writing style: 'Without labouring the point, I would like to make clear that I am not interested in "Advertising Art" or any phase of technique that is separable from the one and only purpose to say something clearly, convincingly, urbanely.'

Rand taught himself to design by designing, and taught himself to write by reading books on art and culture. Unschooled in the formal techniques of writing, he was initially uncomfortable. But if the advertising business (and Bill Bernbach) had taught him anything, it was that being succinct was a virtue. His early texts, therefore, had an advertising cadence. In 'Too Many Cooks', he was pitching and *selling* his notions of design: 'I have no particular credo, except that I must insist on the social responsibility of the advertising artist. He can take the easiest way, the primrose path of popular bad taste; he can truckle to the lower instincts of the herd and for a while, at least, he will secure material rewards. But I do believe, that living and working with the canons of good taste (trust and honesty) he will receive spiritual rewards.'

In an earlier essay entitled 'The Designer's Role', which was later revised for *Thoughts on Design*, he developed the oratorical trope of chaining active verbs together, like punchy headlines in an ad, to achieve greater emphasis. It read like a sermon: 'The designer does not, as a rule, begin with a preconceived idea. His idea is the result of subjective and objective thought, and the design a product of the idea. In order, therefore, to achieve an honest and effective solution he necessarily passes through some sort of mental process … Consciously or not, he analyses, interprets, translates … He improvises, invents new techniques and combinations. He coordinates and integrates his material so that he may restate his problem in terms of ideas, pictures, forms, and shapes. He unifies, simplifies, eliminates superfluities. He symbolizes … abstract from his material by association and analogy. He intensifies and reinforces his symbol with appropriate accessories to achieve clarity and interest. He draws upon instinct and intuition. He considers the spectator, his feelings and predilections.'[51]

Sales of the first edition of *Thoughts on Design* were brisk among designers. It also became a critical success, which both surprised and elated Rand, yet cautioned him not to get too cocky. All the reviews were more or less similar: 'Paul Rand has set an example for a generation of young advertising artists,' wrote Percy Seitlin in *American Artist*; 'The example of his work accomplished this even before he wrote this book.'[52] Even *Time* magazine, in December 1946, proclaimed, with a minor reservation, that 'Some ads (like Wheaties') are good for a laugh, some (like Packard's) are good for a sigh, and some (like Listerine's) for a shiver of apprehension, but very few are good just to look at … Paul Rand [has] packed 102 of his best jobs (plus a few stilted pages of art philosophizing) into *Thoughts on Design*.'[53]

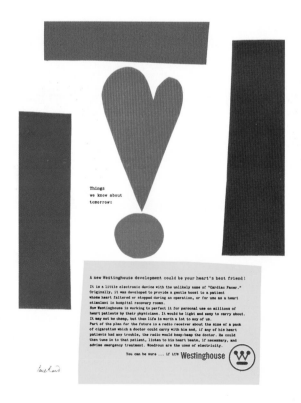

Westinghouse,
advertisements, 1962–71
Long after Rand left the
advertising agency he
continued to produce the
occasional ad. Although
originally asked only
to act as a consultant
on Westinghouse's
'institutional' (non-retail)
advertising, he could not
help but do them himself.
With the armature of a
consistent typographic
style, Rand developed a
wide range of conceptual
and formal variations.

Things
we know about
tomorrow!

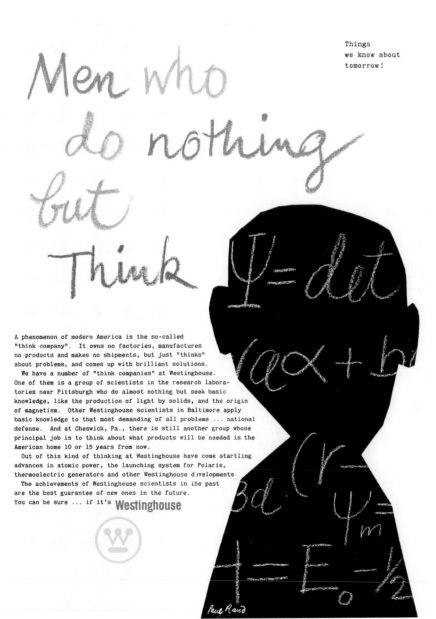

A phenomenon of modern America is the so-called
"think company". It owns no factories, manufactures
no products and makes no shipments, but just "thinks"
about problems, and comes up with brilliant solutions.

We have a number of "think companies" at Westinghouse.
One of them is a group of scientists in the research laboratories near Pittsburgh who do almost nothing but seek basic
knowledge, like the production of light by solids, and the origin
of magnetism. Other Westinghouse scientists in Baltimore apply
basic knowledge to that most demanding of all problems ... national
defense. And at Cheswick, Pa., there is still another group whose
principal job is to think about what products will be needed in the
American home 10 or 15 years from now.

Out of this kind of thinking at Westinghouse have come startling
advances in atomic power, the launching system for Polaris,
thermoelectric generators and other Westinghouse developments

The achievements of Westinghouse scientists in the past
are the best guarantee of new ones in the future.
You can be sure ... if it's **Westinghouse**

Rand was not sanguine about the parenthetical jab in the *Time* review. While he disregarded criticism about his design, his uncertainty about writing made him highly sensitive. And although he continued to write short essays after the publication of *Thoughts on Design*, he did not entertain writing a sequel until almost forty years later. He decided instead to focus on the field in which his mastery was unchallenged – design. He would always proudly say that the 1940s and early 1950s was his most prolific period.

Ironically, one of Rand's most conceptually convincing advertisements failed in its mission, yet it stands out in the minds of all his former colleagues as the true synthesis of his artistic aspirations. In early 1954 Weintraub bought the back page of the *New York Times* to catch the attention of thirty-one top executives of Radio Corporation of America (RCA), which was in the process of selecting a new agency to replace J. Walter Thompson Co., and therefore assume the $10,000,000 of annual billings. Rand was apprised that General Sarnoff, RCA's chief executive officer, was once a Morse code operator. And this triggered an unprecedented idea. In the best attention-getting tradition, Rand designed a full-page ad that featured outsize international Morse code symbols, which said 'RCA!, we want your business', with copy that read, 'an important

message intended expressly for your eyes is now on its way to each one of you'. Onofrio Paccione remembers seeing the ad on Rand's table, 'so beautifully sharp, so brilliant, I was struck dumb', while Frank Zachary recalled that it was quintessential Rand: 'It was not so much wit as humor. The difference between wit and humor is that wit is a function of the brain, humor comes out of the soul. This ad had gut feelings.'[54] Although it revolutionized the manner in which agencies pitched for accounts, it didn't succeed in capturing this particular account because it may have been *too* smart. As reported in *Art Director and Studio News* (March 1954), 'Paul Rand, the AD behind the ad says their switchboard was swamped with calls from people unrelated to the message to find out what the symbols meant.' Weintraub did not get the account because RCA wanted a big agency as a badge of their own stature.

As William H. Weintraub & Co. set its sights on larger accounts, it accepted clients that Rand found impossible to work with. Rand was also getting increasingly restless doing mass-market advertising, so he hired additional art directors, including Alan Hurlburt (later the long-standing art director of *Look* magazine), Onofrio Paccione and Helmut Krone, to work on what he called 'junk' accounts, or clients that objected to his design schemes, such as Maidenform and Revlon (Paccione would later take the Revlon account to his own agency). It was also at this time that Rand met his real nemesis at the agency: Norman B. Norman.

Norman was an 'account supervisor', who came to Weintraub from Procter & Gamble and brought the Revlon account with him. 'He really ruled the roost with the people that worked for him,' recalled Bob Blend.[55] With responsibility for Maidenform and Revlon, among other accounts, he acted more as the clients' representative than an advocate of good design. With Revlon in particular, he acceded to the demanding Charles Revson's every whim, down to the size of the type. Rand worked on Revlon for a time, but then gave it up; rather than an ally, Norman B. Norman became a formidable adversary.

With Norman in place, the agency was virtually divided in two, split between the respectably medium and the high-ticket billing accounts. 'I'm sure that Paul hated this,' continued Blend. Moreover, unbeknown to Rand, Weintraub's finances were faltering. Slowly Weintraub's grip on the agency began to slide, and Norman brought in money men who helped him take over the agency. In quick succession Weintraub departed and Rand was set adrift. 'All I know is that Paul was nixed out,' recalled Blend, who in 1955 became the Head Art Director for the reconstituted Norman B. Norman, Regan, Kumbel agency. After almost fifteen years at the agency, the demise of William H. Weintraub & Co. was hard on Rand, yet he had already lost much of his taste for advertising. 'I don't think he particularly liked it,' attested Gene Federico: 'He proved he could do it. But the positions he got afterward were so much better. Speaking with the heads of big corporations was the way he liked to work. He said it many times, that's the only way he'd get good work done. And, moreover, his time was his own.'[56] In leaving the agency to pursue the next stage in his career, Rand also closed a major chapter in the history of design and advertising.

Thanks in large part to Paul Rand, New York City became for modern art direction what Paris was for modern art at the turn of the century – a wellspring of unrivalled invention. Neither Chicago nor Los Angeles had the same critical mass of talent, nor the business to support it. In New York scores of art directors, many inspired by Rand, had commanding positions at ad agencies and magazine publishers, where they not only made an impact on their respective products but influenced the entire field.

Madison Avenue was Manhattan's Montparnasse.
Rand's style of ingenious conceptual advertising
evolved into what, in 1960, the ad man William
Pensyl termed 'The Big Idea', characterized by
witty visuals, clean design and strident copy-
writing. The Big Idea was an expression of the
unparalleled creative liberation, later dubbed
the 'Creative Revolution', that inaugurated the
overwhelming shift from hard sell to smart
sell. So, in 1955, when the forty-year-old Rand
left William H. Weintraub & Co., he was the
undisputed father of the Big Idea and the
grandfather of the Creative Revolution.

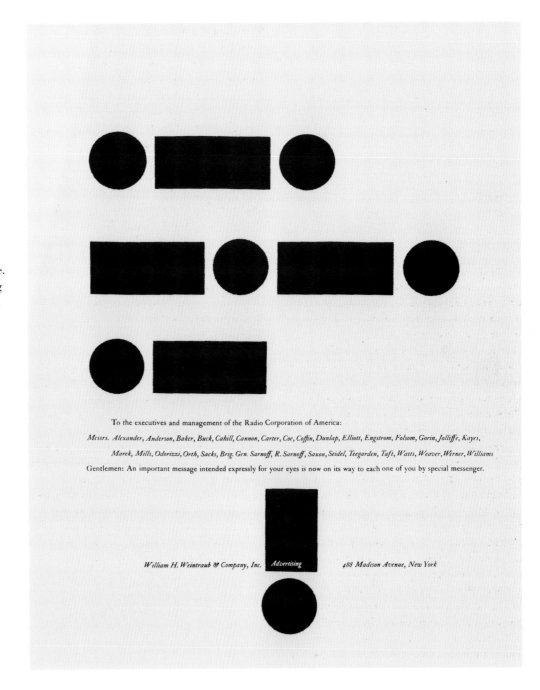

To the executives and management of the Radio Corporation of America:

Messrs. Alexander, Anderson, Baker, Buck, Cahill, Cannon, Carter, Coe, Coffin, Dunlap, Elliott, Engstrom, Folsom, Gorin, Jolliffe, Kayes,

Marek, Mills, Odorizzi, Orth, Sacks, Brig. Gen. Sarnoff, R. Sarnoff, Saxon, Seidel, Teegarden, Tuft, Watts, Weaver, Werner, Williams

Gentlemen: An important message intended expressly for your eyes is now on its way to each one of you by special messenger.

William H. Weintraub & Company, Inc.   *Advertising*   *488 Madison Avenue, New York*

Publishing: The play instinct at work

3

One thing is certain: no matter how successful Rand might have become as a fine artist, he would never have reached the vast audience he has reached, an audience that deserves better than it usually gets – that deserves more Paul Rands.

Percy Seitlin, 'Paul Rand, Commercial Artist: His Fantasy is Boundless', *American Artist*, October 1970

Paul Rand was the consummate graphic designer. It was in his blood; it was his reason for being. 'You have to sacrifice. There's no other way,' he proclaimed; and in fact, Rand forfeited much of his personal life to work. Two of his three marriages ended in divorce (the second marriage resulted in his only child). And as emotionally taxing as this was in his early years, he explained his devotion to his work with the credo, 'design is a way of life'.[2]

When Rand launched his career in the mid-1930s, the term 'graphic design' was rarely uttered. Coined in 1922 by W. A. Dwiggins in an article for the *Boston Evening Transcript* (titled 'New Kind of Printing Calls for New Design'), 'graphic designer' denoted a commercial artist who, like Dwiggins, engaged in a variety of intersecting print disciplines, such as layout, typography, type design and illustration for advertising, periodicals, books and packaging. Yet by the 1930s other classifications, including 'industrial designer', 'designer for industry' and 'modern artist for industry', were more frequently invoked to suggest the commercial artist's elevated standing within the realms of business and commerce. Rand, however, referred to himself simply as a graphic designer. He raised the status of the designation by his association with it, and defined the essence of the profession through the wide range of his work.

Rand was a generalist who believed that everything could benefit from good design, whether an advertisement for Coronet Brandy, a package for Schenley Liquor or a cover of *Direction* magazine. While he claimed to design everything the same way, differences were nevertheless inherent in each project. An advertisement posed a challenge distinct from that of a magazine cover or book jacket.

However, the key to Rand's process was beginning each with the same fundamental concern: imbuing every surface – page, poster, bottle or box – with the same sense of proportion, balance, harmony and, at times, dissonance if the outcome demanded it. Invariably, the solutions would be different, but the problem was always the same – how to arrange diverse elements to achieve aesthetic perfection and clear communication. For Rand, graphic design was a process of conveying messages intelligently, interestingly and wittily. The concepts came quickly and easily, so the challenge was how to achieve clarity and depth in a single entity. Formal questions of space and perspective took centre stage. In the same way that a painter moves paint to achieve an effect, Rand moved type, juxtaposed geometric forms and manipulated colour masses to frame an idea. Intuition was wedded to function, resulting in immaculate graphic design. Admirers commented that when looking at Rand's designs, one never has a doubt whether this line should go that way, whether this shape should not be a little larger or smaller, or whether a green star might not be better than the blue circle.

Most designers could not juggle as many different genres as Rand had mastered by his early thirties. Arguably, he was good at advertising because he conquered editorial space. At the same time, he was an exemplary editorial, book and package designer because he was expert at advertising. By the time Rand joined William H. Weintraub & Co. in 1941 he was already riding the crest of a new wave of graphic design; as agency art director he refocused his energies towards advertising, but kept a strong interest in periodical and book publishing. His temperament would not allow him to be without a project in some stage of execution. When his advertising assignments were securely underway, he did magazine covers, book jackets, packages and textiles. When he had a rare free moment, he designed furniture for his own home. Eventually, he designed his own home.

The freelance publishing assignments that Rand accepted during his tenure at Weintraub are the key to appreciating his increasing eminence during his late twenties and early thirties. Rand claimed that he produced 'the best stuff' between 1941 and 1955, ignoring subsequent achievements in the corporate world. His prolific output was indeed Herculean, given that he designed everything himself; but the quantity is incidental to the quality. He had a knack for hitting the right note virtually every time.

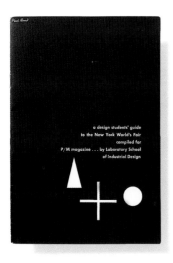

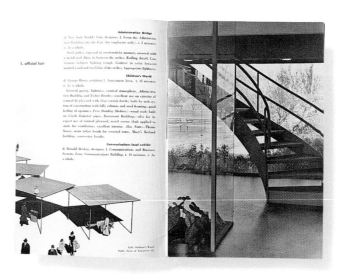

Rand's magazine covers and book jackets (the first jacket appeared in 1944) mark the laboratory phase of his early career. While his advertising for mass-market products defined him as an innovator in the commercial arena, his publishing work cast him as a master of modern form. Moreover, while he had proved that he could sell mass-market products with smart-looking ads, he felt proudest of his publishing achievements because they were the closest he came to pure art, apart from his occasional paintings and collages on canvas (which he ceased doing entirely in the mid-1950s). Rand's publishing work relied more on intuition than forethought, yet each piece was a fully realized conception that addressed all the principles of art and design which had fused into his virtuoso method.

Few magazine covers produced during the 1930s and 1940s were as sophisticated as *Apparel Arts*, fewer still as innovative as *Direction*. Arguably, the only comparable ones were covers for such arts magazines as *Verve* and *Minotaure* (by Matisse and Picasso) and the literary magazine *Transition* (by Miró), which Rand cites as influences. The covers for the graphics trade magazine *PM*, later *AD* (by E. McKnight Kauffer, Lester Beall, Herbert Bayer and others), exhibited similar aesthetics, yet even when compared to these Rand's covers were matchless, owing to the humour of his collage and the economy of his pen line. Created in the spirit of European modern art, Rand's covers were not mere pastiches of Constructivism, De Stijl, Dada or Surrealism, because he did not exploit the past or present as wellsprings of style: 'The idea of imitation is very prominent in Modernism,' he explained, referring to the ideological creed that 'you don't imitate anything.'[3]

In the 1930s mass-market magazine covers were as hard-sell as the advertisements contained inside them. Overly art-directed paintings and drawings were the norm. In order to reach the print stage they had to be sketched out, comped up, and finally passed through a gauntlet of editors before receiving approval to complete the finished art. Few such works survived

without considerable breaches of integrity. Admittedly, Rand did not do covers for those mass-market, news-stand periodicals where this was practised; but when it came to *Apparel Arts* and *Direction*, he simply refused to endure any kind of humiliating sketch and approval procedures. Although he made scores of concept and composition notations for himself, once he decided on the idea, he would not compromise. If the client rejected his comp, he would just move on to the next job.

In the late 1930s there were not as many significant design luminaries in the magazine field as eventually emerged during the 1950s. As Rand was starting out the most eminent was M. F. Agha, the innovative art director for Condé Nast's *Vanity Fair* from 1929 until 1936, who, when it folded, assumed the same position at *Vogue* until 1943. Agha's greatest contribution to magazine history was the modernization of *Vanity Fair*'s interior layouts; he increased the margins, allowed generous white space, introduced sans serif upper and lower case headlines, and commissioned both art photography and artistic cartoons. *Vanity Fair* had strikingly illustrated, poster-like covers by Miguel Covarrubias, William Cotton and Paolo Garretto, among others, and *Vogue*'s *au courant* covers integrated imaginative variations of the masthead

PM, magazine front and
back covers, 1939
This issue of *PM*, for which
Rand designed the covers,
contains the first article
ever written about him.

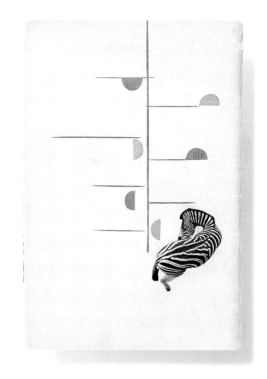

(or nameplate) with stunning photographs. These covers were consistent with the decorative style of the moderne era, and are viewed today as relics of their time. By comparison, however, Rand's compositional simplicity – and emphasis on the singular concept – continues to evoke a sense of timelessness.

Covers for *Fortune*, Henry Luce's lavish business magazine, were also milestones of applied art. The 1929 prototype, designed by the classically inspired advertising designer and typographer T. M. Cleland, included an elegant, shaded serif logotype placed in a frame that sat atop the artwork, which was also situated in a similar frame. The cover format echoed the Neoclassical architecture of Wall Street's financial institutions, while the artful cover images were akin to the murals that hung in their lobbies and rotundas. The cover art generally illustrated the magazine's contents in a monumental manner, while curiously rejecting typical business clichés. Cleland's own illustration for the first issue was a chiaroscuro line drawing that reprised eighteenth-century French book engraving, but *Fortune*'s subsequent covers were influenced by modern European posters – the same posters that had influenced the young Rand. In fact, two of Rand's heroes, the French poster artist A. M. Cassandre and the American

expatriate E. McKnight Kauffer, were among *Fortune*'s cover artists, as were Mexican muralist Diego Rivera and Bauhaus master Herbert Bayer. Although they are graphically strong, in retrospect *Fortune*'s covers were, like *Vogue*'s and *Vanity Fair*'s, essentially products of their time. Later, in the 1940s, after Austrian immigrant Will Burtin became art director, *Fortune*'s covers comprised more collage, montage and photography, but this approach certainly owes a debt to Rand's earlier innovations. Likewise, in the early 1940s, Burtin's (and Lester Beall's) covers for *Scope*, the smartly designed house organ of pharmaceutical manufacturer the Upjohn Company, included collages and montages, which, like *Direction*, were rooted in an abstract idiom. Here too Rand's influence is obvious.

Only *Harper's Bazaar* covers were equivalent to *Apparel Arts* or *Direction* in terms of originality. *Bazaar*'s art director Alexey Brodovitch, a Russian *émigré* who came to America by way of France, had an affinity for European modern art that developed while designing pages in Paris for Deberny & Peignot's graphic arts magazine, *Arts & Métiers Graphiques*, and illustrating advertisements for Madelois department store (in a manner similar to Cassandre). Brodovitch arrived in the United States in 1930 to teach in Philadelphia and moved to New York shortly after, where he rented a space in George Switzer's office (although Rand never directly encountered him there) and became art director for Saks Fifth Avenue. He was a leading proponent of journalistic and art photography before joining *Harper's Bazaar* in 1934, where he developed a distinct design persona based on photography.

Brodovitch and Rand shared many of the same artistic influences. Rand regarded Brodovitch highly, proclaiming that 'he never missed'. Brodovitch's interest in photography as an art form, however, distinguished his method of art direction, which was based on the narrative content of photographs, from Rand's method of designing, which relied on the pure graphic idea. Rand used photographs as tools in,

or components of, his overall design. Conversely, Brodovitch used photographs as dramatic story-telling devices framed by his design. Rand created iconic images. Brodovitch developed movement over many pages. Rand did not acknowledge the integrity of photographs; Brodovitch did. According to Frank Zachary, who worked with both men, 'Paul was intellectual, Brod was emotional';[4] which leads to another comparison.

Rand enjoyed designing magazine covers because it was the most valuable and visible piece of editorial real estate and, moreover, because he exercised total control over this dominion. But when faced with the prospect of designing the inside of a magazine, he had little patience and less interest. Rand's *Esquire* spreads, though innovative at the time, were more like advertisements than coordinated parts of the overall magazine. Since they were done independently from the rest of the editorial section, they were essentially islands of virtuosity in a sea of mediocrity. His interior design for *Ken*, a monthly magazine published by Esquire/Coronet that focused on political events through cartoons and photographs, was a miscellany of disparate pages rather than a unified whole. Even Rand once criticized this work (especially the logo) as misbegotten and best forgotten.

'Paul didn't think much of magazine design, and he himself was incapable of it,' argued Frank Zachary, referring to when, 1948, he began as editor of the short-lived but influential *Portfolio* magazine: 'When I was editing *Portfolio*, I asked Paul to do something in the way of a format, and he just couldn't do it.'[5] Rand designed what Zachary describes as the most beautiful letterhead and promotional brochure that he had ever seen (which are now lost), however, when he approached an editorial page he fussed over all the minute details, such as placement of the page numbers and the composition of the contents page, rather than focus on the magazine's overall pacing. Ultimately, the job of *Portfolio* art director/designer was given to Brodovitch, who did a monumental job. Zachary concluded that Rand was too much the artist, and not enough of the art director: 'He had to do his own thing; he could not manipulate the work of other people. He could only do a set piece.'[6]

Direction ceased publishing in 1945 (it was revived under new ownership a few years later with a mundane cover format), marking the conclusion of this decisive phase of Rand's experimentation. In 1945 he designed a cover for *The Architectural Forum* that more or less echoed his *Direction* aesthetic. But in 1946, while working with Zachary, Rand created one of his most important 'set pieces', the cover for the first (and only) issue of a biannual magazine *Jazzways*, devoted to new modern music. Rand was in heaven with an empty space on which to do anything he wanted – the only prerequisite was to design the magazine's masthead. Zachary had originally proposed that the painter Stuart Davis (a big jazz fan) design a cover to inaugurate the magazine – which at the time was equivalent to the progressive rock magazine *Rolling Stone* in the late 1960s – but decided to give the assignment to Rand (who adored Mozart but admired modern music). Presuming that Rand would do a symbolic illustration using photo collage in the manner of *Direction*, Zachary was surprised by the finished art. The *Jazzways* cover was one of Rand's most improvisational, humorous and audacious images to date: 'He put together the elements of jazz – the players and instruments – but rather than distilling the *essence* of it, he made an *image* out of it all … It is abstract, yet concrete as hell. As I remember it, it was part collage, part drawing, almost like an installation. I was stunned.'[7]

Jazzways owed a spiritual debt to Picasso's *Three Musicians*, a formal one to Paul Klee's childish scrawls, and a tip of the hat to the witty German trademark designers of the 1930s that Rand so admired. With these influences in mind, he reduced the elements of jazz to pure, improvisational symbolism – at once an eye-catching pattern and symbolic representation of the music's ethos. 'A symbol doesn't necessarily mean a trademark, or anything that is simple,' he explained; 'Anything can be a symbol.'[8] This cover not only symbolized the nature of the music, it provided an original approach to illustrative design that rejected heavy-handed rendering. The magazine was not as popular as had been hoped, but it won numerous design awards and, more important, it had profound implications on Rand's later book work.

In graphic design, invention is often eschewed as an anomaly, but Rand's efforts were rarely the result of sheer fluke. 'Originality is a product, not an intention,' Rand proclaimed in *Graphic Wit: The Art of Humor in Graphic Design* (1991).[9] He was always quick to emphasize that his intention was to create good design, not propagate novelty, but his end-products almost always challenged the status quo, in so far as he introduced new alternatives. In this sense, the *Apparel Arts*, *Direction* and *Jazzways* covers were hothouses for his abstract and conceptual methods, which were also applied to his advertising work. Yet these methods were developed even further through the scores of book jackets and paperback covers he produced between 1944 and 1970 (and intermittently thereafter).

Although overshadowed by his advertising and corporate careers, Rand's book jackets and covers are arguably just as significant, and even more crucial in defining him as an artist with a unique vision. Amidst his overall experience, book design was simply a logical expansion of his general practice. This field, however, was particularly mired in mediocrity, governed by marketing conventions, and more often than not indifferent to content. Many publishers scrutinized the interior typography of their books, but surprisingly few were concerned with how their books were wrapped. Jackets were considered necessary evils, the province of marketing departments, designed as advertisements to hook customers into consuming on impulse. Book designers and editors alike referred to them as unwanted appendages of the pristine book. Nevertheless, the jacket was prime for revamping when Rand was hired by a few progressive publishers to help improve their presentations, and, by extension, raise the aesthetic standards of the entire genre.

Ever since dust-wrappers were introduced in early nineteenth-century England, they had not been perceived as integral to book design and binding. Initially they were wrapping-paper coverings with rectangular cutouts that revealed the book's title, designed only to keep dust and soot (the residue of Victorian London's coughing chimneys) from soiling expensive leather covers. In late nineteenth-century America, artwork was introduced onto wrappers, or jackets, as a means to distinguish books and attract the public's attention. Soon, so-called advertising 'blurbs' or testimonials from other writers or critics were printed on the flaps and back of these jackets to entice prospective readers – thus a publishing convention known as 'log-rolling' was born. During the 1920s and 1930s the dust-jacket was additionally spruced up with full colour, stylized paintings and drawings, and titled with decorative lettering. This served as a mini-poster and fulfilled what

become known as the ten-foot rule: that a jacket image must be seen by passers-by from a distance of ten feet, anything less was ineffectual.

The cover image, therefore, was not always motivated by content. Frequently the illustrator/designer would not read the manuscript, but rather scan a summary of the plot and description of its characters. The result might be an eye-catching picture or design that often had little relevance to the narrative. Usually, the jacket was not designed by the same designer as the interior and bore no resemblance to the overall typography of the binding, title page or interior. The jacket was purposefully ostentatious, while the cover and all the other components conformed to the finer points of design. W. A. Dwiggins, one of the rare bookmen who designed jackets *and* interiors, frequently criticized his own jackets as being too vulgar. In fact, a schism developed between jacket and book interior designers that continued well into the 1950s. The latter distanced themselves by belonging to exclusive 'book builder' societies, forcing jacket designers to form their own 'national' Book Jacket Designers' Guild.

Rand believed that book jackets were no different from any other medium that could benefit from good design, and he was convinced that this particular medium had even greater potential as an outlet for art than did advertising or magazines. A book jacket did not have to be slavishly literal; it had to convey moods or interpret content. Not only were graphic symbols the perfect shorthand, but colour, shapes and lettering could also provide the requisite cues. Presumably the designer could have more control if the advertising and marketing experts could be kept at bay; and since Rand was already rather skilled at getting his way, he did not foresee that this would be a stumbling block.

In fact, Rand always worked with sympathetic (i.e. 'good') clients. Wittenborn & Company (later Wittenborn, Schultz) gave him ample licence to push the boundaries of their art book jackets and covers. He used all the methods in his growing repertoire to give each book an individual presence, as well as an overall Wittenborn identity. Advertising taught him the virtue of anchoring concepts to a consistent design element, such as a logo. In the case of the Wittenborn books, consistency was achieved through the use of bold sans serif titles typeset unobtrusively to underscore the contemporary

spirit of the books that he designed. Beyond this, the rest depended on the content of the book itself. Although he was adamant about not being pigeonholed by a particular look, a Rand style emerged. This, however, was hard to pin down. 'Describing Paul Rand's style remains somewhat akin to catching lightning in a bottle,' wrote Allen Hurlburt, who worked as Rand's assistant at Weintraub in the mid-1940s; '[He is] one of the few designers practising today whose work can be identified without his signature.'[10] While Rand himself rejected the notion of a tangible personal style, he acknowledged that a personal *approach* probably developed as a consequence of 'recurrent habits, restraints, or rules invented or inherited, intuitive, or preconceived'.[11] He reduced the complexities of a book to a single idea that either represented the whole or focused on a part of the text. As with his magazine covers, he created symbols that distilled the book's essence.

Rand's earliest jacket for Guillaume Apollinaire's *The Cubist Painters* (1944) was his first attempt at pure abstraction: smudges of colour adorn the jacket, with a simple, unobtrusive line of sans serif type for the title. This jacket was the prototype for the series, 'The Documents of Modern Art'. Not only did it differ from typical American art book jackets, which convention dictated were either all type or showed a detail of a painting – in line with his dictum against copying – but Rand's interpretation did not even mimic the Cubist style. Rather, it evoked the essence of the revolutionary art form. Designing art books in such an 'artistic' way might seem appropriate to the subject, but before Rand it was almost exclusive to European avant-garde designers. By using Bauhaus and Italian Futurist books among other touchstones, Rand developed a vocabulary of shapes and colours that evoked modernity. He also used a medley of antiquated visual elements in collages to illustrate ancient and classical art. For the jacket of *Origins of Modern Sculpture* (1946), he juxtaposed two silhouettes – an ancient sculpture and Brancusi's sculpture of an egg (a pun on 'origins') – divided by a small line of sans serif type. Through this iconic pairing he astutely summarized centuries of artistic evolution.

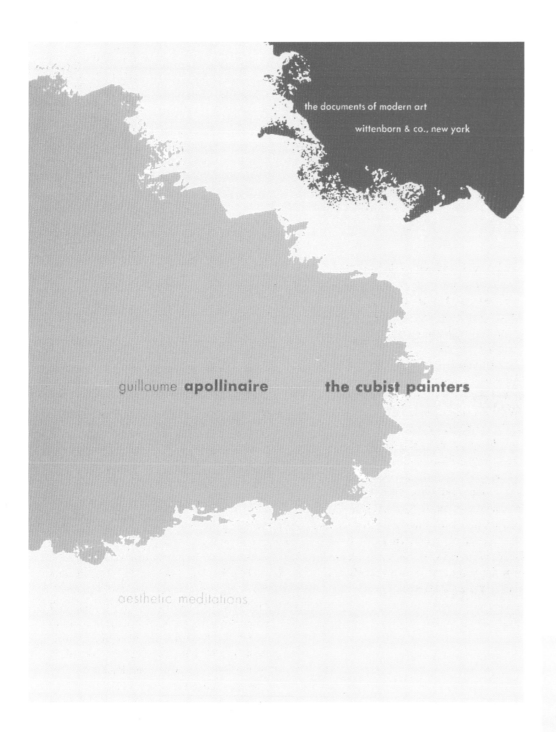

DADA, book jacket, Wittenborn & Company, 1967
Rand abhorred pastiche, so much so that even the jackets on books about specific periods in time were recast using his own graphic vocabulary. Although *DADA* had a distinctive typographic style, Rand's own interpretation of Robert Motherwell's book was rendered in his own contemporary approach.

Right:
Origins of Modern Sculpture, book jacket, Wittenborn, Schultz, 1946
Most art book jackets showed details of either an iconic painting or of a sculpture. Rand preferred to make an editorial statement in this instance: a montage that shows the formal similarities between representational and abstract art.

Origins of Modern Sculpture

In 1945 Rand was commissioned to design jackets for Alfred A. Knopf Inc., one of New York's most prestigious small literary publishers. Alfred Knopf, himself a design-aware bookman with a penchant for fine typography and illustration, kept his eyes opened for new talents that could give his publishing house its distinctive graphic image. Rand was invited to join an eclectic repertory of classical and modernistic designers, including W. A. Dwiggins, Rudolf Ruzicka, Ernest Reichl and Warren Chappell. As part of his initiation he was asked to do a version of Knopf's Borzoi logo, the sleek Russian hound whose running silhouette was stamped on every spine and was rendered by the other designers in pen and ink or woodcut, usually in a traditional manner. Rand graphically reduced the elegant canine to a few simple straight lines at right angles, with a full stop for an eye. Prefiguring his later makeovers of venerable corporate logos that began in the mid-1950s, this was a textbook example of Rand's ability to redefine a visual problem and devise an alternative solution that pledged allegiance to the original form. Although it shocked his colleagues, Knopf was quite taken with the audacity of the design, whose radical transformation of the mark retained its essential mnemonic quality. Rand's Borzoi was used exclusively on his own jackets at the time, but decades later it is still found on many current Knopf books.

Like the Borzoi logo, Rand's first jacket for Knopf, Thomas Mann's *The Tables of the Law* (1945), raised eyebrows at the time of publication. It was certainly Knopf's most reductive jacket, and ironically, given the book's biblical theme, it was also the publisher's first truly modern jacket. The image was a dramatically lit, silhouetted photograph of the head of Michelangelo's *Moses*, partially covering the stacked lines of gothic headline type, which like a billboard screamed out, 'The Law'. The solid brown background colour did not fill the entire image area but, like a window blind, stopped before reaching the jacket's bottom, leaving a channel of empty white space that gave an illusion of three-dimensionality against the base of the photograph. The jacket's *ad hoc* quality gives the impression that Rand cut and pasted the art and type together in an instantaneous burst of creative energy, reminiscent of a Dada collage. In fact, he laboured over his solution until he achieved the appearance of an accident. Everything was precisely composed, yet slightly off kilter.

Manipulating ragged cuts of paper and torn photographs, often using an informal, hand-scrawled script, Rand's jackets and covers were not so much mini-posters as small playthings. Perhaps in another life he would have been a toymaker, because he loved the magic of combining shapes, colours and objects into sculptural cartoons. Yet there was a serious side to this: 'I use the term "play", but I mean coping with the problems of form and content, weighing relationships, establishing priorities', Rand explained years later in *Graphic Wit*. Each book title offered him the stimulus and rationale to play with or manipulate a multitude of forms, from drawing to collage, from lettering to type. There was never a preordained format or formula. Curiously, the only real precedent for his jackets were the package labels he designed for Schenley Liquors which, a critic noted, contain 'the same elements of gaiety, grace, and surprise as his advertising'.[12]

Left, below:
Borzoi Books, logos,
Alfred A. Knopf, 1945
The publisher, Alfred A.
Knopf, asked all his book
designers to reinterpret
his Borzoi logo and all
rendered it in a more or
less conventional manner
(for example by Warren
Chappel, left). Rand,
however, could not resist
reducing the sleek
creature to a few lines
with a dot for the eye
(right).

Below and below, right:
The Tables of the Law,
book jacket and case
covering, Alfred A.
Knopf, 1945

The first book jacket and
book designed by Rand
for Knopf was the
publisher's most
contemporary. Rand used
Michelangelo's sculpture
of Moses placed against
a modern typographic
treatment. The binding
was composed of ancient
glyphs, resembling a Paul
Klee painting. The interior

was restrained in the
classical tradition, but
nonetheless contemporary.
The author, Thomas
Mann, was pleased with
the result and said so in
Rand's own inscribed
copy.

Rand's book jackets for Alfred A. Knopf never adhered to a rigid style but were always recognizable as his. The signature gave it away, of course, but even more distinctive was his use of found objects, cut papers, and minimal typography. His jackets of the late 1940s and early 1950s helped to alter the standards of the genre.

Clockwise from top:
American Son, book jacket, Alfred A. Knopf, 1954
Traps, book jacket, Alfred A. Knopf, 1956
The Fervent Years, 1931–41: The Story of the Group Theatre and the Thirties, book jacket, Alfred A. Knopf, 1945

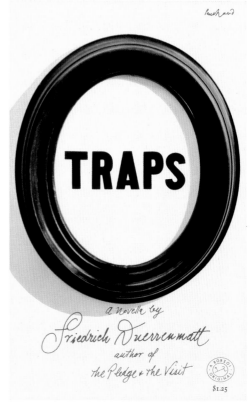

Clockwise from top left:
The Second Man, book jacket, Alfred A. Knopf, 1956
The New Borzoi Book of Ballets, book jacket, Alfred A. Knopf, 1956
Leave Me Alone, book jacket, Alfred A. Knopf, 1957
The Lost Steps, book jacket, Alfred A. Knopf, 1956

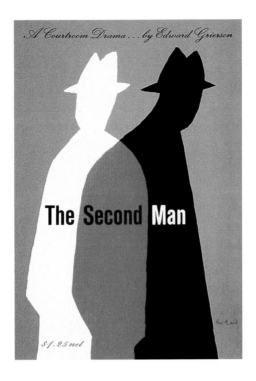

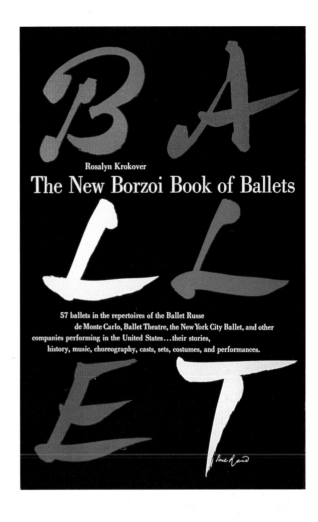

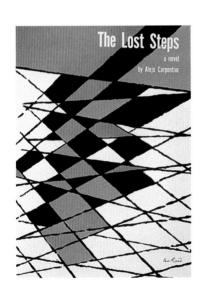

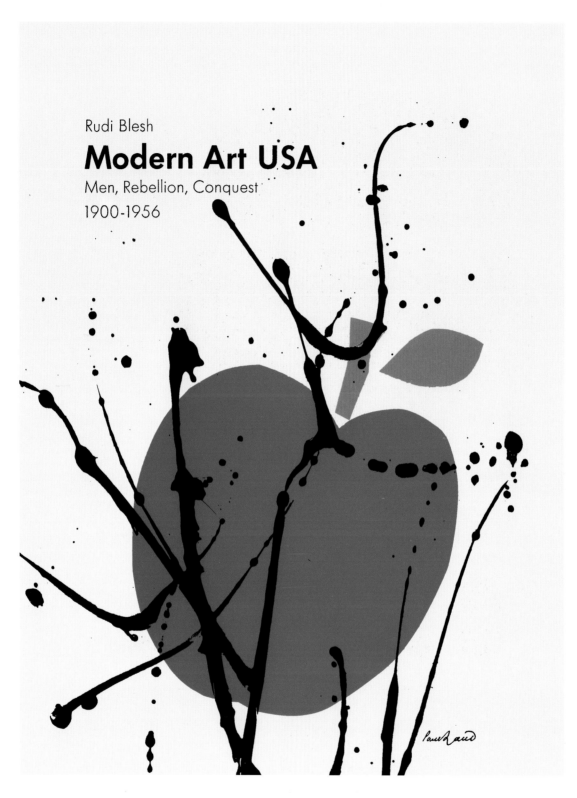

Rudi Blesh

Modern Art USA

Men, Rebellion, Conquest

1900-1956

Modern Art USA: Men, Rebellion, Conquest, 1900–1956, book jacket, Alfred A. Knopf, 1956 Rand's jackets and covers were both mini canvases and mini posters. He composed the limited image area for maximum impact. He also did not distinguish between hardback jackets and paperback covers. Rand rejected the convention that dictated that paperbacks be more commercial and cluttered with marketing copy. These two examples employ the same basic attributes for the same purpose: to capture attention through provocative forms.

Caligula
and 3 other
plays

Albert

CAMUS

Awarded the Nobel Prize for Literature in 1957

Including:

The Misunderstanding

State of Siege

The Just Assassins

With a New Introduction

Below:
Leave Cancelled, book
jacket, Alfred A. Knopf,
1945
One of Rand's earliest and
most audacious book
jackets, this romantic tale of
lovers torn asunder by war
is symbolized by the floating
image of Eros shot with
bullet holes. Influenced by
artist's books of the 1920s,
Rand's decision to die-cut
the holes was not about
novelty but function in the
service of the idea.

Right:
Paul Rand, 1970
(photographer:
Milton Ackoff)
Rand is seen signing a
poster of his Mencken
cover, which was shown
at his 1970 retrospective
exhibition at the IBM
Gallery in New York.

Far right:
H. L. Mencken,
Prejudices: A Selection,
book cover, Vintage
Books/Random House,
1958
This was one of Rand's
favourite covers. 'What
else could I do with such
a lousy photograph?' he
asked rhetorically. The
answer: he made it into
a paper doll that under-
scored the essence of the
pontificating social pundit.

Scores of jackets and covers illustrate Rand's
play principle at work, but two of his favourites,
created twelve years apart, show how his
experiments evolved. The first was a jacket for
Nicholas Monsarrat's *Leave Cancelled* (Knopf,
1945), a tragic tale of lovers separated by war.
The second was for James T. Farrell's *H. L.
Mencken: Prejudices: A Selection* (Vintage 1958),
an analysis of the acerbic social critic's most
biting essays. For *Leave Cancelled* Rand
requested that 'bullet' holes be die-cut through
the cover photograph of Eros, the god of love.
The technique was unheard of with a trade book
at that time – indeed everything about this
jacket was so unprecedented and fanciful that
Alfred Knopf's wife was reported to have called
the final result an 'expensive extravagance'.
Rand also designed the binding, which featured
an embossed line drawing of the broken hands
of a clock, symbolizing the protagonist's
premature return to the battlefield. Rand took
his inspiration from European avant-garde art
books, but he also prefigured contemporary
artists' books in the introduction of tactile
bookmaking materials that added drama and
expression to the entire package.

leave
cancelled
by nicholas
monsarrat

Rand was more limited in what he could do for the paperback cover of *H. L. Mencken: Prejudices: A Selection*. The budgets for paperback covers were even smaller than for hardback jackets; consequently the printing options were fewer. However Rand recalled that his solution was built into the raw material he was given. Starting with a 'lousy' photograph of Mencken, he magically produced a comic image that became a virtual logo for the writer. 'What could one do with a bad portrait of the guy?' Rand explained in *Graphic Wit*. 'I cut up the photo into a silhouette of someone making a speech, which bore no relation to the shape of the [original] photo. That was funny, in part because of the ironic cropping and because Mencken was such a curmudgeon.'[13] The result was a kind of paper doll in the satiric form of an oratorical statue. The ragged contours of the cut photograph dictated that a hand-scrawled title and byline be dropped out of irregularly cut and randomly positioned colour boxes. Each of these elements was crude, but in total the pieces fitted perfectly together. The Mencken cover echoed the raucous informality of Futurist and Constructivist book covers from the 1920s, but was far ahead of its time in American trade publishing of the 1950s.

A Bell For Adano,
advertisement, 1945
Occasionally, Rand would
design book ads for Alfred
A. Knopf. For this one
he photographed hands
ringing a bell at St Patrick's
Cathedral, New York,
and then made a multiple
exposure.

In addition to jackets and covers, Rand created an occasional advertisement at Alfred Knopf's personal request. One such for John Hersey's *A Bell for Adano* (1945), with two hands pulling on ropes that cut through the length of the ad, was a dynamic composition in a genre where text-heavy and pictorially weak ads were common. Frank Zachary was with Rand when he conceived and created the artwork, and recalls that this process was typical of his hands-on method. When Rand did freelance work that required photography, for example, he rented a cubicle in a photographer's studio over Schrafft's Restaurant on Fifth Avenue. As Zachary related:

'Paul always did everything himself … He shot a photo of the dangling rope at St Patrick's and once in the darkroom he took the negative of the static ropes, pulled it through the enlarger just enough to get the effect of movement and then laid on the type.'[14]

The entire exercise was completed very quickly because Rand was totally confident that his idea worked. 'Paul once told me that when he was presented with a problem,' Zachary continued, 'the first idea that came to his mind was the solution. No matter what he did after, he always came back to that. It was always the first idea.'[15]

At Knopf, Rand's ideas were never questioned. Harry Ford, production manager and art director from 1947 to 1959, recalls: 'We bent over backwards to give Paul what he wanted because he was so good.'[16] Booksellers were 'bowled over', competitive publishers were also impressed, although 'since most publishers were set in their ways, few wanted to copy what Rand did. Nevertheless, there was widespread agreement that his method was revolutionary.'[17]

Of course not all of Rand's jackets and covers were equally visionary, and a few may seem laboured today. The tendency for simplification that made the Mencken cover so startling sometimes resulted in imagery that was too facile. Nevertheless, Rand defined a standard for the conceptual jacket and cover genre that other designers ultimately followed.

A BELL FOR ADANO

A novel endearing as it is important, which has stirred the hearts of thousands of readers.

Selected by eight out of ten of the nation's leading critics as "the best novel of the year."

Credited by TIME MAGAZINE with "a clean sweep of critical and popular honors for the year."

Chosen by *Harry Hansen* and *Orville Prescott*, in annual summaries, as "the best novel of the year."

Declared an "Imperative" by the Council on Books in Wartime.

An immediate success in its stage version: "one of the finest war plays you will ever see," says *Howard Barnes* in the NEW YORK HERALD TRIBUNE..."a new bell which probably will be shaking the theatre district for some time to come," says *Lewis Nichols*, NEW YORK TIMES.

"Likely to stay for the duration."... LIFE MAGAZINE.

John **Hersey's**
"terrific little masterpiece"
A Bell for Adano...
is on sale at all
bookstores at 2.50
It is a *Borzoi* Book
published in New York by
Alfred A. **Knopf.**

By the late 1940s, there were two primary methods of book jacket design: modern and calligraphic. The former was reductive, the latter was fussy. In contrast to Rand, George Salter was a prolific jacket designer who did innovative work in his native Germany in the 1930s, but in America during the late 1940s and 1950s he was well known (and very prolific) for a calligraphic style that exemplified a mannered school of lettering, which Rand mildly disparaged: 'I never did calligraphy … But handwriting is an entirely different kind of thing. It's part of the syndrome of Modernism. It's part of that asceticism.'[18] At a time when many people believed that modern art was cold, intellectual and accessible only to an educated élite, Rand made it seem friendly and accessible. As the designer and design historian Louis Danziger explained: 'He did this largely through colloquial, idiomatic, humorous and witty images. Using his own handwriting was not only economical and expedient but contributed to that "friendliness".'[19]

Below left:
Wake Up, Stupid, book jacket, Alfred A. Knopf, 1959
This seemingly *ad hoc* cover was not so easy to produce. Rand worked hard to get immediacy.

Below:
Zen and Japanese Culture, book cover, Bollingen Series, 1958
This is one of Rand's most subtle visual puns in which the lettering is like a typical Japanese brush drawing of a mountain and landscape.

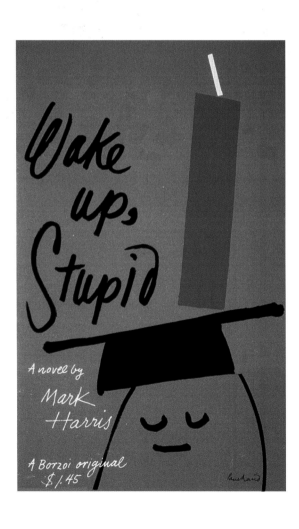

Below:

The Revelations of Dr Modesto, book jacket, Alfred A. Knopf, 1955 Rand used amorphous forms to suggest the plot and evoke a sense of mystery.

Right:

A Fine Frenzy, book cover, Alfred A. Knopf, 1959 Rand perfected his handwriting style on covers for *Direction* and continued to employ the method on book jackets and covers to underscore the informality of his artwork.

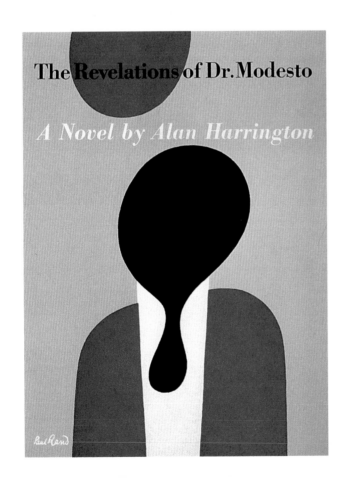

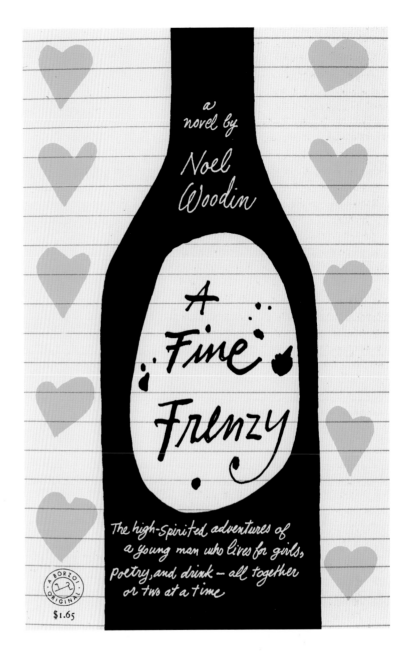

This page:

The American Essays of Henry James, book cover, Vintage Books/Random House, 1956
Rand makes a commentary on James' dual literary life by repeating his profile as a silhouette.

Poetics of Music in the Form of Six Lessons, book cover, Vintage Books/Random House, 1956
A homage to Picasso, Rand's portrait of Igor Stravinsky is drawn on a musical notepad.

The Captive Mind, book cover, Vintage Books/Random House, 1955
Rand loved masks of all kinds. To illustrate Czeslaw Milosz's book, this image evokes a sense of imprisonment.

Opposite page, clockwise from left:
The Transposed Heads, book cover, Vintage Books/Random House, 1959
Rand would always draw ideas from the texts and inspiration from art history. This book is a synthesis of Indian and European art.

The Social History of Art, book cover, Vintage Books/Random House, 1957
Sometimes his covers and jackets were just basic visual elements, which were determined by the content of the book as well as the limitations of the budget. Book work, incidentally, was notoriously badly paid.

The Road to Xanadu, book cover, Vintage Books/Random House, 1959

Wagner as Man and Artist, book cover, Vintage Books/Random House, 1962
Rand had a passion for the history of letter forms. Although he used only the most functional serif and sans serif typefaces (and his own handwriting) for titles, he found that the sculptural quality of certain antique typefaces was well suited to illustration.

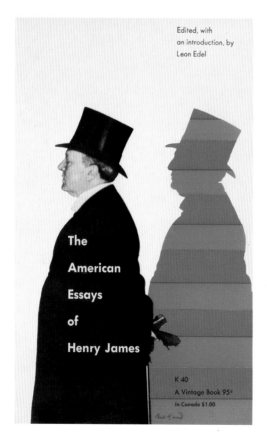

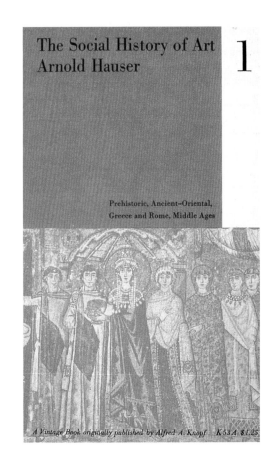

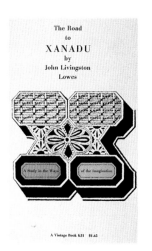

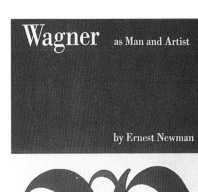

The Anatomy of Revolution

Crane Brinton

A Vintage Book
K44 $/25
in Canada $/35

Paul Rand

The Anatomy of Revolution, book cover, Vintage Books/Random House, 1956
This cover is typical of the way in which Rand reduced a huge topic, revolution, into a demonstrative logo.

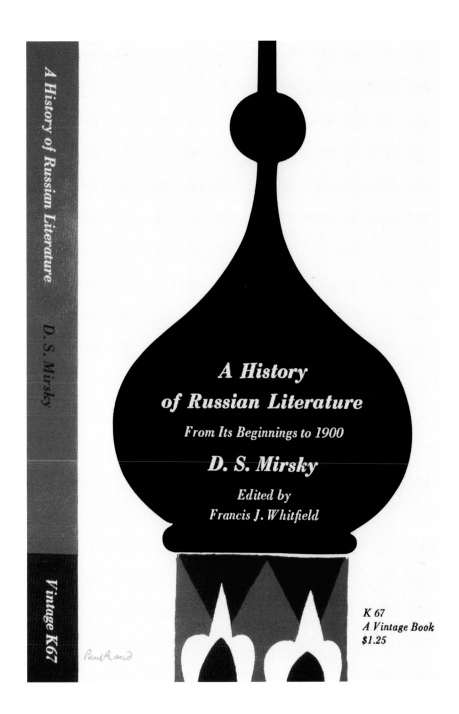

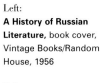

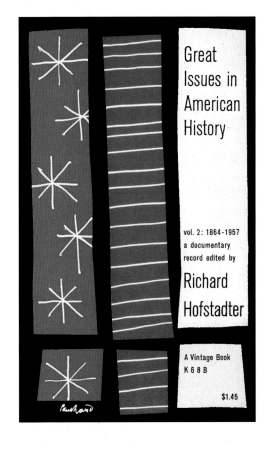

Below:
Plato: An Introduction, book jacket, Bollingen Series LIX.1, Pantheon Books, 1956

Right:
Art and Illusion, book jacket, Bollingen Series XXXV.5, Pantheon Books, 1956
While his other publishing clients used various designers, Rand was Bollingen's exclusive designer for over a decade. Around the same time that he was beginning to develop a consistent identity for IBM, he was also developing a 'character' for this publisher.

Although the Knopf (and later Vintage, Doubleday, Atheneum, Harvard and Harvest Books) jackets and covers were ostensibly illustrative, Rand continued his exploration of pure abstraction with jackets produced between 1956 and 1964 for the Bollingen series, published by Pantheon Books. Using colour fields, geometric and amorphic shapes, and random splatters combined with his distinctive scrawl, these jackets were more akin to small canvases than conventional wrappers. And while they were overtly less playful than his other, mass-market jackets, they were no less eye-catching – and in a way even more enduring.

The Bollingen Foundation was founded in 1947 by the Andrew W. Mellon family to encourage the teachings of, and publish works by, the psychoanalyst Carl Jung. In addition to Jung's own books and essays, and those by Jungian scholars, Bollingen also supported art and social histories, notably E. H. Gombrich's *Art and Illusion*, and published papers presented at the prestigious A. W. Mellon lectures. Pantheon Books, a small publishing house, was run by the literary visionaries Helen and Kurt Wolf with Jacques Schifrin, who had emigrated from Germany to New York and published important European authors. Pantheon's role was to package and distribute Bollingen's books on a

regular schedule. Rand was introduced to Pantheon's production editor, Wolfgang Sauerlander, by Flora Gross, a freelance production expert and designer (and later director of the American Institute of Graphic Arts who had commissioned Rand to design the AIGA's current logo), which began a very fruitful relationship. Sauerlander was an avid supporter, and made certain that Rand never had to hawk his ideas to the editors. There was no Rand concept that he could not successfully explain to the Bollingen people, or a Rand jacket that was ever killed. In return for their trust, Rand developed an unmistakable identity that underscored the serious aim of Bollingen while highlighting the accessibility of the list. Rand did the Bollingen jackets until 1964, when the series moved from Pantheon to Princeton and a new designer was hired.

Bollingen Series LIX 1
Pantheon Books

PLATO
An Introduction

Paul Friedländer

PLATO
An Introduction

Paul Friedländer

Art and Illusion

E. H. Gombrich

The A. W. Mellon
Lectures in the Fine Arts, 1956
Bollingen Series xxxv/5
Pantheon

This page:
Evangelical Theology,
book cover,
Doubleday/Anchor Books
*c.*1960
The Future of an Illusion,
book cover,
Doubleday/Anchor Books
*c.*1960
**Of Time, Work, and
Leisure,** book cover,
Doubleday/Anchor Books
*c.*1960

Opposite page,
clockwise from top left:
The Acquisitive Society,
book cover, Harvest
Books, 1955
Six Nonlectures, book
cover, Atheneum, 1962
**The Diplomats:
1919–1939,** book cover,
Atheneum, 1963
Love Against Hate, book
cover, Harvest Books,
1959

Rand's book jackets and
covers – for a variety of
publishers – were based
on the idea of the book,
not the identity of the
house. These examples
show a wide range of
methods for designing
paperback covers.

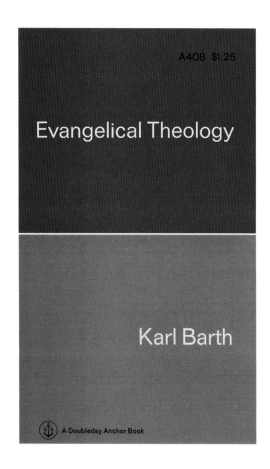

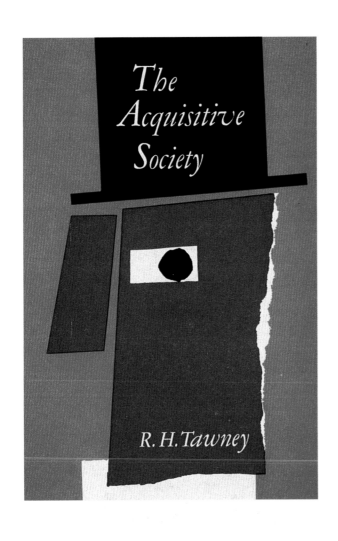

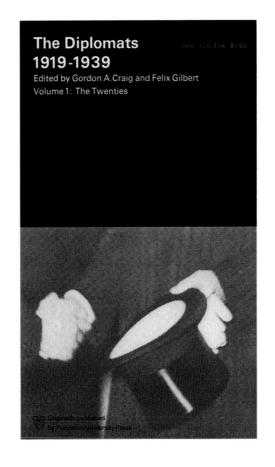

Clockwise from top:
Seamarks, book jacket,
Bollingen Series LXVII,
Pantheon Books, 1958
Shamanism, book jacket,
Bollingen Series, LXXVI,
Pantheon Books, 1964
The Living Symbol, book
jacket, Bollingen Series
LXIII, Pantheon Books,
1961
**Paracelsus: Selected
Writings,** book jacket,
Bollingen Series XXVIII,
Pantheon Books, 1962

Rand was never called
upon to design jackets
for mass market fiction –
it was not his style – but
this abstract approach was
well suited to taking the
pedantic edge off books of
serious scholarship.

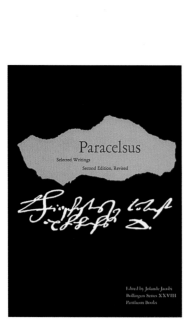

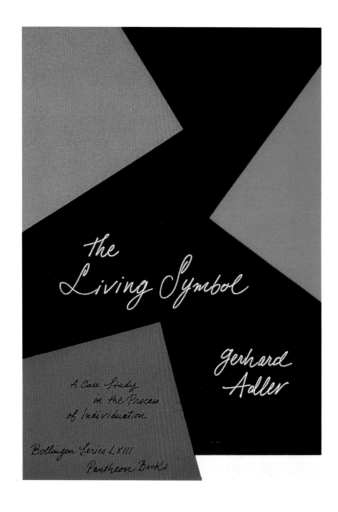

Clockwise from below:
Mudra: A Study of Symbolic Gestures in Japanese Buddhist Sculpture, book jacket, Bollingen Series LVIII, Pantheon Books, 1960
The Archetypal World of Henry Moore, book jacket, Bollingen Series LXVIII, Pantheon Books, 1959
The Portrait in the Renaissance, book jacket, Bollingen Series XXXV.12, Pantheon Books, 1963

Rand used photographs and paintings not only to add a level of information to his design, but as a graphic focal point. In these jackets the image is a prop to suggest the themes within.

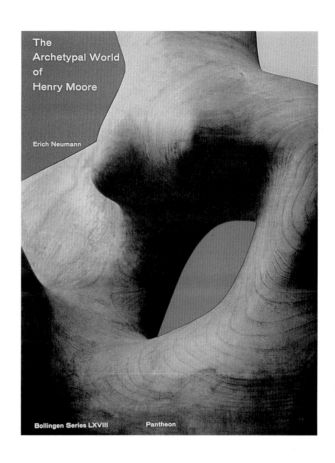

The
Archetypal World
of
Henry Moore

Erich Neumann

Bollingen Series LXVIII   Pantheon

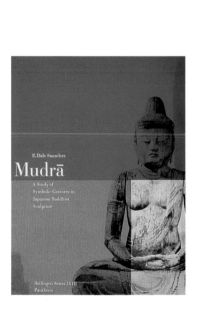

E. Dale Saunders

Mudrā

A Study of
Symbolic Gestures in
Japanese Buddhist
Sculpture

Bollingen Series LVIII
Pantheon

The A. W. Mellon Lectures in the Fine Arts, 1963

The Portrait
in the Renaissance

by John Pope-Hennessy

Bollingen Series XXXV.12
Pantheon

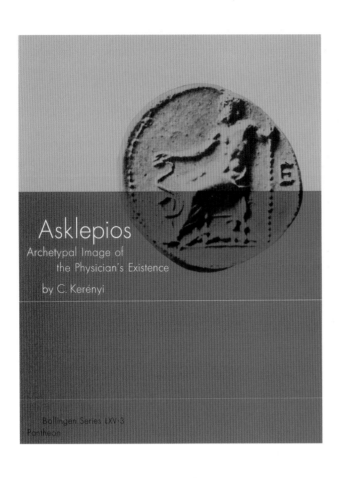

Asklepios: Archetypal Image of the Physician's Existence, book jacket, Bollingen Series LXV.3, Pantheon Books, 1959
Prometheus: Archetypal Image of Human Existence, book jacket, Bollingen Series LXV.1, Pantheon Books, 1963
Eleusis: Archetypal Image of Mother and Daughter, book jacket, Bollingen Series LXV.4, Pantheon Books, 1963

For this series of archetypal images Rand developed a somewhat untypical (for him) grid on which he layered transparent colour over a representative image from antiquity.

Eleusis
Archetypal Image of
Mother and Daughter
by C. Kerényi

Bollingen Series LXV· 4
Pantheon

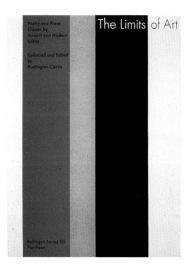

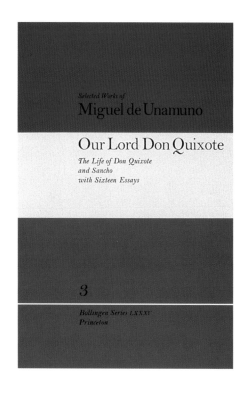

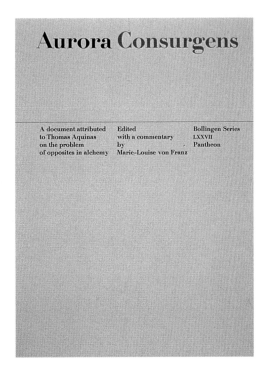

Aurora Consurgens

| A document attributed to Thomas Aquinas on the problem of opposites in alchemy | Edited with a commentary by Marie-Louise von Franz | Bollingen Series LXXVII Pantheon |

On Quality in Art

By Jakob Rosenberg

Criteria of Excellence Past and Present

The A. W. Mellon lectures in the Fine Arts 1964 Bollingen Series XXXV.13 Princeton

The A. W. Mellon Lectures in the Fine Arts, 1959 Bollingen Series XXXV.8 Pantheon

Naum Gabo   Of Divers Arts

Opposite page, clockwise from top left:
The Limits of Art, book jacket, Bollingen Series XII, Pantheon Books, 1960
The 'I' and the 'Not-I', book jacket, Bollingen Series LXXLX, Pantheon Books, 1965
Our Lord Don Quixote, book jacket, Bollingen Series LXXXV, Pantheon Books, 1967
The Great Mother, book jacket, Bollingen Series XLVII, Pantheon Books, 1963

This page, clockwise from far left:
On Quality in Art, book jacket, Bollingen Series XXXV.13, Pantheon Books, 1967
Aurora Consurgens, book jacket, Bollingen Series LXXVII, Pantheon Books, 1966
Of Divers Arts, book jacket, Bollingen Series XXXV.8, Pantheon Books, 1961
To offset the limited budgets for Bollingen jackets, Rand was given freedom within the parameters of the material. Compared to jackets and covers for Alfred A. Knopf and others, these appear somewhat conservative, but nevertheless enabled Rand to test both the formal and playful sides of his personality.

Among the modern designers with whom Rand had an affinity, and perhaps a healthy rivalry, Alvin Lustig, an American-born designer of books, magazines, textiles and sign systems, was the most prolific. Lustig (along with Herbert Bayer) was also invited by Alfred Knopf to design jackets. But Lustig had made his name starting in 1940 as a designer for the small literary publisher New Directions (which shared the same floor as Pantheon Books). At that time he was making imagery from hot-metal typecase 'furniture', using a similar method to that of Russian Constructivist books by El Lissitzky and Alexander Rodchenko. By the mid-1940s, however, when he was designing all the jackets in New Directions' 'New Classics' series, Lustig had combined modern type with abstract line drawings, or what he called symbolic 'marks', which owed more to the work of such artists as Paul Klee, Joan Miró and Mark Rothko than to accepted commercial styles. Like jazz improvisations, these non-representational images signalled the progressive nature of his publishing house. During the late 1940s he introduced collage/montage and reticulated photography, evoking surrealistic fantasies. And in the early 1950s he developed a series of paperback covers for Noonday and Meridian Books using only gothic and slab serif typography. Rand and Lustig clearly shared certain traits, since they were both fluent in the language of Modernism – each had a similar preference for contemporary typefaces and child-like scribbles – but each interpreted Modernism in their own ways, and no doubt competed for who could alter the form faster. Some insist it was a dead heat.

Rand always enjoyed a good conquest, and he considered book design a territory that was ripe for invasion. In 1945, without previous experience in book design – a craft that was jealously guarded by traditional typographers and compositors – he began designing bindings, title pages and entire books, which in concert with other modernist book designers contributed to changing the standards of design and production. In the 1940s and 1950s production managers usually ruled over the interior design of books, while in some publishing houses respected designers held control. Nevertheless, the traditional sensibilities governing bookmaking, which dated back to seventeenth-century Italian printers, frequently prevailed. Books were often designed to reference the period evoked by the text; so that an early nineteenth-century theme was designed in an early nineteenth-century manner, or at least using a revivalist typeface. Rand's initial foray into these guarded precincts was with the biblically inspired *The Tables of the Law*, for which he also designed the jacket.

Since Rand was a functionalist, he respected those rules that contributed to legibility, and his interior book design was clean and handsome. His typography illuminated the theme of the book, but it was void of allusions to the past. In *Books For Our Time* (1951), the first major exhibition and catalogue of contemporary interior book design sponsored by the AIGA, Rand's work was featured among others who challenged taboos and conventions. While snobbishly ignoring the jacket entirely, the editor Marshall Lee's analysis of Rand's design for *The Tables of the Law* captured its essence: 'The arrangement of rules on the half title page induces the notion of the tablets, contains a numerical allusion to the ten commandments, and, together with the symbols on the binding, establishes an air of timelessness appropriate to the subject that antedates any historical typographic style.'[20] Referring to this book as a practical example of modern design theory, Rand maintained in a 1945 essay in *Book Binding and Book Production* that, 'The designer might be guided somewhat in the way he plans the book from the description of the bygone era, but to simulate that period is absurd.'[21]

Goodbye, Columbus and 5 Short Stories, book cover, Meridian, 1959 Rand illustrated Philip Roth's sexually obsessive novel eloquently. This was his first idea, but getting the right lips took him days.

Rand's House, Weston, Connecticut, *c.*1970 Rand, with his wife Ann, designed his own house in Weston, where he lived and worked from 1952 until his death. A paean to Modernism, the design is clearly influenced by the architect Marcel Breuer, to whose designs Rand had built his previous residence in Harrison, New York.

While Rand refused to adhere to outdated rules and modes of composition, he never entirely rejected classical design, especially venerable typefaces, when deemed appropriate: 'It is a mistake to think that the modern typographer does not have a healthy respect for tradition,' he wrote in *American Printer* in 'What is "Modern" Typography?' (1948). He was quite fond of Garamond Old Style, as Eugene M. Ettenberg, a printer and typographer, observed: 'He has, as we have come to expect of him, used the face [Garamond Old Style] in the least traditional of ways. Always legible, he has used it playfully, experimentally, tossing it back and forth.' By the late 1940s Jan Tschichold had renounced the New Typography as too rigid (which caused some of his followers to accuse him of an unforgivable betrayal), but Rand was more liberal in his own variant of Modernism, as he wrote in *Thoughts on Design*:

'Disputes arising between the two schools of typographic thought, the traditional on the one hand and the modern on the other, are, it seems to me, the fruits of misplaced emphasis. I believe the real difference lies in the way "space" is interpreted: that is, the way an image is placed on a sheet of paper. Such incidental questions as the use of sans serif typefaces, lower case letters, ragged settings, primary colours, etc., are at best variables that tend merely to sidetrack the real issue.'[22]

He was also more sanguine about the choices one makes as a designer of the printed page and allowed for deviation based on purpose and function: 'I know people who have religiously used only sans serif, who suddenly switched to Times Roman. The reason they switched to Times Roman is for the same reason they used sans serif. They considered sans serif very functional, devoid of doodads and ringlets and hair curlers.'[23]

When compared to the iconoclasts of traditional book design, Rand was the epitome of tolerance. He respected traditionalism, yet maintained an unfaltering adherence to modernism. Yet in breaking from traditional methods he challenged the leaders of early twentieth-century book design to prove they were contributing to contemporary practice rather than simply supporting nostalgic conceits. In 'What is "Modern" Typography?', Rand argued that, 'One cannot deprecate the contributions made by such men as Goudy, Rogers, Dwiggins, Cleland, etc. To say, however, that any of these men are creative in the vernacular of the twentieth century is certainly an error in classification. For these men, who are perpetuating the past, are in a sense, historians … [They] have made little or no contribution to the understanding of the plastic arts in relation to our new, dynamic conception of space.' Rand was respectful of his elders, yet he also carved out a critical position and fervently defended it.

A few years after Rand's first published salvo, W. A. Dwiggins counter-attacked in a letter to Knopf's production manager, Sidney A. Jacobs:

'It's the work of these Rand fellows and the Bauhouse [*sic*] working in Chicago at advertising typography which is not anything like book typography. These people use type masses as grey elements in a picture technique without any concern for the movement of the narration, or the author's dramatic intention. They think they are interpreting the author's intention, but I am sure they are fooling themselves.'[24]

Dwiggins sarcastically labelled these moderns 'the Books In Our Time Boys', referring to the 1951 AIGA Fifty Books of the Year exhibition (which, ironically, included work by Dwiggins himself), and accused them of 'destroying the function of books'. In the final analysis, however, these 'Rand fellows' made a formidable impact on book design.

Rand's approach to book design borrowed more from modern architects and thinkers such as Le Corbusier and Mies van der Rohe than venerable bookmen. 'The immediate assumption is that the designer is thinking in architectural terms,' wrote the typographer Will Ransom in a critique of *The Tables of the Law*.[25] Rand's tectonics were rooted in an invisible grid inspired by Le Corbusier's proportional systems and adhered to the tenets of balance and harmony. Rand made a distinction between jacket and cover art, which was eclectic and free, and book design, which required structure and order. The jacket satisfied the artist's wants, while the interiors engaged the craftsman's skill. Unlike a magazine format, book typography allowed Rand to fuss as much as he wanted with the details, including the running feet and heads, the margins and indents. Book design required a

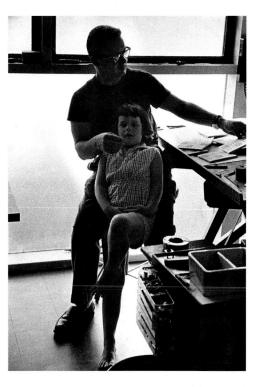

Left:
Rand's Yard, c.1970
(photographer unknown)
Rand not only designed
the exterior and interior
of his home, he
landscaped the grounds
as well. This is one of
the many environments
he created outside the
window of his studio.

Below left:
Rand's Studio, c.1970
(photographer unknown)
Rand worked in a small
studio in his home
surrounded by light boxes,
stat cameras, and an
eclectic array of visual
influences.

Below:
Paul and Catherine Rand,
c.1957
(photographer: Joe
Watson)
Rand sitting at his drawing
board, with his daughter
Catherine, in his studio in
Weston, Connecticut.

disciplined arrangement of design elements.
'The primary object of spatial divisions,' he
wrote, 'is to avoid using so many different sizes
of type, by varying space units.'[26] When order
was paramount, everything else followed.

Rand nevertheless railed against the 'lack of
inventive, experimental spirit' in book design
during the 1940s and early 1950s. He continually argued that if a book is being produced for
present-day consumption 'it should be designed
in our manner'. Yet he objected to efforts by
designers who were self-consciously modern.
Citing a flagrant example of this in his review
of the 1951 AIGA Fifty Books show, Rand
lamented that a book designer succumbs to
faddishness, 'with the mistaken notion that a
face like Futura automatically bestows a modern
appearance. But to design in the traditional
style, using a modern face, is like building a
Gothic church with glass bricks … The result
is "modernistic".'[27] He deplored those books,
and all other design, where style prevailed
over functionality; he also emphasized that,
'You always have to keep a step ahead of the
other guy … Which doesn't necessarily mean
that you're advancing. It may mean that you're
going to go back to Victoriana. This is also true
of typography. Today, you revive Cheltenham,
you revive Bookman, you revive all sorts of ugly
Victorian faces for no reason other than to be
different from your competitor. Basically, it's
for the birds.'[28]

Book design allowed Rand to evolve and
codify his typographic and layout principles.
Even in advertising he experimented with book
typography – he never used screaming banner

headlines when a line of 14 point Akzidenz or
Garamond would work just as well. Although his
work as a book designer is overshadowed by his
eminence as an advertising art director, the
book experience enabled him to crystallize
principles of modern design not only through
his work, but also in his writing. The following
'commandments of book design', which he
published in the *AIGA Journal* (Spring 1951)
represent the beginning of a formal doctrine of
Modernism that would evolve into what might
be called 'Randism':

1 Designing is not capricious arrangement.
2 Freedom of expression is not anarchy.
3 Understanding of the nature of new
   materials is not an exercise in novelty.
4 Functional form is not streamlining.
5 Order, discipline and proportion are not a
   Greek monopoly.
6 Simplicity is not nudity.
7 'Space' does not mean empty space, nor is
   'space articulation' the arbitrary placement
   of things in a void.
8 Sensitivity is not fussiness nor is it
   preciousness.
9 Glass bricks do not a modern house make.
10 Lower case letters and sans serif do not make
   modern typography.
11 Montage is not synthesized confusion.
12 Cropping and bleeding are not the
   prerogative of a Bluebeard.
13 Texture is not exclusively a physical
   experience.

When Rand left the Weintraub agency in early 1955 he had no shortage of freelance advertising work. The Compton Agency, which assumed the El Producto account, wanted him to continue with the campaign, and some international advertising agencies feverishly knocked at the door. But Rand was increasingly weary of the advertising business. While deciding what to do next, he briefly started painting (but stopped, reasoning that it was necessary to be totally devoted to either fine or commercial art). It is likely that his book jackets and covers supplanted easel painting. As it turned out, illustrating children's books also engaged him as the easel had not.

In 1956, the year that he was named design consultant for IBM, he designed and illustrated *I Know a Lot of Things*, the first of four children's books written by Ann Rand, his second wife, all published by Harcourt Brace and World, Inc., for the legendary children's book editor, Margaret McEldery. This was followed by *Sparkle and Spin* (1957), *Little 1* (1962), and *Listen! Listen!* (1970), comprising a fairly extensive footnote to Rand's publishing *oeuvre*. While each book tapped into Rand's previous design and illustration experiments, they focused them on a specific, if mysterious, audience that he had not previously addressed.

So much of Rand's imagery already revolved around simple, childlike forms that doodling and playing with cut paper was a meditative experience. Remove the cigars from the El Producto advertisements and the fanciful paper cut-outs could easily have been created as children's book illustrations. Likewise, what child would not warm to the artwork of the haughty bird on the jacket of *The Stork Club Bar Book* by Lucius Beebe? These silly scribblings were peculiar to Rand's impish sense of humour, hence it was only a matter of time before he, like El Lissitzky, Kurt Schwitters and George Grosz before him, created a book for the very audience from whom he drew such inspiration.

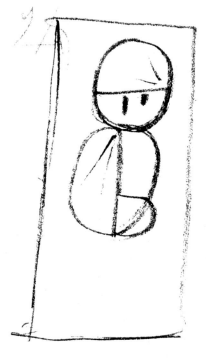

Opposite, clockwise
from top:
Untitled, oil on canvas,
1954
Self portrait, felt pen,
*c.*1944 (used for
announcement at Weston
Arts Center)
Cathy, pen and ink, 1964
Untitled (Child with arm
in a sling), pencil, date
unknown

Below and right:
I Know A Lot of Things,
gouache, sketches for
children's book, 1956
Rand loved to paint, but
realized that he did not
have the temperament
to be a Sunday painter.
Although he ceased
painting seriously in 1955,
he continued to be a
compulsive doodler and
prolific sketcher.

The opportunity arose when Gerald Cross, then production manager at Harcourt Brace and World, suggested to McEldery that Rand would be very well suited as a children's book illustrator. McEldery knew of Rand's reputation and invited him to submit an idea, which his wife Ann, an architect by training, wrote, about a child's capacity to learn and know. Rand was not initially comfortable with the children's book genre and took baby steps before finding his equilibrium. In fact, McEldery found that the first set of illustrations were too sophisticated for children, and offered suggestions for alteration that included further simplification of the characterizations, which, she said, Rand accepted surprisingly well and made the changes. Given the notoriously low fees paid to children's book artists, ultimately his greatest challenge, however, was not finding the best imagery (or visual personality) but to create reproducible, finished art without spending precious hours doing hand-cut colour separations.

Below left and below:
The Stork Club Bar Book, book jacket, Rhinehart and Company, 1946
Untitled, pencil, 1946

Opposite page:
I Know a Lot of Things, book jacket and interior spreads, Harcourt Brace and World, 1956
Considering the playful quality of Rand's drawings and paintings for 'adult' books, it is surprising that he was not commissioned to illustrate children's books earlier in his career. In 1956 he illustrated his first of four, authored by his second wife, Ann.

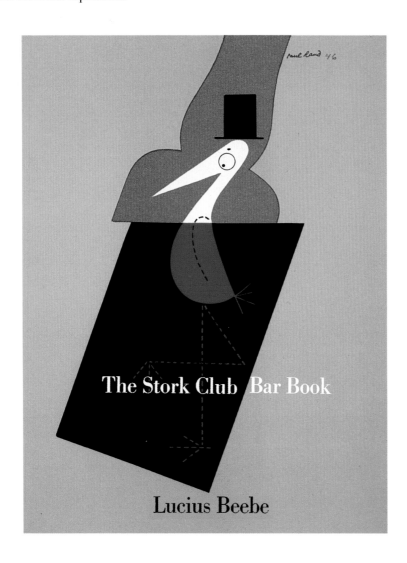

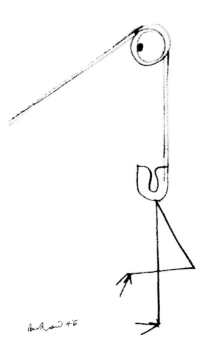

I know
a lot
of
things

Ann & Paul Rand

and climb a tree
high as the sky
to watch a bird fly by
and an acorn drop
kerplop kerplop

And even an ant
could carry
a load on his back
big as a berry

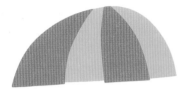

Oh

I know

such

a

lot

of

things,

but

as

I

grow

I know

I'll

know

much

more.

I Know a Lot of Things,
interior page and
spreads, Harcourt Brace
and World, 1956
Rand was a born
children's book illustrator.
He not only had a sixth
sense for what visually
excited a child's interest,
he honestly enjoyed
making the images.

or wave hello   to a mush

Of course I know
a horse can pull
a wagon full
of wood.

who's just a little fellow with a big umbrella.

I know that I can
hide
in a
cozy
cave

Eventually, he found a method of making his images on overlays that could be stripped in by the printer. The cute artwork for *I Know a Lot of Things* was therefore more tentative than the virtuoso *Sparkle and Spin*, a word book published the following year, which was chosen as one of the 1957 *New York Times* 'Ten Best Illustrated Books of the Year'.

Once his technique was assured, Rand relished illustrating books that he would complete in one long sitting. Ann Rand had found a voice that engaged four- to six-year-olds, and Rand had found a *métier* that captured the imagination of all ages. *Sparkle and Spin* earned other awards and was lavishly praised by the *New York Herald Tribune Book Review*:

'In their first handsome, original picture book [the Rands] have a child boast of all he knows. In their second, *Sparkle and Spin*, dedicated "to all children who like ice cream", they offer them knowledge about words, what they are for, the

Sparkle and Spin, book
jacket (left) and interior
spreads, Harcourt Brace
and World, 1957
A year after *I Know a Lot
of Things* was published
to good reviews, the duo
came out with *Sparkle
and Spin*, in which Rand
integrated illustrative
and design elements
even more than in the
first book.

A word is a thing
you heard or saw
or can even draw a
picture of.
Words are the names of objects
like book and doll and chair
or of animals
like bird and dog and bear.

Words are "Yes I will"
and "No I won't,"
but they are polite too
like please and thank you.

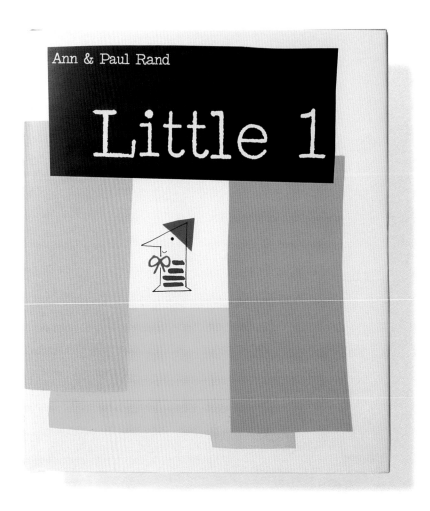

different kinds of words, what they can do "and surely you've found words sometimes sound exactly like what they're supposed to be". Ann Rand writes in short sharp rhymes and rhythms worded with a clever awkwardness that suggests the child's own speech.'[29]

Whatever field Rand worked in, the results nourished all other genres. His collages and drawings for book jackets were already fairly loose and expressive, but working at virtually the speed of unconsciousness on children's books offered even more freedom to exercise his ever-present play instinct.

Four years after Rand's divorce from Ann in 1958, they teamed up again in 1962 to write and illustrate the number book *Little 1*. The eponymous comic character wistfully asks in rhyming phrases if he cannot join two pears, three bears, four bees and other groups up to nine fish, only to be turned down indignantly. He is about to resign himself to a lonely fate, when to his delight, a circling hoop replies more cordially: 'Don't you know a circle that's empty inside is the same as a zero? Just stand here by me and then you and I can be ten.'

By 1962 Rand was already far along in his pioneering corporate work, and though he continued to execute book covers and jackets, it appeared that he used *Little 1* as a kind of respite from his many rigours. Again, he completed the

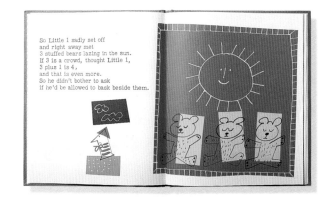

Little 1, book jacket (left) and interior spreads (pages 134–7), Harcourt Brace and World, 1962 Another five years passed before the third book, *Little 1,* was published. Ann Rand had perfected her narrative voice in this counting book, while Rand continued to do what he always had done – create delightfully witty characters (not unlike his marks for major corporations) aimed at the young.

"I'd like to be 2 like you,"
Little 1 said, smiling at 2 yellow pears
that lay in a dish.
"Go away," said the pears.
"2 is company,
but 2 plus 1 is 3,
and that would be
a crowd."

Little 1 was in such despair
he hardly dared
to stare into a big glass bowl
and tell 9 frisky fish
it was gayer when 10 could swish.
He felt no surprise
that each fish blew a bubble
and not one took the trouble
even to reply.

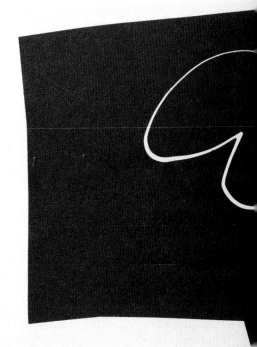

Little 1 was ready to cry
when a bright red hoop
came looping by.
"Hi!" cried the hoop with a smile.
"Come and play for a while."
"But I'm only 1," said Little 1.

Listen! Listen!, book jacket (below) and interior spreads, Harcourt Brace and World, 1970
Eight years after *Little 1*, Rand illustrated his last children's book, *Listen! Listen!*, a book of sounds. He enjoyed the serendipity of working with cut paper. For one thing, this method did not take him long, and this book was completed in less than a week.

Some sounds are scary
and some are nice.
I like the scritchity-scratch
of mice,
but my mother
takes a broom and very soon
Whoom!
that mouse
is out of the house.

I like the whir
that the wings
of a hummingbird make
when it flies,

and the Pssssssst!
of fireworks as they
sputter in the sky.

26 · 27

basic illustration in a single sitting, resulting in
wonderfully light-hearted images. Yet the book
as a whole received mixed reviews, with the
trade press serving librarians (at that time the
largest market for children's books) complaining
about its defects as a teaching aid.[30]

Eight years passed between the publication of
Little 1 and *Listen! Listen!* by Ann Rand, a book
of sounds illustrated with paper cut-outs and
pictorial typography. The double-page spreads
with 'talking type', owed a debt to Italian
Futurist onomatopoeic poetry and El Lissitzky's
word and symbol children's book *Story of Two
Squares*, but it also gave rise to a trend in
imaginative typography in children's books that
exploded in the late 1980s. Rand never felt the
impulse to write and illustrate his own children's
books, nor did he agree to illustrate other
authors', though he was persistently asked.
His books are an addendum to his career, but
like most of his accomplishments, they made an
impact on popular culture (he lived to see the
long out-of-print *Sparkle and Spin* and *Little 1*
republished in 1994).

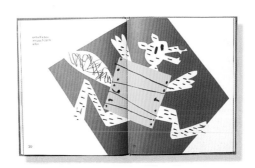

Rrrroooaaarrrrr!

12

13

But the noise I like
the very best
is early morning before sunrise
because then
(when I keep my eyes tight shut)
I can hear
the world wake up.
It's a wonderful mixed-up sound.
From far and near
from air and ground,
it comes from all around.
Listen...

30

31

Now that's not a door
because a door goes wham!
if you slam it,
nor a dog,
and as for a cat,
it certainly isn't that.
A bear would growl
and a wolf would howl.
None of you knows
what that roar was.

14

15

By the time *Listen! Listen!* was published, Rand was firmly established as a master of corporate Modernism, but despite the high-pressured consulting for multinational companies, Rand never lost his passion for books and book jackets. Of course, many of the art directors he had worked with left the publishing houses where he enjoyed sinecure, and he received fewer, if any, commissions from their successors. In 1984, however, he decided to return to book design as an 'auteur', when he revived the essays from his first book, *Thoughts on Design*, and added others to an entirely new volume, *Paul Rand: A Designer's Art*. At the age of seventy, he was still in control of his medium and message.

Little 1, final page,
Harcourt Brace and
World, 1962
Rand said that his work
for children was not
formally or even concep-
tually different from any
of his other work. Many of
his subsequent corporate
projects were obviously
influenced by these books.

Thoughts on Design was completely recast
and redesigned by Rand, who also supervised
the printing. He selected a flexible cover rather
than a rigid one, 'to make it more friendly'. The
pages were arranged in sequences for surprise
and rhythm: 'I try to keep material in contrast
so you don't fall asleep – a black page, then a
gray one, then a blank one,'[31] he explained. At
least fifty per cent of the book was changed at
the printing plant because, 'that's part of the
design process; being in complete control of
production is essential for an artist'. Where
Thoughts on Design was elegantly reserved, *Paul
Rand: A Designer's Art* was audaciously
reserved. In the former, the type framed black-
and-white illustrations (of his advertisements
and magazine covers) were reproduced in the
manner of an art catalogue. In the latter, type
and colour images (predominantly of his own
work) fused together in a seamless narrative.
Rand had become more of a story-teller,
using design elements to advance his tale. The
book jackets for *Thoughts* and *A Designer's Art*
also revealed Rand's maturity. The earlier one
was a photogram of an abacus (the same design
was also made into furniture cushions and
drapes), an abstract image that symbolized the
sum and substance of design; the latter was
text only, the title in white Univers dropped out
of a black background; the only colour –
rainbow-like bands reminiscent of his children's
books – was reserved for the spine. This might
be construed as a sly commentary on the state
of contemporary jacket design, a critique of the
decorative tendencies that prevailed, and an
example of how Rand's book design embodied
principles that ensured good design.

In Rand's lexicon, 'contrast' is a powerful
word. As if to provide a coda to Rand's publishing legacy, Patricia Allen Dreyfus summed up
his process as, 'the contrast between the
expected and the unexpected, between rough
and smooth, simple and complex, line and
mass, negative and positive space, up and down,
photography and artwork … tight and loose,
thick and thin, representation and symbol,
movement and repose, colour and black-
and-white.'[32]

If Rand left one lesson behind for book
designers it was that good design is a curative,
not a cosmetic.

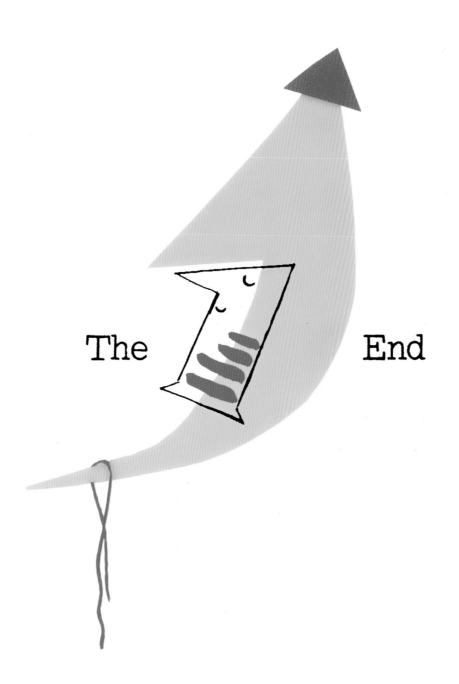

The End

Corporate Identity: Good design is good business

4

He almost single-handedly convinced the business world that design was an effective tool. Anyone designing in the fifties and sixties owed much to Rand. We went from being commercial artists to being graphic designers largely on his merits.

Louis Danziger, 1996

Paul Rand was simultaneously a giant in the advertising industry and the victim of unscrupulous advertising men. When, faced with financial ruin, William H. Weintraub sold his embattled agency, he collected ample profit and callously left Rand to fend for himself in a hostile environment, with the firm now headed by Norman B. Norman. Despite Rand's growing disillusionment with advertising, his forced resignation from the agency was a shock to one who had known few obstacles on the road to success. At forty-one-years old he was on his own, and those who knew him in 1955 agreed that it was his darkest moment.

Advertising taught Rand many important lessons, not the least of which was that it was better to be his own boss. Although he did not seek either partnership nor parity with Weintraub, Rand was never totally sanguine about being an employee. Prior to Weintraub's demise, Rand had already decided to limit his time at the agency to three days a week, with the balance devoted to working on freelance projects from his home in Harrison, New York (which incidentally was built to designs by Marcel Breuer), where he did everything with one assistant. While he also refrained from participation in the leading professional clubs and societies, he made a few social relationships with kindred designers that proved useful in getting referrals. So by the time of the Weintraub débâcle Rand was professionally prepared to face the summary end of his sinecure. Nevertheless, he was embittered enough to initiate a lawsuit that earned him a modest monetary settlement. By the end of this ordeal he accepted that a large burden had been removed from his shoulders and was ready to enter the next phase of his career.

A few of Rand's peers feared that their professional lives were jeopardized by the vicissitudes of business and fashion, and turned from graphic design to the fine arts. One or two achieved success, but most aspiring painters never really made greater contributions through painting than through graphic design. While Rand also briefly turned his attention to the easel, he knew that graphic design was his true calling. He rationalized that only 'The guy who can really make it work is the real artist. The other side of the coin is to be a Sunday painter, which is the most depressing idea there is … Because it means that the rest of the week is futile.'[1]

Art was Rand's inspiration. Yet, at this turning-point in his career, it was a means not an end. 'That graphic design is generally considered a minor art has more to do with posturing than it does with reality,' he later explained in *Paul Rand: A Designer's Art*; 'The paucity of great art is no more prevalent among designers than it is among painters.'[2]

Rand's practice was motivated by the aesthetics of art, but by 1956 his career took a sharp turn from art-based graphics for advertisements, magazine covers and book jackets to the more circumscribed realm of corporate communications.

Post-war corporate culture

In the decade following the end of the Second World War multinational corporations started to spring up in the United States, Europe and Asia. Many of the energy, technology and information conglomerates that had extolled their progressive aspirations at the 1939 New York World's Fair developed during the early post-war years into forces of industrial innovation, introducing products that both changed and defined the second half of the twentieth century. Advertising agencies handled most of the marketing and public relations for these corporations, but did not generally develop the unified graphic systems that provided a consistent visual identity. By the mid-1950s, the so-called 'ID business' had become the fastest growing and most lucrative graphic design speciality in the world.

Germany was the wellspring of modern corporate identity, and during the early 1900s Peter Behrens, a typographer and architect with stylistic roots in *Jugendstil* (Art Nouveau), designed factories, offices and the graphic design system for AEG (Allgemeine Elektritäts-gesellschaft), Germany's largest electrical products manufacturer. His sway over the conception and application of a uniform 'house style' was so complete that historians refer to him as the grandfather of modern corporate identity. Behrens' graphics programme centred on a logo that dictated the typographical scheme for all the company's printed materials, from calling cards to letterheads, from catalogues to posters, from packages to labels. Although illustrative trademarks were traditional business identifiers dating back to the nineteenth century, Behrens' innovative integration of the mark in all forms of coordinated printed matter had far-reaching implications, particularly on Rand's later work.

By the late 1920s, the Bauhaus propagated the concept of systematic design based on the use of universal design elements. Although the term 'Bauhaus style' was rejected by strict Bauhausians, who eschewed style as a bourgeois concept, the school's coordinated typographic design programme spearheaded by László Moholy-Nagy and Herbert Bayer amounted to nothing less. By the 1930s, modern and modernistic design identities were routinely employed by most German companies, and German designers, notably Wilhelm Defke and F. W. O. Hadank, took the lead in abstract logo and trademark design. Of course, the most memorable identity system of the twentieth century was developed under Nazi auspices. The swastika, the charged symbol of the Nazi Party and the Third Reich, was the cornerstone of an interconnected system dictated by strict formal rules. It left an indelible mark.

As mammoth conglomerates colonized the post-war commercial world, theories of corporate communications developed, and corporate design consultancies prospered. Standardization and integration resulted in the clarification of corporate missions. Industry's need for communicating distinct identities to the public and congruent messages to employees gave rise to a design methodology known as the 'International Typographic Style', which was based on mathematical grid systems that provided consistent frameworks for arranging type and image. Earlier in the century graphic design for business was an ostensibly *ad hoc* exercise subject to the vagaries of individual designers and the whims of their clients. Subsequently, the newer doctrine of systems design required that designers adhere to precise formulas laid down in house style manuals.

Swiss and German designers of the post-war period were the most vociferous proponents of the new rationalist method. Followers of *Neue Grafik* (New Graphic Design) synthesized Bauhaus notions of functionality and Dutch De Stijl's advocacy of a universal art of absolute clarity to create a distinct corporate design vocabulary. Advocates of the International Style, also referred to as the Swiss School, believed that tectonic design structures could frame a variety of messages that would also allow for startling dynamics between visual and textual elements. Yet, since the method was rooted on a principle of strict uniformity, which encouraged conformity, the International Style was alternately praised as bringing order to a chaotic environment and criticized for reducing visual communications to predictable formulas.

Effective corporate identities did not, however, conform to a single rightness of form but were created with imagination and vision. Since these design systems were not ephemeral, they required considerable financial investment from corporate leaders, which mitigated against too many standardized solutions. One of the earliest advocates of modern corporate identity, the Container Corporation of America, Chicago's largest corrugated box and paper container manufacturer, was among the first American companies to introduce a uniform design system which, in concert with innovative institutional advertising – employing many of the world's avant-garde artists and designers (including Rand) – telescoped the image of a progressive company. The founder and chief executive of CCA, Walter P. Paepcke, was convinced by former *Bauhäuslers* Herbert Bayer and László Moholy-Nagy that good design was not simply a veneer but an integral component of the 'corporate culture', which like any national culture was comprised of symbols and icons.

During the late 1940s, the Columbia Broadcasting System, headed by Frank Stanton, was a trail-blazer in corporate identity for the radio and television industry. Stanton hired art director William Golden whose CBS 'eye' was the centrepiece of an identity programme that included an array of innovative advertising and promotion. This symbol had a huge influence on the modern ID business when it was introduced in 1951, and remains one of the world's most indelible trademarks.

Despite the need for integrated design systems, most American business leaders were slower to embrace the concept than were Europeans. Corporations rising from the ashes of war were more in need of fresh new identities than American concerns that flourished during the war. Indeed, the most remarkable modern identity system at that time belonged to Olivetti, the Milan-based business machine company founded in 1908, which was one of Europe's most internationally renowned firms, for both its superior products and its innovative graphic design. Design director Giovanni Pintori's attention to every detail, from logo to advertisements (including two by Rand), to retail store outlets, to products designed by progressive designers, enhanced the reputation of a far-sighted firm and leading competitor in the world market.

Right and far right:
Paul Rand, 1958
(photographer unknown)

Below:
Olivetti, advertisement, 1953
Rand created a few ads for Olivetti, the Milan-based business machine corporation. Its ambitious design programme was the inspiration for Thomas J. Watson Jr's decision to revivify IBM's total visual identity.

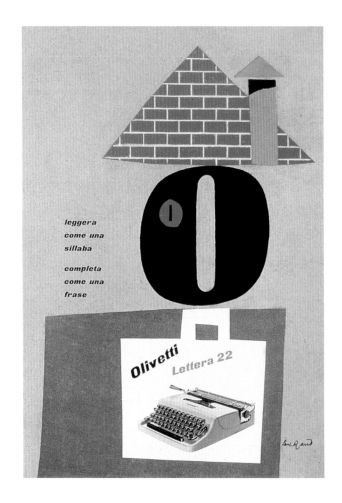

leggera
come una
sillaba

completa
come una
frase

Olivetti Lettera 22

IBM

Olivetti was doubtless on the mind of Thomas J. Watson Jr, the scion of International Business Machines (IBM), founded by his father in 1914, when he invited a fellow Second World War glider pilot, Eliot Noyes, an architect and industrial design consultant from New Canaan, Connecticut, to assess the overall status of IBM's network of manufacturing plants and its array of products. In a 1975 Tiffany/Wharton School lecture titled 'Good Design is Good Business', Watson acknowledged that what originally sparked his interest in design was a 1955 letter from an IBM manager in Holland who wrote, 'Tom, we're going into the electronic era and I think IBM designs and architecture are really lousy.'[3] This wake-up call, combined with having seen Olivetti's ultra-contemporary New York City showroom (replete with a working typewriter on a podium outside its front door on Fifth Avenue), just blocks from IBM's stolid, traditionally appointed, mahogany-panelled headquarters on 57th Street and Madison Avenue, inspired the young executive to question the image that his company presented to the public. Watson made a pilgrimage to Milan to meet Adriano Olivetti, the Medici of the design programme that included buildings, offices, employee housing, products, brochures and advertisements. He later wrote that it was then that he decided to 'improve IBM design, not only in architecture and typography, but colour, interiors – the whole spectrum'.[4]

'Watson asked Noyes "Do you think it's possible that IBM could look like the kind of company it really is?",' recalled Marion Swannie; who, after graduating in 1945, wrote advertising copy and purchased artwork for IBM brochures, eventually rising to manager of the IBM graphic design department until retiring in 1975 (when she became Rand's third wife). Deciding to expand IBM's development into fields of electronics and computers with the long-term goal of dominating the market required that Watson invest in a design programme equal to the aspirations of the company. Although he admittedly did not possess design acuity, he realized that the company was in need of an encompassing makeover. Since Noyes devoted a large amount of his time to revivifying IBM's buildings, products and visual communications, Watson too became a Medici of corporate design. '[G]ood design must primarily serve people, and not the other way around,' he wrote. 'It must take into account human beings, whether they be our employees or our customers who use our products.'[5]

IBM already possessed a corporate mark – a globe that sat atop a nondescript line of type – designed anonymously in 1924. By the 1930s the stand-alone monograph IBM became the familiar 'call letters' of the company and began appearing on stationery in a Beton Bold Condensed typeface (with the words 'Trade Mark' set in an obtrusive gothic face below). 'However, there was no consistent graphic identity strategy followed throughout the corporation,' according to Tom Hardy, IBM Program Design Manager from 1988 to 1991. 'For example, IBM world headquarters in New York continued to display the 1924 globe even after the Beton Bold IBM version was in use on printed materials.' Prior to 1956, apart from some people responsible for communications inside the company, there was no dedicated internal graphic design staff, and most graphic materials were farmed out to freelancers.

The lack of a central internal direction of the company's visual character became Eliot Noyes' first major hurdle.

Noyes, who is credited with coining the term 'corporate design', was socially acquainted with Rand from Cape Cod and Martha's Vineyard, where a group of artists and architects spent summer vacations. Rand's second wife Ann, a former assistant to Mies van der Rohe, cultivated these social relationships. The otherwise reticent Rand was content to hobnob with kindred modernists. 'Ann and Paul were at our house having dinner, when Eliot first asked Paul if he would be interested in working for IBM,'[6] recalled Helen Federico, who had worked for Rand at the Weintraub agency. Although Noyes was well aware that Rand had never done a complete corporate system before, he was impressed by the logos and trademarks that Rand had created for Weintraub's clients – especially the advertisements that built a brand identity for Smith, Kline, French pharmaceutical laboratories, and the identity campaign for El Producto Cigars that amounted to his first independent corporate design programme for the Consolidated Cigar Company. In addition, the 1954 full-page 'Dot-Dash' advertisement in the *New York Times*, intended to win over RCA to the Weintraub agency, was what Allen Hurlburt described as 'an appropriate indicator of that point in the Rand career where corporate design began to supersede advertising'.[7]

Both Rand and Ann quickly developed
a detailed proposal for IBM that became the
blueprint for the initial redesign. Rand was
aware that corporate design programmes had
been carried out in Germany, and was familiar
with the Hochschule für Gestaltung in Ulm, the
spiritual repository of the Bauhaus, where
these programmes were an integral part of the
curriculum. He was also introduced to an influential teacher and designer there, Max Bill,
a Swiss-born former Bauhaus student, whose
scientific and methodological approach to corporate communications took the idiosyncrasy
out of corporate design. Rand to some extent
modelled his efforts on Bill's rational approach,
while at the same time injecting idiosyncrasy
when appropriate. 'Paul and Ann wrote an
impressive proposal – a big book with pictures
in it – which explained how the identity thing
worked. Paul said that a full scale identity
programme centres around graphics but added
that it should be instituted in stages,' explained
Marion Swannie, who was chosen by Rand
in 1956 to coordinate and facilitate his efforts.
'I don't think the proposal was submitted
directly to Watson. Paul just did it, and the vice
president at IBM in charge of the project at that
time, Gordon Smith, said "It looks fine to me".'[8]

Rand was never given a specific assignment
from Noyes or any IBM manager to start the
programme off with a new logotype. Instead,
during the process of designing brochures for
different divisions, Rand decided to clean up the
logo. 'The first job, as I recall, was a loose-leaf
binder that somebody needed for some function.
That's when Paul did his first IBM,' said
Swannie about the incremental shift that made
Rand the spark that ignited the engine of
change throughout the corporate culture.[9] 'It
was clearly understood that the most rapid and
conspicuous means to begin showing a shift in
the expression of IBM was through the medium
of graphic design, having relatively low costs
and quick turn-around,' added Tom Hardy. 'I
recall Paul telling me that one of the very first
applications of the new IBM logotype design
was, on matchbook covers. The reason was that,
during the fifties, matches were ubiquitous and
it was a way to introduce the new image quickly
and repeatedly.'[10]

Both the IBM logo and the corporate motto,
'Think', coined by Thomas Watson Sr, were set
in a Beton Bold Condensed typeface that was
fairly current in the 1930s yet by the 1950s
looked archaic. Reasoning that this style was too
familiar throughout the company to change in
one fell swoop, Rand was nevertheless disturbed

that the Egyptian-style slab serif exuded an aura
that was not in sync with Watson's progressive
aspirations. 'IBM was a very conservative organization, especially when Mr Watson Sr [who died
in late 1956] was alive, and it was obvious that
anything that you did had to be what you perceived as something that they would accept,'
Rand reasoned.[11]

'I perceived that something that they would
accept would be pretty close to what they
already had. Incidentally, I wasn't interested
in doing beautiful stuff just to put in my file …
They had a slab serif, so I used a slightly
different slab serif. But it didn't occur to me,
nor would I have done the stripes at the time.
Because if I had done it, it never would
have passed.'[12]

IBM Electric Typewriters,
advertisement, 1950
Before Rand joined IBM
the company did not
have a uniform design
programme. Ads, such as
this one, bore little
relationship to the
company's other printed
materials.

Right and far right:
IBM Annual Report,
cover and inside spread,
1957
Rand's responsibilities at
IBM grew gradually over
time, but before long his
presence was felt on
everything from business
cards to annual reports.

Below right:
Fair, brochure cover, 1964
Rand designed this Dada-
inspired circus motif for a
brochure distributed at
the IBM Pavilion at the
New York World's Fair.
He also used this image in
his children's book,
Sparkle and Spin.

Of course, Rand was right to wait a few
more years before introducing the most enduring
iteration of the IBM logo – the striped version –
because, as Marion Swannie recalled about that
first subtle change, 'Nobody said anything about
it. There was no, "Gee, that's terrific", because
it wasn't that different from what everybody
was used to seeing.'[13] Rand had switched from
Beton Bold Condensed to a more hard-edged
slab serif, City Medium, designed in 1930 by
the German designer Georg Trump and based
on a 'Constructivist' model. It was, however,
an interim solution. 'I was learning on the job,
really,' Rand admitted. 'The first logo I did
for IBM I thought was for the birds! I kept
changing the drawing all the time, because
it was never perfect. I didn't change it so that
it was noticeable, but I changed it so that it
was noticeable to a guy who knows how
to do lettering.'[14]

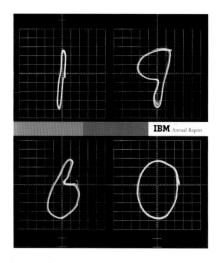

Thomas J. Watson Jr declared in the 1976
Tiffany/Wharton lecture that 'Experimental
design carried beyond disciplined control, often
becomes nonfunctional, wasteful, and expensive.
Good design has to meet functional requirements. It has to serve as good background and
be subordinated to the human and machine
activities it supports.'[15] And this was a textbook
description of Rand's method in the early years
at IBM. He was certainly cautious, but nonetheless anxious to set the wheels of progress in
motion. Noyes made Rand the point-man of
change, and together they planned the design
policy for the long term. While Rand initially
unified the graphics, Noyes took the Queen
Anne legs off the IBM accounting machines
and redesigned the electric typewriter. More
importantly, however, he initiated a strategy to
modernize product design and plant architecture
(hiring Marcel Breuer and Eliel Saarinen as
his architects). In addition, in 1958 Noyes named
the industrial designer Charles Eames as a consultant with the objective of employing Eames'
visionary ideas about industrial film-making
and museum exhibitions to further enhance
IBM's image. Charles and his wife Ray Eames,
who jointly headed their consultancy, ultimately
conceived a major exhibition on the history of
communications as seen through the IBM lens

that was mounted at IBM's world headquarters
at 590 Madison Avenue. They also developed
educational 'history wall' timelines and a
spectacular ground-floor showroom, as well as
designing pioneering multi-image-multiscreen
displays for the IBM pavilion at the New York
World's Fair in 1964. Noyes also briefly invited
Edgar Kaufmann Jr, an art expert who wrote on
design issues and was affiliated with the Museum
of Modern Art, to consult on the IBM
programme. But the majority of new ideas came
from the interchange between Noyes, Eames and
Rand. For Rand this was the most stimulating
association of his career.

IBM had sold products for decades and
invested a huge amount of money in merchan-
dizing and information materials. Most of it
emanated from the central office where Marion
Swannie hired freelancers, including designer/
illustrator Milton Glaser and typographer
Freeman Craw. But at the company's manufacturing sites throughout the United States and
Europe groups of artists were more or less
grinding out whatever needed to be done to
satisfy the requirements of the particular region,
whether it was an instruction manual, in-house
newsletter, or announcement for the plant
bulletin board. Rand's biggest challenge was
not convincing the IBM executives about the
rightness of his designs, but rather setting
standards that would be dutifully followed
throughout the company.

'We decided that the first thing to do was to get in touch with these other locations to show them what Paul expected of them,' recalled Marion Swannie about the gruelling coordination process. 'Paul did key pieces, such as the executive letterhead, the calling card, and many other things that everybody in the company would be using. Initially, we took them on a road show to the units that already had some sort of art-related functions.'[16] Determining the strengths and weaknesses of the existing decentralized 'communications' departments and educating the 'designers' was not an easy task. Prior to instituting a standardization manual, Rand, who was no more comfortable speaking before groups at IBM than he had been at the Weintraub agency, gave detailed presentations explaining the virtues of the new design system. The initial response was usually encouraging, but the results were often disappointing. Draughtsmen and cartoonists who had for years assumed responsibility for in-house posters and announcements resisted change. Swannie remembers 'a guy in Poughkepsie who drew a little Indian character called Ogiwambi on plant posters,'[17] which exemplified the kind of obstacles they encountered. Although IBM leadership gave Rand its official support, they resisted firing or transferring these employees, preferring to somehow assimilate them into the design programme.

Under the circumstances, Rand insisted that it was necessary to centralize output with an internal staff of graphic designers. 'Paul hired people who understood his aim,' explained Swannie. 'So we built up a staff of graphic designers who worked every day in New York City designing IBM brochures, and they began to do some very nice things that represented the quality that Paul wanted for the company.'[18] Rand worked on IBM projects from his home, first in Harrison, New York, and later in Weston, Connecticut, but maintained an office at IBM headquarters in New York where he worked at least one day, and often as many as five days a week. In addition to doing specific jobs, Rand counselled designers and made sure that the new design scheme was circulated throughout the company. When IBM's White Plains plant launched a Design Center, he held frequent discussions and critiques there. He also undertook regular reviews of work at his home in Weston, where designers would gather around the dining table surrounded by icons of Modernism, or under the bright fluorescent lights at Gold's Delicatessen (Rand's favourite local eatery), nervously bracing for Rand's sometimes stinging criticism. 'Obviously parts of this programme had to be enforcement, like "Here is the logo; use it!",' recalled Swannie. 'But a lot of it was simply encouragement.'[19]

To help them propagate the faith, Rand enlisted experts to teach IBM staff members about the techniques of printing and nuances of paper and type, believing that design was only as effective as the production. Alvin Eisenman, a book designer and director of the design programme at Yale University, was one of the consulting lecturers who provided 'educational hours' at each location. Other lecturers were also hired to expound on their specialities. The design programme soon took on a momentum all of its own, and ultimately graphic design, which came under the auspices of a sympathetic and encouraging Vice President of Communications, Dean McKay, became one of three main design laboratories – the others were product design and architecture.

Left:

The IBM Logo, booklet inside pages, 1990
Rand continually maintained a watchful eye on the use of the logo. In the pages from this late edition of one of his many design manuals, he discusses the evolution from the original City Bold to the striped versions.

Below:

IBM, logo (striped version), 1962
Rand was not officially commissioned to redesign the logo, but he determined it needed to be changed. The striped version was added to the i.d. system because he felt there was a problem in the sequence of the letters, going from narrow to wide without any pause or rhythmic cadence.

The IBM logo was the centrepiece of the programme. 'A trademark is the signature of a company as opposed to the signature of an individual,' Rand wrote in 1950. 'It should as closely as possible embody in the simplest form the essential characteristics of the product or institution being advertised. It should be easy to identify, and it should serve to glorify the merchandise in question, which is often dull and utilitarian by nature.'[20] Of course, the IBM logo was not exactly like the illustrative character marks he had designed during his advertising days, but it still had to represent the essence of the company. Initially, Rand decided that he would use the City type family to tie the company together, using it as the standard display type. But eventually he decided that Bodoni was a more graceful and functional typeface. Moreover, as the designers used the new logo on various media, further modifications were required. It was clear that the logo was still in an evolutionary stage.

IBM was so influential that its call letters symbolized the technological revolution of the 1950s and 1960s. Like Kleenex for tissue, Frigidaire for refrigerator and Xerox for photo-copier, IBM was synonymous with computers (and, of course, electric typewriters). 'But Paul believed that people shouldn't feel hit over the head by this company,' explained Swannie, 'and felt that the IBM logo in solid form could be a hit in the head depending on the way it was used.'[21] As a result of its numerous different applications, the logo became more condensed, solid and heavy, so Rand decided it was necessary to add an outline version, setting it in two weights, light and medium. Meanwhile, he zealously sketched logos as if searching for the Holy Grail. Eventually he introduced the striped version, because he thought that the stripes gave the logotype a sort of a legal sense, like scan lines on a banknote, and it defused the impact of that big, heavy IBM, which really could become a problem. 'And did become a problem in some cases,' added Swannie. 'IBM was a very big force in the world, and a lot of people did not like that.'[22]

Throughout the process Rand did not forsake tradition but valued serendipity. He once admitted that El Producto's logo was set in stencil for no other reason than he did it in

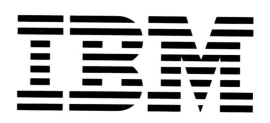

Left:
IBM, doodle,
date unknown.
The stripes on the logo
suggested the lines on a
cheque or bank note used
to thwart forgeries. But
one IBM executive, upon
seeing it for the first time,
said it reminded him of a
prison suit. Rand thought
that this was not out of
the realms of possibility as
this doodle indicates.

Below:
IBM, rebus doodle,
date unknown.
One of many small
sketches for a rebus by
Rand that challenged the
sanctity of the IBM logo.

stencil. 'So, too, IBM could have been done the same way, and I could have manufactured all sorts of reasons.'[23] But when he finally decided on stripes, the rationale owed more to common sense with a touch of poetry:

'It came about because I felt that the letters in themselves were not interesting enough. I felt there was a problem in the sequence, going from narrow to wide without any pause, without any rhythmic possibility. You know, DA-DA-DA, DA-DA, DA-DA-DA … It was just DA-DA-DA-DA … It went up in the sky, and you couldn't come down. I got the idea for the [stripes] by projecting the notion of a document that you signed that uses a series of thin parallel lines to protect the signature against counterfeiting. And I thought, "Well, if that's the symbol of that kind of authority, then why don't I make the letters into stripes or into a series of lines." That's what I did. And it not only satisfied the conceptual problem, but also satisfied the visual problem of tying the three letters together which tended to fall apart … Since each letter was different, the fact that all the lines were the same was the element of harmony that brought them together. It's since been used to symbolize the computer industry, and that's only because it's been used by IBM. There's nothing inherent in horizontal lines or vertical lines that says 'computer' except what you read into it because of association with a good company.'[24]

Watson and Noyes were Rand's patrons, and Dean McKay was a rock of support. Consequently, Rand was not anxious about having his ideas accepted throughout the company.

Nevertheless, when two versions of the striped logo (eight lines and thirteen lines, one bold, the other more discreet) were introduced to a group of managers in 1962, someone around the table suggested that it looked like a prison uniform (a concept that must have struck Rand as funny because he doodled on a notepad at the time a striped IBM with prisoners' heads). Noyes, however, discounted any criticism, assuring the managers that Rand knew exactly what he was doing. The logo was subsequently accepted without debate.

Rand ensured that IBM's new mark was not misused or abused. 'In our daily work we have all had an opportunity to employ, study, criticize, or exercise our talents or authority in the use of the IBM logo,' announced Rand before a Washington DC seminar, one of many held for IBM designers from around the United States.

'None of us, however, has *not* had problems relating to the use of the logo: as a question of propriety or legality, or as a matter of aesthetics or mechanics. As opposed to a pictorial device, a logo is read, not just looked at. By their very nature, letters are generally less visually absorbing than pictures. Since the logo has little to do with elucidating a particular content, the designer is often in a quandary as to what to do with it, where to place it, how big, how small, how light, how dark. As a result, sometimes the logo is simply left out or made so small as virtually to disappear, or is so organized as to conflict with its neighbouring text and pictures. For the competent designer, these problems offer interesting challenges. The logo provides him with potentially effective design possibilities: elements of scale, contrast and visual interest. For the businessman it makes possible a means of identity, a stamp of authority, and an invaluable communications device. The problems we face in using the logo are essentially problems of design and business judgment, universal problems unique to no one.'[25]

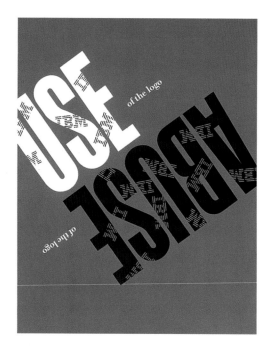

Rand took a proprietary interest in his creation, and remained the keeper of the logo throughout his tenure, authoring and designing two important documents, *IBM Logo Use and Abuse* and *The IBM Logo* – the latter a story illustrating innovation by showing the logo's flexible applications. Once the logo was established, only Rand retained the right to alter it in any way, and even this was not a divine right. Once, when Rand made a rebus out of the logo (a poster with brightly coloured, witty renderings of an eye, a bee and the striped M), management thought that this would be an invitation to in-house designers to engage in tomfoolery. They also claimed that 'it wasn't IBM and failed to recognize that in one fell swoop Paul had humanized the corporation', stated Louis Danziger.[26] To Rand's surprise, distribution of the poster was forbidden for some time. It has since become a classic example of whimsy in the service of the corporation.

Left:
Use of the Logo/Abuse of the Logo, brochure cover, 1990
Rand's job was to establish the design law and police it too. The imposition of absolute adherence took years. This brochure shows both the latitude and constraints of the programme.

Right:
Eye, Bee, M, poster, 1981
Rand designed this rebus as an announcement for an in-house IBM event, The Golden Circle Award, but its distribution was temporarily prohibited by managers who feared it would encourage staff designers to take liberties with the logo. Eventually, Rand prevailed and it has become one of his most popular posters.

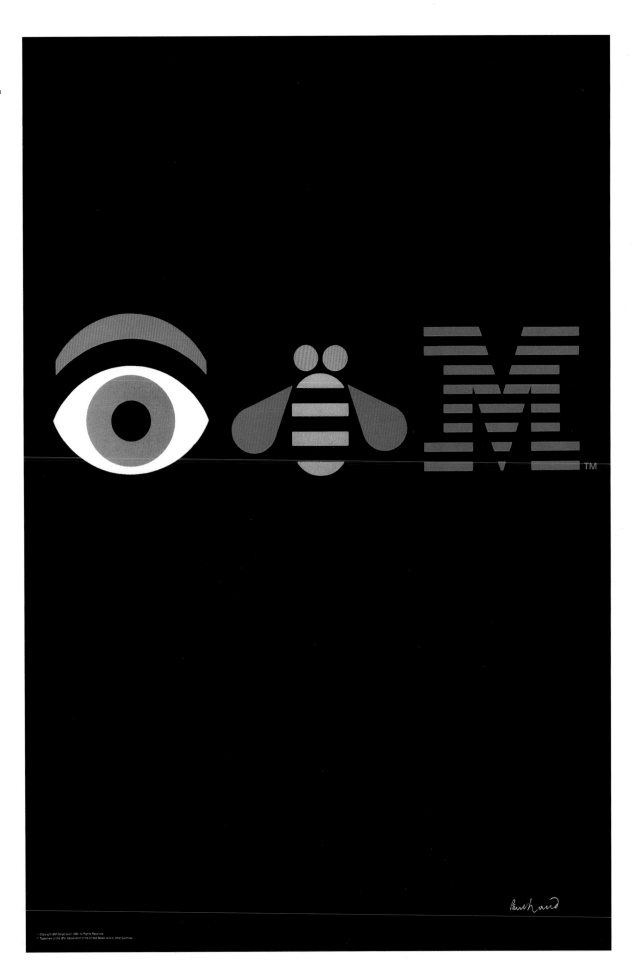

Rand's fundamental approach to corporate identity was deliberately at odds with corporations conforming to overly standardized rules and regulations. While he adhered to basic structural consistencies, he rebelled against routines that ensured mediocrity. He argued that, while a framework was necessary, it should not inhibit the designer. 'There's a natural need for order,' he explained:

'Whether you like it or not, you live by a system. Even if you think that systems are stupid, you have breakfast every morning, and you go to the john, and you go to sleep, that's a system … [But] people mistake a system for something that has to be adhered to … You have to edit a system. Otherwise, you may as well walk around in a striped suit.'

He further detested imitation: 'Every logo that some designers do has stripes,' he chided. 'Now, there has to be something wrong with that concept. It's just not possible to do everything with stripes. Except that stripes have become symbolic of the latest in technology.'[27]

Rand acknowledged the influence of European design on his work, but, as Tom Hardy insisted, he developed his own design vocabulary or 'Paul Rand look'. 'I'm sure he would hate that term, yet I don't mean a consistent visual style, but rather a consistency of simplicity, directness, clarity, uniqueness, appropriateness, relevance, beauty, and very often playfulness,' said Hardy.[28] Rand would agree that working for IBM made him more conscious of contemporary methods, the most influential being Swiss design:

'When I was first aware of what the Swiss were doing, I used to ridicule it … I really felt that stuff was cold, and all the other clichés people use to describe Swiss design. But then I changed completely … Granted, there is a lot of lousy, very stiff and very cold stuff. But there is no counterpart to Swiss design in terms of something that you can describe, that you can follow, that you can systematically understand.'[29]

He once said that Swiss design was to graphic design what Cubism was to art, and he borrowed Swiss methods that were appropriate to his practice, such as the grid. 'I don't sit down and start with grids – although I do grids all the time,' he explained: 'Sometimes maybe I don't use them, or maybe I don't use them properly, but who cares? I want to know I can always start the margin in the same place, and then use my different vertical and horizontal nodal points for different things. And that's a help! You wouldn't know it after it's done, but that's the way I did it.'[30]

In 1959, articles in national business and trade magazines cited the 'new look' of IBM and praised its flexibility. 'This new look of IBM did not depend upon sameness,' emphasized Tom Hardy, 'but followed a theme of quality and creative appropriateness. In other words, the consistent corporate image of IBM was *good design*.'[31] This rather nebulous term became something of a mantra for Rand and a watchword for a generation of designers who came of age in the late 1950s. 'Good design adds value of some kind, gives meaning, and, not incidentally, can be sheer pleasure to behold; it respects the viewer's sensibilities and rewards the entrepreneur,' wrote Rand in *Design, Form, and Chaos*,[32] describing the era when designers honestly believed that good design was synonymous with good citizenship. Clarity in visual communications became a social service. The modernist credo of social responsibility had shifted from concern for the individual to concern for the individual through the beneficence of the corporation; with the corporation as the patron of good design, designers believed that the individual would benefit. The top management at IBM certainly held this view too, and in addition to propagating good design practices, the company maintained an art collection (administered by Swannie) and mounted public exhibitions (designed by Rand) that were consistent with its belief in cultural responsibility.

Nevertheless, IBM was not unlike an army of occupation in post-war Europe during the late 1950s and 1960s. Plants and offices were established as beachheads in England, France, Germany and Switzerland to extend its influence and increase its profits throughout the world. And design was its primary weapon. But rather than adhere to a central plan, each country's graphic design department was comparatively autonomous. The IBM house style was used arbitrarily, if at all, with varying degrees of accomplishment. 'Everything was growing in IBM at that time, but nothing was in place,' Marion Swannie said about the disparate talents throughout the European design offices.[33] Rand and Swannie made frequent trips to Europe, where they held seminars on design philosophy and application. According to Swannie:

'In Europe there are more highly educated designers, generally speaking, than you would find in the labs in the United States. Nevertheless, the education level was different between the locales. There were good designers in Germany and Switzerland, which you could predict because the training in those countries was good, but there were lesser lights in England and France.'[34]

The Europeans insisted that their graphics should be different from the United States, because both their languages and business cultures were different. But Rand did not favour independence without controlling safeguards. As flexible as the identity was, it required consistent management. Rand realized IBM needed to have a European consultant in graphics and named Josef Müller-Brockmann, one of Switzerland's foremost proponents of *Neue Grafik*, to the job. In addition, Karl Gerstner, whose advertising agency GDK was a leading firm in Europe, ministered to various design needs, from type direction to advertising design.

As IBM grew, Rand expanded his purview, cautiously exploring new terrain and making it his own. His first packaging assignment came in the late 1950s from IBM's Typewriter Division to design carbon paper and typewriter ribbon boxes, a small job that had a significant impact.

IBM Typewriter Ribbon,
packages, *c.*1959
The first major change
in package design was
requested by the Typewriter
Division. To humanize the
product Rand used a
carnival-like colour palette
and offset the logo with his
emblematic script.

Rand used the logo prominently set against the distinctive 'IBM blue' with type set in complementary reds and purples. The logotype was supplemented by the informal Rand-scrawled script used on his book jackets and covers. Eliminating the stolid business-as-usual aura from IBM's products and replacing it with carnival-like graphics humanized the merchandise *and* the corporation. Soon, other divisions requested package designs that were similar yet distinctive. Rand obliged by introducing a controlled range of identifiable colour variations, logo applications, and package shapes and forms. For one package, colourful IBM logos were

randomly sprinkled like confetti to give the sense of informality. For another, vertical rows of alternating rainbow colours gave off a festive glow. And it worked, too. IBM was not perceived by the public as the monolithic giant it was, but as an accessible provider of quality machines and products.

In the early 1980s IBM's Office Product Division decided to open retail Product Centers, and its chief, Dick Young, gave Rand complete discretion to design a showroom prototype that would be adopted throughout the United States. 'The project involved the design of the complete environment including furniture, lighting,

interior wall treatments, floor coverings and product displays, together with graphic items such as identification symbols, signs, shopping bags, binders, business cards, stationery, etc.,' Tom Hardy explained about this mammoth undertaking, which was Rand's first comprehensive three-dimensional design commission.[35]

Left:
IBM Tote Box, package,
1983
Unlike the orthodox
European Modernists
who maintained limited
palettes, Rand loved
colour. Keeping the IBM
logo constant, he
introduced colourful
patterns and shapes,
including this carnival-
like confetti motif.

Below:
**IBM Wheelprinter Starter
Pack,** packages, 1983
The carnival motif
contributed to making
IBM a pioneer of
'user-friendliness'.

Right:
IBM Modem, packages,
1985–7
Rand continued to design
packages for over a
decade. The logo served
as an anchor for num-
erous colour variations
such as these. He wrote:
'Placement of the logo is
often arbitrary and thus
baffling to understand its
relationships to other
elements ... To use a logo
properly, a knowledge and
experience in typography
is invaluable.'

Overleaf:
IBM Product Center,
interior design, 1981
In the early 1980s Rand
was asked to design the
prototype for IBM's retail
stores where he was not
only responsible for the
graphics (packages and
signs) but also the displays
which featured working
products.

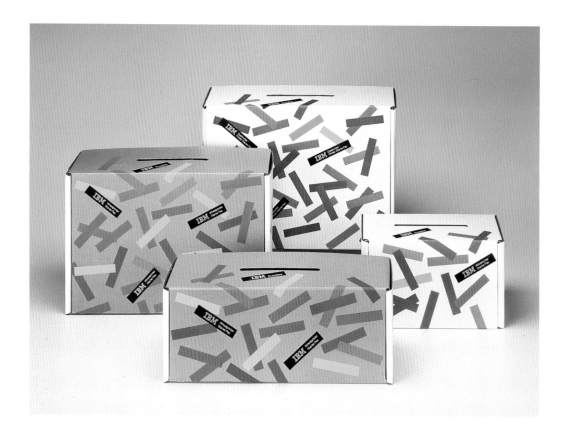

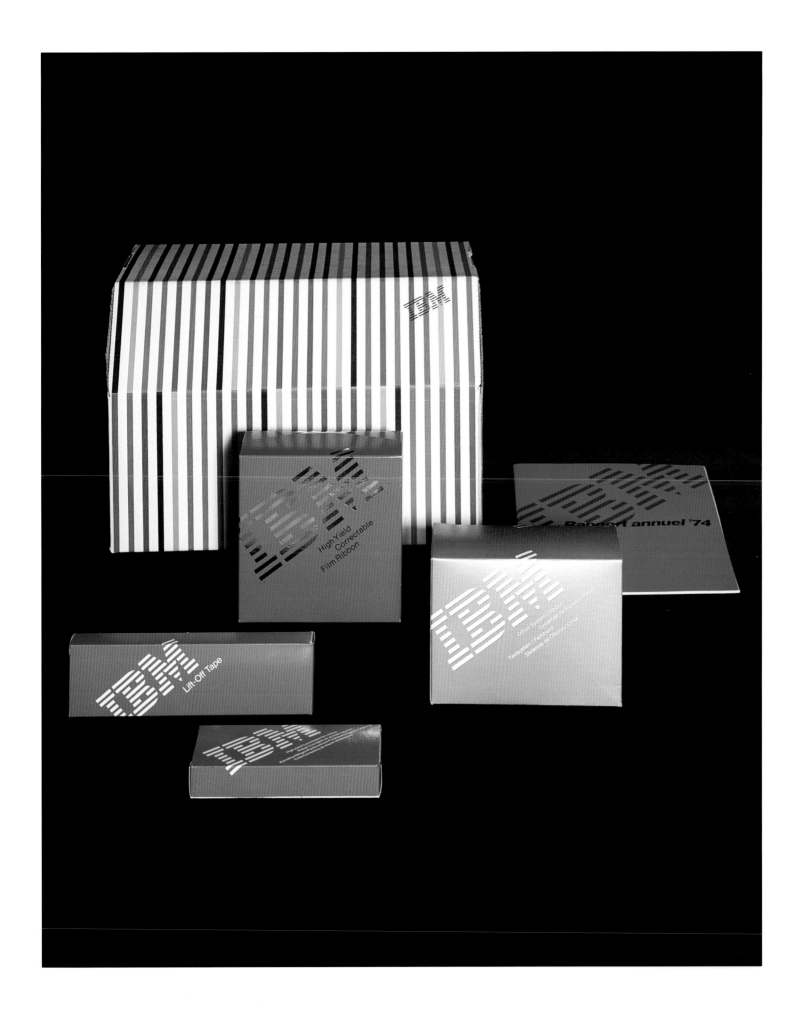

Coordinating the system around IBM's logo and house style, Rand energized the overall look through bright colours and lively geometric forms. Furthermore, he conceived of interactive displays that enabled customers to play with the machines. The stores were very well received by the public, but internally the powerful Real Estate and Construction Division, which held responsibility for architectural commissions, resented the influence in this area of the Office Product Division. A political rivalry ensued that, unbeknown to Rand, included him because he was in the employ of Dick Young. It was at this time that Rand, who insisted that he had no other agenda than to 'work with good clients', realized that corporate politics could impinge on his ability to make good design.

Rand eschewed corporate infighting and focused his energies on IBM's graphic repertoire, which was increasing at such a fast pace that a manual was needed to provide guidelines for the 'IBM look'. Rand was impressed by the innovative presentation books produced in programmes at Ulm, which not only provided guidelines for corporate standardization but also explained through integrated text and visuals the evolutionary rationale for specific design decisions. Similarly, he believed that an impeccably reasoned account of IBM's design process would serve as an invaluable guide for the growing army of IBM designers. With didactic precision and poetic rhythm Rand wrote and designed manuals for IBM's internal use that showed the breadth and flexibility of the programme.

Below:
IBM Design Program,
folder, 1984
Rand enjoyed using geometric forms whenever possible. This colourful folder, one of his favourite works, was used at a Design Program seminar at which Rand spoke.

Right:
The IBM Logo: Its Use in Company Identification,
cover and inside spreads from brochure, 1996
Rand was the keeper of the logo and protector of the mark, responsible for a variety of manuals designed to maintain quality and consistency among IBM design offices. In an address to IBM designers in 1981 Rand stated: 'A logo can shout or whisper, be discreet or assertive; it can be decorative or plain, straightforward or elaborate,' but, he added, 'a logo must always be authoritative.'

Design Program

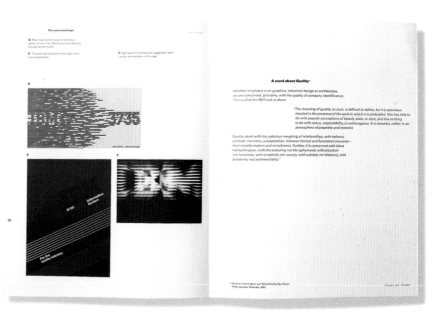

Rand's standard of excellence for IBM expressed his total dedication to design. His belief in the rightness of form had not diminished since his advertising days, and his intolerance for management interference had hardened with age, while his very 'direct presentation style' resulted in periodic conflicts with IBM's middle managers. He was a tough critic, an independent thinker and by no means a 'yes man'. 'These traits, desirable in consultants, can naturally cause conflicts with some corporate management-types, who are political and in positions of authority, yet indifferent to the value of design,' remarked Tom Hardy:

'Paul fondly referred to them as Philistines. And I think every person that worked with Paul had some type of conflict at one time or another. But that was expected if you understood his total immersion in the design process. Those of us who greatly respected his brilliant work, and who also had the privilege of experiencing the personal side of Paul, considered the conflicts we encountered as learning experiences from a genius.'[36]

Rand was certainly not shy – some thought him downright arrogant – when it came to expressing his opinions about design, especially to IBM managers. There was no grey area, no room for compromise. He resisted bad work, and more vehemently resisted people who could not understand the difference between good and bad. 'I was terrible,' he admitted:

'I had a hard time with many people. But there is no *ad hominem* relationship. It's just that I love good work, and I know certain people in big business are put into jobs that have no idea what the job is, and they immediately become authorities. They become authorities over me, and I've been doing it for more than fifty years. They've been doing it for five years, and they can approve or disapprove my work, which is outrageous. I resist that, and therefore I am a pariah. And yet people who are really intelligent don't give me a hard time.'[37]

Design: Paul Rand

"He who stops being better

stops being good"

Oliver Cromwell

IBM Excellence Plus

The concept of quality is difficult to define, for it is not merely seen, but somehow intuited in the presence of the work in which it is embodied.

Quality has little to do with popular notions of beauty, taste, or style; and nothing to do with status, respectability, or luxury. It is revealed, rather, in an atmosphere of receptivity, propriety, and restraint. Paul Rand

Resource Management:
Energy and
Materials Conservation
Ridesharing
Environment Protection

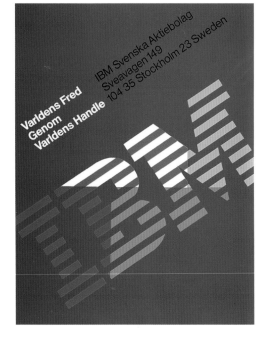

Varldens Fred
Genom
Varldens Handle

IBM Svenska Aktiebolag
Sveavagen 149
104 35 Stockholm 23 Sweden

Left:
IBM, packaging, *c.*1980
Although each European country in the IBM orbit had its own design and language concerns, as shown here with this package for Sweden, Rand's basic design theme was strictly followed.

Below left:
Customer Support Center, poster, *c.*1980
Rand maintained a large graphic vocabulary for the equally large number of projects that he worked on himself, such as these coloured squares which appear frequently throughout his work.

Below:
Awards Conference,
poster, 1982
The mask is a recurrent theme and prop in Rand's work.

IBM
Customer Support Center

1982
Customer Service Division
Awards Conference
March 31-April 3. April 4-April 7
Fontainebleau Hilton
Miami Beach, Florida

Golden Circle, poster,
1981
For this IBM sales
conference in Kauai,
Hawaii, Rand developed
integrated print pieces,
including posters,
identity tags and folders.

May 5–9 '81

Golden Circle

Kauai Surf Hotel
Hawaii

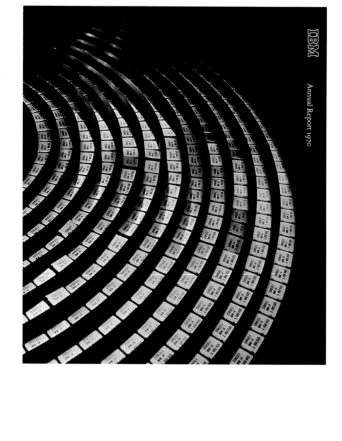

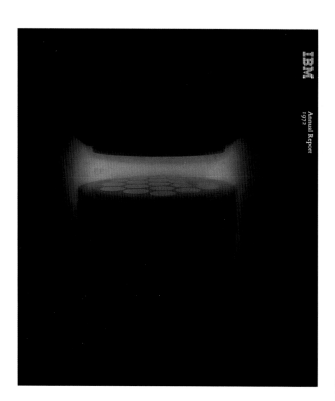

Left (clockwise from
far left):
IBM Annual Report,
cover, 1972
IBM Annual Report,
cover, 1970
IBM Annual Report,
cover, 1980

Below and right:
IBM Annual Report,
cover and inside
pages, 1981

Bottom right:
IBM Annual Report,
cover, 1991
Throughout his tenure,
the annual report was one
of the many components
of corporate culture over
which Rand exerted a
strong creative influence.

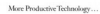

More Productive Technology...

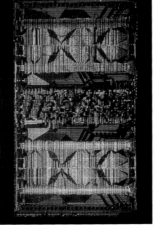

1991 Annual Report

When Eliot Noyes died in 1977, he was not replaced as chief design consultant. Charles Eames died a year later, and although Ray Eames continued to consult for IBM until her death ten years after that, Rand was the only full-time, outside design consultant until he recommended that industrial designer Richard Sapper be brought aboard to design IBM products. By the mid-1980s, Thomas J. Watson Jr had distanced himself from day-to-day operations, and while younger company executives continued to support the design programme, Rand's role slowly began to change. By 1987, at seventy-three years old, he became IBM Graphic Design Consultant Emeritus, and although he continued focusing on major corporate identity components – logotype usage, packaging and revision of house style items such as stationery and signs, as well as special design projects – Rand's allies were retiring in quick succession. Consequently, shifts in divisional- and corporate-level policies took a toll on his ability to function as well as when he had Noyes' and Watson's total support.

'Everyone assumed that the design programme would be a way of life at IBM,' explained Marion Swannie (who became Marion Rand in 1975 and retired from the company).[38] However, starting in the late 1980s with the advent of the personal computer, IBM management made some disastrous business decisions – notably the continued emphasis on huge and costly mainframe computers – that enabled competitors in the personal computer field to gain market dominance over this former Goliath. As revenues declined, a new management team forced IBM to become a much leaner company. Pressure to alter the product lines and focus more on no-nonsense marketing concluded in diminished emphasis on design. Initially, there was no direct decision to end the design programme, but personnel changes in positions of influence had devastating effects. Rand believed that it was important to educate new managers, but the marketing experts insisted that they should dictate design policy. As the company began its precipitous decline, new management discontinued the corporate art collection and exhibitions and closed IBM's prestigious 57th Street gallery.

The Medician culture that Thomas J. Watson Jr had vociferously supported was summarily dismantled. Lip service was paid to the design programme, but in the internal power struggle, Rand's influence diminished further. He remained on retainer, and if anyone wanted his advice they could come see him at his home in Weston. 'But people took sides,' recalled Marion Rand, 'there were those who wanted to work with Paul and those who wanted to work within their own power structure.'[39] In 1991 IBM offered Rand a new consulting contract that he refused to sign, citing irreconcilable differences with middle management and inaccessibility to top management. After almost forty years, Rand reluctantly announced that he would no longer consult for IBM, leaving behind a design legacy that both underscored a progressive corporate culture and gave graphic design increased credibility.

Below:
Paul Rand, 1970
(photographer: Milton Ackoff)
Rand oversaw the hanging of his exhibition, 'The Graphic Art of Paul Rand', at the IBM Gallery.

Below left:
75, poster, 1989
Rand loved to use his logos (especially the IBM one) as confetti, thereby adding wit to the application.

The Graphic Art of Paul Rand, poster, 1970
Much of Rand's work looks serendipitous, such as this hand balancing a spinning-top, used to announce his exhibition; but nothing is ever left to chance. This image appeared earlier in his children's book *Sparkle and Spin*.

Westinghouse and Cummins

Being graphic design consultant for IBM during its glory years might have been enough responsibility for most large design firms, but for the indefatigable Rand it was just one part of his solo practice. Rand was dedicated to IBM, but he was not shackled to it. During these years he never actively sought work; he nonetheless acquired some of the most prized corporate commissions American business could offer. In 1959 Eliot Noyes tapped him again to be graphic design consultant for Westinghouse Electric Corporation, with responsibility for its new logo, identity, packaging and institutional advertising. Then in 1961 he was named design consultant for the Cummins Engine Company. In addition to his continuing work in book and book jacket design, and children's book illustrations, in 1961 he crafted the United Parcel Service logo, and in 1962 the American Broadcasting Company logo. When many of his peers had retired, he was at the top of his form.

The design programme launched by Rand for Westinghouse is as historically important as the IBM legacy. Westinghouse was a huge corporation with plants and offices throughout the world; it developed transistors, power generation equipment, electronics and atomic reactors. Yet its antique logo was originated at the turn-of-the-century by founder George Westinghouse. It was a block W in a circle with a bold, lozenge-shaped bar underneath with the word Westinghouse chiselled inside, and although it was frequently updated, none of the iterations were any more modern than the original. Realizing that the company was not presenting a realistic image to the public, an internal analysis was ordered by Westinghouse management in 1959, resulting in an indictment of corporate design practices in a white paper titled *Image by Design*. 'It was a voluminous report, accompanied in meetings by scores of colour slides,' recalled Dick Huppertz, who was Coordinator of Corporate Design in 1960 and Manager of the Westinghouse Corporate Design Center from 1964 to 1973:

'There were many management meetings which startled a lot of people, because we showed how old-fashioned Westinghouse looked everywhere, including packaging, products, print applications, architecture, interiors and the trademark itself – everything bespoke a company that was out of the Oliver Twist era.'[40]

This rude awakening forced Westinghouse president Mark Cresap to act decisively. Impressed by IBM's successes, he hired Eliot Noyes in 1959 as Consultant-Director of Design, responsible for graphic identity, architecture and product design. Noyes recruited Charles Eames to work on products and displays and Rand to redesign the logo and graphics. The logo process took Rand a few months, although he claimed that he devised the mark within thirty minutes. Dick Huppertz recalled that the initial presentation was an extraordinary event because Rand presented only one solution – a circle with the W, the points of which were topped with three dark circles suggesting the look of an electronic circuit board, with a dark black lozenge underneath (a remnant from the old logo). The presentation was not made with conventional slides or display boards, instead Rand distributed a small book that traced the development of the mark and some applications in a prototypical form. 'He had a genius,'

Below:
Westinghouse, logo, 1960
Realizing that a radical departure would meet resistance, Rand combined elements of the old logo (the circle and underline lozenge) with the circuit board W. Upon seeing it one executive said it looked like a pawnbroker's symbol. Criticism aside, it was accepted without question.

Below left:
Alphabet, specimen of Westinghouse's gothic typeface, 1961

Right:
Westinghouse, animated sign, 1962
Rand did not foresee the animated potential of the logo when he first designed it, but the possibilities for bringing it to life soon became perfectly clear.

Right, below:
Proposal for the new Westinghouse trademark and logo, sketch, 1960
This preliminary pagination for Rand's presentation booklet is but one step in a long process.

abcdefghij klmnopqrst uvwxyz123 4567890&

commented Pete Seay, who headed the Westinghouse design programme during the late 1960s, 'because he took the old logo, and keeping all the elements in it – the circle, the "W" – made it a completely new thing.'[41] But Huppertz viewed the presentation with some alarm: 'Having come from this heavy block "W" with the underscore and the word "Westinghouse" often wrapped round it, going to something that had a bit of a cartoon character – what I referred to as a face with mouse ears – seemed to be too radical a departure.'[42]

'Whenever you present anything new to a bunch of Midwestern engineers like those at Westinghouse, they get startled,' acknowledged Seay.[43] Attendees at this meeting were indeed so dumbfounded that, after a brief silence, Cresap asked Rand if he had done any other variations. Rand responded with a blunt 'No'. The ensuing murmurs sounded like a plague of locusts, until one executive chimed up that the logo looked like a crown, another called it pawnbroker balls, and yet another said that it resembled a 'Negro's face'. But before opening the critical floodgates any wider, Cresap turned to Noyes and asked him how to determine whether this was the right solution or not. Noyes replied firmly: 'I'll tell you how we decide it. I am your design consultant, and we got the best man to do it, and I say this is good and you should approve it.' Cresap adjourned the meeting and ten minutes later announced that it was approved. 'It would never have passed if we hadn't had someone as strong as Noyes,' Seay concluded.[44]

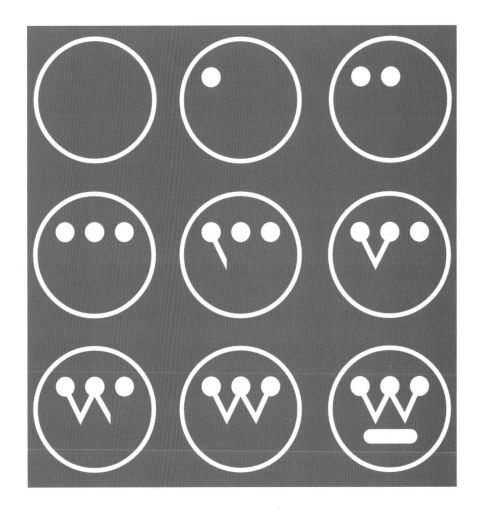

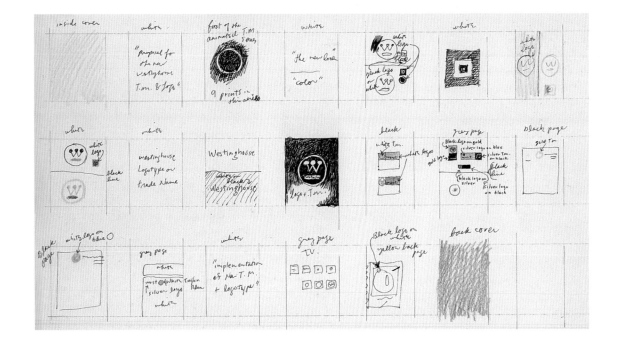

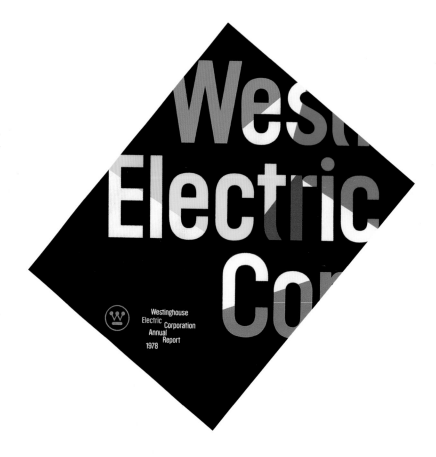

Noyes' recommendations were always accepted. And under his auspices Rand's role as design consultant became almost as absolute as it was at IBM. But Westinghouse, which was headquartered in Pittsburgh, Pennsylvania, was an even more diversified corporation with more outposts and more autonomous managers, who were not always inclined to follow design regulations. To remedy this, in 1961 Rand was asked to develop an initial design manual as an attempt to systematize corporate identity and put an end to the poor standards that pervaded the company. Entirely developed by Rand, it was the first example of how the logo could be used in myriad forms. All the different versions of the old circled W were shown by way of comparison, and Rand included a frontispiece introducing an animated version of the new logo (as it eventually appeared on two huge electronic signs in Pittsburgh and on the Long Island Expressway approach to New York City), that reminded Pete Seay of a Charlie Chaplin-like figure. Rand left no application to chance, showing how the mark could be used on business forms, mailing labels, parts labels, cartons, packaging, shipping banners for use on railroad cars, and a vehicle programme for various trucks. He further showed it in conjunction with the slogan, 'You Can Be Sure If It's Westinghouse.' At the end of the manual, there were binder covers and business cards, and even a matchbook cover. Rand further took great pleasure in designing signs – illuminated dealer signs, building signs, and water tower signs.

Nevertheless, there were difficulties in enforcing compliance, and, according to Huppertz, it took a number of years for the old to be replaced. One of Huppertz's roles was to get Rand to appear at various meetings, seminars and workshops, where he would critique work (including regular advertising critiques in the early days to make sure that the mark was being used properly in ads). 'But Paul couldn't help himself but critique the quality of the advertising itself, which was rather traumatic,' Huppertz added.

'I had to have very thick skin in those days. Because I would bring Paul in for a review, and there would be all the key people there, including outside agency people, and the people whom they reported to in the specific division. Paul wouldn't mince any words. He would say, "This stuff looks like a bunch of crap. This is garbage, this is terrible." He didn't give a damn about whose feelings he was hurting or whose toes he was stepping on. But he always followed this up with constructive criticism about how it could have been better. However, by this time, many of the people in the room were so incensed about his manner that by the time I got back to Pittsburgh people would call me up and say, "Who is this guy? What does he think he's doing?"'[45]

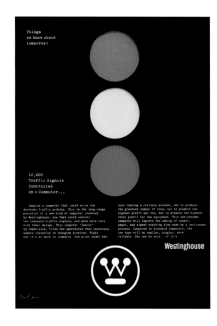

Below left:
Westinghouse,
advertisement/poster, 1962

Left, and this page, clockwise
from left:
Westinghouse, covers for
annual reports, 1978, 1974,
1971, 1979
Many designers worked for
the Westinghouse Design
Center, which produced in-
house, promotional and
packaging materials. Rand
consulted on these pieces
but reserved the annual
report covers – and some of
the institutional advertising –
for himself.

Rand was draconian when it came to quality. If the designer he was criticizing listened and learned Rand was patiently helpful. But when confronted with excuses, he saw red. 'Paul was sometimes like a truck, just barrelling through a group of people,' continued Huppertz. 'And I had the very difficult task at times of trying to smooth everybody's feathers at the end and telling them that this was all for the good. But they were used to the typical corporate people never making a clear statement, sort of weaseling their words.'[46] Rand believed that clarity was as important in design management as it was in good design. He also felt that if *he* could do it well in a short amount of time, so should everyone else.

With the success of the Westinghouse logo, Rand proceeded to design the entire panoply of corporate materials. But his real opus was the redesign of Westinghouses' retail light-bulb packaging. Commissioned by the Lamp Division in Bloomfield, New Jersey, to revamp their dated packages printed in orange and blue with the old circled W logo, Rand seized on one very important detail. The type indicating the wattage was so small that the consumer could not distinguish one bulb from another without close

scrutiny. So this became the focal point of the redesign. Rand made wattage the dominant graphic element, with the logo used more discreetly. However, since he liked to retain a little linkage with the past in building brand identity, the blue colour used by Westinghouse while making it much more contemporary, became known as 'Westinghouse electric blue'.

By 1968 Eliot Noyes determined that Westinghouse needed a design lab to centralize both experiments and quotidian work in architecture, product and graphic design. Huppertz developed the fundamental proposal that was submitted to the new president of Westinghouse, Donald Burnham, who also strongly supported the Design Center and encouraged good design in general. Rand was the chief consultant and the 'inevitable interviewer', recalled Grant Smith, first manager of the Graphic Design Department at the Design Center in 1969. Smith recalls that Rand had to approve all the designers they hired:

'If the person responded defensively or in any kind of insecure way, Paul's tiger came out … He had an instant eye, and when he saw a piece of work that he didn't think held up, or didn't have an idea in it, he would ask a couple of questions, and if the person tried to defend it, the interview was over. He couldn't stand somebody who bluffed. He hated pretence.'[47]

Colleagues believe that it was in the mid-1960s, while consulting for Westinghouse, that Rand became an enthusiastic proponent of Swiss-style design grids. In 1965 Rand hired Ken Hiebert, a designer and design educator, to work on identity guides, brochures and books that were done on precise grid structures. 'When Rand saw the sketches [for these books] he was very excited at the possibility of learning more about the use of grids.'[48] Yet Rand wanted to develop his own vocabulary for referring to the grid. What Hiebert referred to as micro- and macro-units of a grid (micro referring to the unit based on type-size plus leading; and macro referring to the larger blocks embracing multiple lines of type) Rand found too technically offputting. 'He liked calling the micro-grid the "baby grid",' recalled Hiebert. 'He was easily overwhelmed by brilliant Swiss and German grid manifestations, but his own language didn't fit the technical substrate. He kept it in very simple, humane, often childlike terms. In no case did he want to get bogged down with the technical.'[49]

Rand's interest in such systems had been stimulated by Le Corbusier's Modulor and the Japanese tatami mat system, but pure geometry was one of the most critical influences on his later work. 'How can you argue with geometry?' he declared.[50] According to Hiebert, this was a major factor in his shift from the more whimsical and ephemeral drawing style of the earlier work to the systematic 'corporate Rand' of the 1960s. In addition to grids, Rand also started using more Swiss-derived typefaces, Helvetica and Univers, to define Westinghouse's look. 'Basing typography on a unit grid, and letting that extend into the modules constructed for a page, were ideas that Paul practised at Westinghouse, and extended to other work,' confirmed Grant Smith.[51]

With Westinghouse's 120 divisions worldwide, 'it was hard for anybody to really get their arms around this monster,' commented Reid Agnew. 'It was very easy for somebody to go off and do their own thing, and Paul would complain bitterly about when he saw a smiley face on the Westinghouse logo or whatever people were apt to do. But even Paul recognized that it was too big for any one person to control, though he certainly tried.'[52]

Rand exercised as much control as possible, given that he had two other major consultancies and more freelance work than his one assistant could handle. However, he never missed a quarterly visit to Westinghouse's office in New York to review the design work *en masse*. If it was a particularly important project or one that was uncertain, the work would also be taken up to his home in Weston where he held his legendary critiques. He also designed the annual report covers on his own, while the designers on staff produced the interiors. Rand further officiated over the redesign of the corporate sign system, and the packaging system from semi-retail to corrugated shipping cartons, as well as small but highly visible investors' guides.

In the 1970s, Westinghouse was hard hit by a nuclear fuel crisis. The corporation had constructed the first commercial atomic power plant near Pittsburgh and others around the country. When the company sold plants and reactors to regional utilities, they guaranteed to maintain the plutonium fuel rod prices at a very minor price increase over a period of years. When the cost of plutonium suddenly soared on the world market, Westinghouse was stuck with dozens of utilities with contracts for low-cost fuel. Consequently, Westinghouse adopted a big austerity programme to counteract the huge drain caused by these contractual arrangements. Departments that were not considered essential were cut back or eliminated, and the Design Center was one of the early casualties. Donald Burnham also retired as president at this time, and the Design Center was consequently detached from its top management sponsorship. With dwindling support, the contracts with outside consultants were not renewed. Although Rand was subsequently called upon to produce designs until the early 1980s, his position was significantly eroded. Once again, good design was sacrificed to corporate mismanagement.

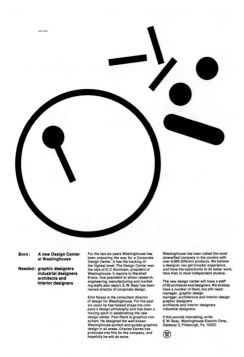

Far left:
Westinghouse 75 Watt, package, 1968
Westinghouse's original lightbulb packages were not very appealing or informative. Rand's solution was to simplify the package, introduce the 'Westinghouse Electric Blue' colour scheme and display the wattage in large type, which, after all, was the consumer's most immediate concern.

Centre left:
Westinghouse Colortone Floodlight, package, 1968

Left:
A New Design Center, advertisement/poster, 1968
With characteristic wit, Rand deconstructed his own Westinghouse logo design in this recruitment pitch for designers for the corporate Design Center.

Westinghouse,
illuminated sign, 1968
The Westinghouse logo
evoked different images
for different people, but
for Rand it was a mask,
like Charlie Chaplin's
tramp face, which inspired
the animation of this
electric sign, constructed
in both Pittsburgh and
New York.

Many of Rand's so-called 'good clients' had
their Achilles' heels. But Cummins Engine,
founded in 1919, remained the most enduring
of Rand's business associations (in fact, one
week before he died, the Cummins people asked
Rand to review some designs related to the 1996
annual report, which Marion Rand brought to
the hospital). In 1961 Eliot Noyes introduced
Rand to Cummins Engine president Irwin Miller,
who from the 1960s to the 1970s, revived his
corporate town, Columbus, Indiana, with buildings designed by Eliel and Eero Saarinen, Kevin
Roche, Richard Meier and I.M. Pei, among
others. Miller also realized that the venerable
company needed a modern graphic and
product design overhaul along the lines of IBM.
Initially, however, Rand worked only on the
annual report because, under the auspices of the
Marketing and Advertising Department, another
designer had been commissioned to redesign the
Cummins logo. The proposed redesign looked
curiously like a 'C' in the shape of a hot-dog,
elongated and rounded on both ends, and was
coloured sausage brown. Miller was not keen
on this, so, after continuing to use the old logo
(a crossed rectangle) long after it was proven
ineffective, he announced that it was time to
give Rand the assignment.

Below left
and bottom left:
Cummins, logos (English
and Japanese), 1973

Below:
Cummins, presentation
book, 1973
After some trial and error
Rand presented what was
termed by Cummins
staffers as 'the half-essed
logo' to Irwin Miller, president of Cummins Engine
and patron of good design.
Rand developed a system
that was both identifiable
and expandable.

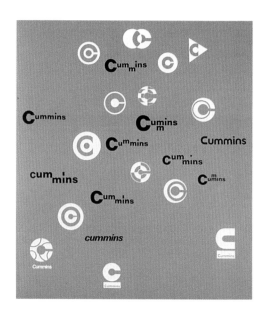

Below:
Cummins, logo as shown
in *From Lascaux to
Brooklyn*

Right:
Cummins Annual Report,
cover, 1975

Below right:
Genuine Cummins Parts,
packages, *c.*1974
Rand developed a design
system that governed
all Cummins printed
materials and packages
and continues today
with little variation.

'We always gave Paul a very clear definition
of the problem, then turned him loose,' said
Randy Tucker, who coordinated graphics at
Cummins Engine and worked closely with Rand
for almost thirty years. 'The key to this problem
was in understanding that Cummins was a
one-product company – diesel truck and tractor
engines – and because the product is under a
hood, the logo is not visible to the general
public.'[53] Miller therefore wanted Cummins' full
name to be overtly part of the logo. Yet Rand
was not initially given these instructions by the
Marketing Department, and so played with some
abstract ideas that didn't have the Cummins
name in it. 'Once he understood the problem,'
related Tucker, 'he solved it in his mind within
a half-an-hour at most.'[54] Nevertheless, 'the half-
essed logo', as Tucker called it because part
of the 's' was outside the dominant 'C', was not
immediately used.

Cummins, annual report covers, 1969, 1976, 1977, 1979, 1981, 1986
Rand's covers for Cummins Engine annual reports were simple and eloquent. Most covers incorporated the logo either as the defining motif or ancillary image.

The logo languished for a year or so because Miller was unhappy with the colour options offered by Rand – a tan and a Wedgwood blue. Miller had absolute discretion when it came to design; but Tucker recalled that, 'one thing about Irwin in design matters was he never said "It's got to be this way." His view always was, if it wasn't right, don't tell the designer what *is* right, just say, "Why don't you try again."'[55] Nonetheless, Miller indicated to Rand that he preferred yellow from the visibility standpoint. Rand agreed, but added that Cummins' competitor had already claimed yellow for themselves. Caterpillar was well known for its yellow tractors, so Rand sampled red, green and blue. 'He came out here for a presentation with a letterhead printed up in these various colours,' Tucker remembered, 'and before showing it to Irwin he predicted that he was going to choose Yale blue, because Miller had graduated from Yale. And Paul was absolutely right.'[56] Despite the pseudo-scientific talk about the power of logos, Rand knew that in all matters of taste and aesthetics, personal prejudice intervened. 'What's important for me is that I know that [a logo] is appropriate,' Rand explained. 'Why the client decided it was the right decision is unimportant because the reason has nothing to do with *reason*. And since you can't deal with unreasonable facts or people, you just forget about it.'[57]

Irwin Miller's view on art and design was always accepted as the final word, not only because he was the chairman, but because he showed good taste and judgement. Apart from the logo, there was only one other time in over thirty years that there was any disagreement between Miller and Rand. Tucker relates that:

'Before Irwin got his glasses changed, there were times when he thought that the annual report was too hard to read and I remember Paul made some adjustments – somewhat grudgingly. But other than that, he had Irwin's absolute confidence. Moreover, we were a great client because we were predictable, and accepted Paul's word on design issues pretty much as law.'[58]

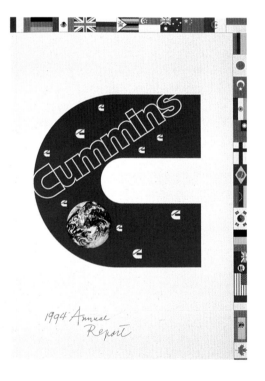

1994 Annual Report

1994 Annual Report
Cummins Engine Company, Inc.

Right:
UPS, logo on truck, 1961
Prior to Rand's
involvement, various
designers failed to
redesign the UPS logo
satisfactorily. Rand
decided to retain the
shield believing that it had
symbolic significance for
the men who wore it. He
replaced the typeface and
added the 'gift' box atop
the shield. Before showing
his proposal to UPS, he
asked his young daughter,
Catherine, for her opinion
– according to Rand
she said: 'That's a
present, Daddy.'

Far right and below:
Paul Rand, 1990
(photographer unknown)
Going through his UPS
job bag at his home in
Weston, Connecticut, Rand
showed off different
versions of the logo. While
he created dozens for
himself, he only showed
one to the client.

UPS

During the late 1950s and early 1960s,
numerous sophisticated designers were assuming
larger roles in corporate communications and
setting their own laws. The veteran Lester Beall
had created a landmark identity for International Paper, and various newcomers – including
Brownjohn Chermayeff Geismar, Rudolf
DeHarak, Louis Danziger, Massimo Vignelli
(then at Unimark) and others – were
contributing to the widespread acceptance of
corporate identification. But one of the key
reasons that Rand was called upon so frequently
by American businesses was his uncanny ability
– or rather obsession – to inject wit and
whimsy into the corporate vocabulary. As
difficult as it was to reconcile business's need
to turn over large profits with the humanization
of their images, Rand possessed the knack that
the mammoth identity design offices, such as
Lippincott and Marguiles, Landor, and Unimark
did not have. He created systems (or at least
logos) that were humanistic, if not playful. One
prime example of this was his redesign of the
United Parcel Service (UPS) logo.

Before approaching Rand, UPS had commissioned different designers to redesign their
original logo, a shield with initials set against a
brown background. Many of the proposed
solutions eschewed the shield as too antiquated.
Although Rand also thought it should change,
he was told that it must be retained. 'So, that
was the end of it,' said Rand, knowing that the
UPS employee shareholders, who would ultimately have to vote on the logo, viewed it as a
badge of their authority. 'The shield was also a
good transitional phase,' he reasoned. 'It wasn't
so abrupt, so there was some recall for the old
one.'[59] Rand's challenge was to transform the
shield into a modern image. He streamlined the
contours, introduced balanced gothic lower
case letters, and placed an outline of a package
with a bow on the top of the shield as sort of a
crown. 'I didn't try anything else,' Rand proudly
admitted. 'In fact, when I brought it to the
client, I handed him a rolled up photostat,
he looked and said, "You got anything else?"
I said, "No, that's it." And he didn't know how
to respond.'[60]

Rand had a week to sketch out the different versions of the logo for himself, but, as was his custom, he showed the one that made the most sense – to him. Rand had an informal way of testing his designs: 'I always used myself as a measure. I also used other people. Not experts, but rather simple people, like my eight-year-old daughter when I did UPS … I said, "Catherine, what's this?" and she said, "That's a present, Daddy" – which was perfect. You couldn't have rehearsed it any better.'[61]

In the late 1990s the logo is still in currency as Rand originally designed it, despite his offer years later to revise those parts of it that had bothered him since its inception. 'I would redraw the bow and take the point out of the shield,' he explained:

'I don't like pointed shields, never did. The only reason I used it in the first place was that it is a familiar way to show a shield. But I prefer one with a rounded base. Though at the time, if I had used a rounded base, somebody could have said that it looked like a pocket; I just didn't want to go through that at that juncture.'[62]

Below:
ABC, logo, 1962

Below left:
ABC, sign, 1962
Rand designed logos for
endurance. 'I think permanence is something that
you find out,' he once said.
'It isn't something that you
design for. You design for
durability, for function, for
usefulness, for rightness,
for beauty. But permanence
is up to God and time.'

ABC

One year after introducing the UPS mark, Rand
was commissioned to develop a logo for the
American Broadcasting Company (ABC). Again,
he was brought in after other designers had
tried and failed. So, of course, it had to be
completed in haste. ABC ranked third of the
three national networks and had an equally
third-rate logo in which the letters ABC were all
set in capitals. Realizing immediately that ABC
was a naturally rhythmic combination of forms,
Rand proposed that they be set in a lower case
gothic typeface similar to Futura, basing his
design entirely on equal circles that comprised
the negative space of the three letters, and
dropped it out in white from a black circle. It
was simple, direct, full of character, and
accepted immediately without debate.

In the late 1980s, however, ABC was purchased by Capital Cities, a media conglomerate,
which in an attempt to signal the change of
ownership demanded that the Rand logo be
altered or scrapped. Once again, various designers
were called upon to better the original (Rand
was not invited to participate), and new versions
included such tropes as stylized stars and eagles
(to emphasize the American in ABC). But none
could equal the simplicity of the existing mark.
After the failed attempt at change was over,
a bemused Rand commented: 'It was a great
mistake, not because it was the greatest logo in
the world, but even a bad logo shouldn't be
changed except for very good reasons. Because
a logo doesn't represent a company. The company represents the logo. If you're a lousy
company, your logo is useless, no matter how
well designed. If your logo is good, and you're
a good company, you have an ideal situation.
If the company is bad, it's a bad logo. So the
idea of changing a logo without recognizing the
importance of the change is stupid.'[63]

Rand railed against the cult of logos that
prevailed from the 1960s onwards and argued
that there was no mystique, except that a good
mark had to be intelligent to work efficiently.
'The reason I wasn't upset about the ABC thing,'
he further explained, 'is that I thought they
would have a hell of a time improving on it.
Somebody can do something better, obviously,
but in respect to its own form, it's perfect. You're
dealing with four circles. I mean, it can't be bad.
Circles are circles. If somebody comes up with
hexagons or triangles, that's possible to do, and
initially, at least, it will imprint in people's
mind the fact that the logo has been changed.
People will be aware of it more – only because
it's been changed.'[64]

Ford

Rand was responsible for scores of logos and marks that continue to dot the commercial landscape. But not all of his proposals were accepted. In 1966, at a time when many venerable companies were experiencing redesign fever, the Ford Motor Company considered changing its familar Ford script inside an oval nameplate. Rand was invited to make a proposal, which resulted in one of his most interesting presentation books, replete with a new logo and scores of sample applications. 'We spent a lot of money printing the book. It was a very elaborate affair,' he recalled. 'My approach to the problem was that what Ford had was perfectly good, but it was old-fashioned. It was not in keeping with the present technological era.'[65] So Rand modernized the script by removing the curlicue swash and streamlining the Art Nouveau elements. And ironically, the lettering looked quite similar to some of the fontography produced at the outset of the current digital era. But Henry Ford III rejected the proposal on the grounds that it was too radical a departure, even though it was more consistent with the contemporary design of Ford's automobiles.

Left, above:
Ford, logo, *c.*1900

Left, below:
Ford, logo proposal, 1966

Below:
Ford, pages from presentation booklet, 1966

Commissioned to re-examine the identity of the Ford Motor Company, Rand decided that the Model T-era logo could benefit from some updating. Although he retained the script, he streamlined the mark, which was shown to the client in a presentation book that extolled the past, whilst at the same time promoted change. The new logo was ultimately rejected by Henry Ford III.

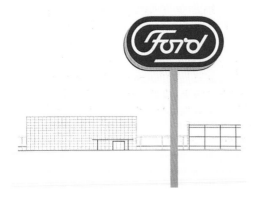

The Limited

In 1988 Rand was commissioned to design the logo for The Limited, a large chain of retail clothing stores based in Columbus, Ohio. His solution was a chain of horizontal and vertical linking lines, with 'The' meeting 'Limited' at a right angle. The two dotted 'i's in Limited form the 'm' and look as though they are shaking hands. Rand's signature use of alternating primary colours was one variation, the 'L' standing alone was another. Again he developed a presentation book that traced the logo's evolution. But what he did not reveal was his testing method:

'I showed this thing to the plumber, who was under the sink, and I said, "What does this say?" He read it. And I knew that it was right … Then I showed it to my maid, and she read it. Then I showed it to my accountant and he read it. I figured if these three people can read it it's got to be foolproof! My wife read it, and she thought it was ingenious. I never heard her describe anything that I did like that before.'[66]

However, Rand did not deal directly with the chairman, but rather an enthusiastic, secondary manager. After deliberation The Limited's Chief Executive rejected the mark without giving a reason.

Below:
The Limited, logo, 1988
Rand complained that the name of the clothing stores chain, 'The Limited', did not suggest an easy solution and so he sketched many ideas before transforming the M into a couple holding hands

Below left, bottom and right:
The Limited, pages, presentation booklet, 1988
Rather than talk at the client, Rand's presentation booklets spoke to the client – clearly and simply – about the rationale behind the solution. As this presentation reveals, it was also an opportunity for Rand to show the various applications of the logo on tags, bags, and other corporate materials.

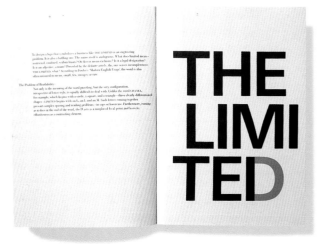

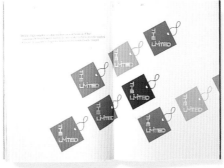

NeXT

By the late 1980s the logo business was gigantic: hundreds of large and small design firms produced logos, marks and full-scale identity systems for businesses throughout the world. Many of these firms were catering to the burgeoning computer companies of Silicon Valley. While the majority of these young corporations were seeking out equally young designers, Steven Jobs, the founder of Apple Computer Company, sought special dispensation from IBM to have Rand design the logo for his new educational computer company, NeXT. 'Paul understood the purpose and power of logos better than anyone in history,' explained Jobs about his decision to pay $100,000 for the mark in 1986. 'He was also the greatest living graphic designer.'[67]

It is difficult enough to invent a meaningful corporate logo, sign or mark to express conventional business issues without having to depict the future as well. However, that is what was demanded of Rand when he was commissioned to design a logo for NeXT. Although NeXT's new product was cast in secrecy, the corporate name alluded to its futuristic positioning – not simply a *new* computer, but the *next wave* of information-processing for the educational market. With only a few clues, Rand was given a month to devise a logo that would embody as much symbolic power as the memory of a silicon chip.

'Logos are *aides-mémoire* that give you something to hook on to when you see it, and especially when you don't see it,' explained Rand. Yet the problem with the word 'next' was that it was not depictable. 'What are you going to show? A barber shop with somebody pointing, "You're next"? It's simply not describable in typographic terms.'[68]

Graphic devices that represent the future, such as the arrow, were made meaningless by overuse, but the NeXT computer was contained in a black cube, which gave Rand the idea he needed. He decided to frame the word in a cube to evoke the product itself. However, at the time the logo was introduced to the public, the computer's form was completely secret. 'It was understandable only as a cube, nothing else,' he explained. 'But without that reference point, I would have had to devise something out of the blue.'[69] The NeXT logo was successful in part because the cube was symbolically related to the product itself, but Rand insisted that the shape was only important in sparking the idea. 'Some reference was made to it being like a child's block,' he continued. 'I really think that is one of its virtues and part of its charm. However, the logo is not designed to be charming, it is designed to identify.'[70]

Rand had to sell the mark to Jobs, and devised a two-pronged strategy. The first was to present only one logo, which underscored his own confidence in the solution and deflected indecision on the part of the client. The second was to 'speak' only through a presentation booklet, titled 'The Sign of the Next Generation of Computers *for Education ...*' which concisely explained the rationale and showed the applications of the logo. At the beginning of this limited (fifty copies at the time, later reprinted in a much larger quantity at Jobs' request), idealistic document, Rand announced his premise: 'What should a logo for Next look like?' he asked in text set in Caslon. This led to a concise narrative that condensed decades of communications history into ten minutes of reading time. First he introduced the concept of type itself:

'Choosing a typeface as the basis for the design of a logo is a convenient starting point. Here are two examples: Caslon and Bifur. Caslon is an alphabet designed as far back as 1725 by William Caslon. It appears to be a good choice because it is both elegant and bookish, qualities well suited for educational purposes.'[71]

He described the nature of his faces – the quirks and virtues – and concluded by admitting, 'Attributing certain magical qualities to particular typefaces is, however, largely a subjective matter.'

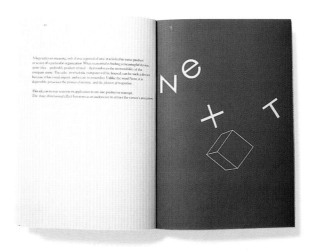

Left:

NeXT, logo, 1986
Steven Jobs kept a tight lid on the design of his new educational computer. Yet Rand cleverly incorporated the image of the top-secret black and square product into a distinctive mark.

Below left and below:

NeXT, pages from presentation booklet, 1986
IBM put Rand on the map, but NeXT brought him the most publicity, not only for his large fee ($100,000), but for the presentation booklet that convinced Steven Jobs of the rightness of the solution. In this veritable textbook of logo design, Rand explained the decisions that supported his type choices and how these simple letters were transformed into a mnemonic mark.

Next he defused the client's desire to sample a variety of typefaces:

'One reason for looking at a number of possible typefaces is to satisfy one's curiosity. Another, and perhaps more meaningful one, is to study the relationship of different letter combinations, to look for visual analogies, and to try to elicit ideas that the design of a letter or group of letters might inspire.'[72]

He offered some examples that were intended to pique the reader's interest, with this warning: 'Personal preferences, prejudices and stereotypes often dictate what a logo looks like, but it is *needs*, not wants, *ideas*, not type styles which determine what its form should be.'

Then Rand took a representative typeface and set it in capitals to explain why this particular iteration was unsuccessful: 'Set in all capitals, the word NeXT is sometimes confused with EXIT, possibly because the EXT grouping is so dominant. A combination of capitals and lower case letters alleviates this problem.' And after winning the argument, he provided a textbook example of a more successful application:

'Here are some possibilities which explore the use of lower case letters. The "e" is differentiated so as to provide a focal point and visual contrast among the capital letters which, otherwise, consist only of straight lines. Happily the e also could stand for: education, excellence, expertise, exceptional, excitement, e=mc2, etc.'[73]

This brief lesson in typographic style led into an explanation of how a mark should function: 'Ideally, a logo should explain or suggest the business it symbolizes, but this is rarely possible or even necessary. There is nothing about the IBM symbol, for example, that suggests computers, except what the viewer reads into it. Stripes are now associated with computers because the initials of a great computer company happen to be striped ... A logo takes on meaning, only if over a period of time it is linked to some product or service of a particular organization. What is essential is finding a meaningful device, some idea – preferably product-related – that reinforces the company name. The cube, in which the computer will be housed, can be such a device because it has visual impact, and is easy to remember. Unlike the word Next, it is depictable, possesses the *promise of meaning,* and the *pleasure of recognition.*'[74]

Rand talked about the cube's versatility: 'This idea in no way restricts its application to any one product or concept. The three-dimensional effect functions as an underscore to attract the viewer's attention.' Once established that the cube was the appropriate form, Rand addressed the basic structure of the logo:

'Splitting the logo into two lines accomplishes several things: it startles the viewer and gives the word a new look, thus making it easier to separate from common usage. And even more importantly, it increases the letter size two-fold, within the framework of the cube. For small space use, a one line logo would have been too small to fit within this same framework.'[75]

Rand showed that readability was not affected because the word was too simple to be misread: 'Moreover, people have become accustomed to this format with such familiar four-letter word combinations as Love.'

He concluded his primer with a practical analysis:

'The adaptation of this device to miniaturization – tie tacks, charm bracelets, paper weights, stickers, and other promotional items is endless. It lends itself as well to large-scale interpretation – signs, exhibits in the shape of cubes, in which the actual exhibit is housed, as well as exhibit stands. For printed matter, its infinite adaptability and attention-compelling power is self-evident.'

At the presentation, Rand did not utter a word, he just sat silently watching as Jobs read. 'The book itself was a big surprise,' Jobs recalled, 'I was convinced that each typographic example on the first few pages was the final logo. I was not quite sure what Paul was doing until I reached the end. And at that moment I knew we had the solution ... Rand gave us a jewel, which in retrospect seems so obvious.'[76]

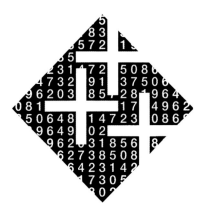

Below left and far right, above:
Irwin Financial Corporation, preliminary design and sketch,1990

Below: **Irwin Financial Corporation,** logo, 1990

Right, and far right, below:
Irwin Financial Corporation Annual Report, covers, 1990, 1992
Before deciding upon the final logo, Rand sketched numerous variations for his own amusement. Inevitably, the client was only presented with the one that he wanted them to see.

Irwin Financial
Corporation

Annual Report 90

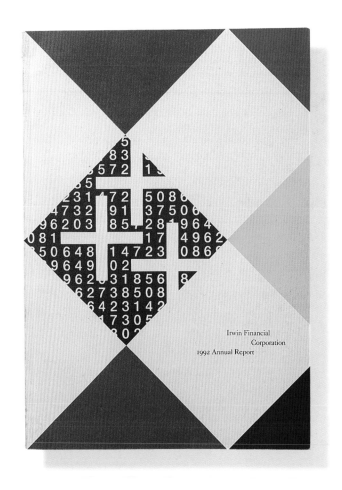

Irwin Financial
Corporation
1992 Annual Report

English First, logo and
pages from presentation
booklet, 1994
In this presentation
booklet Rand explained
the wrong typographic
decisions before revealing
his hypnotic design, and
its many applications, for
the final logo.

A B C D E F

G H I J K L M

N O P Q R S

T U V W X Y

Z A B C D E

F G H IJ K L

M N O P Q R

What you have just seen is the embryo of a graphic idea.
The most trying part of any design problem, especially the design
of a logo, is to find an idea that visually epitomizes
an enterprise of some sort, and that is also both appropriate and
visually arresting. Formalizing, pinning it down on paper, is the
next most difficult step.

The sound idea/pattern serves a clear purpose. It is
conceptually and graphically appropriate; it provides a visual
device that is both decorative and mnemonic, and
is easily incorporated as an organic and inseparable part of
the logo. The pattern provides a needed contrast to the
straight lines of the EF; the italics add emphasis.

EF Education
First

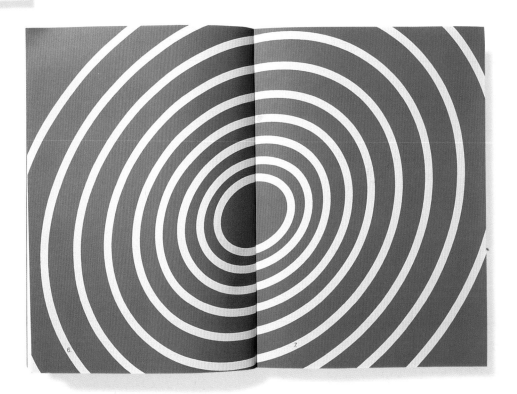

Here are some preliminary trials: with the exception of
the simplest logo, showing the E and F as a single letter, the other
designs are defining or descriptive ideas that relate to the
business of language, the alphabet serving as a springboard.

However, these ideas were abandoned, not because
they were inappropriate, but because they were imperfect.
Since the EF logo will be used in tandem with other
words as an active part of a particular design, it was felt that
the transition between the EF and accompanying
words was not sufficiently smooth; the alphabet seemed
to get in the way.

HUB TV, development of logo as shown in *From Lascaux to Brooklyn* Rand used the satellite dish as the motif for this decidedly animated logo for HUB TV. The only problem was that, after the presentation was accepted, the company name was changed to USSB. Rather than scrap the solution, Rand simply solved the problem anew.

Far right:
USSB, logo, 1995

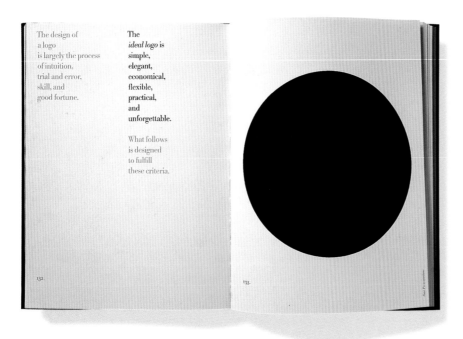

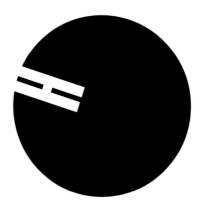

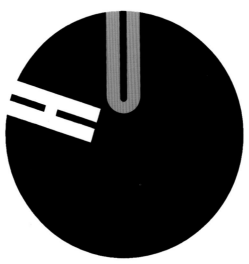

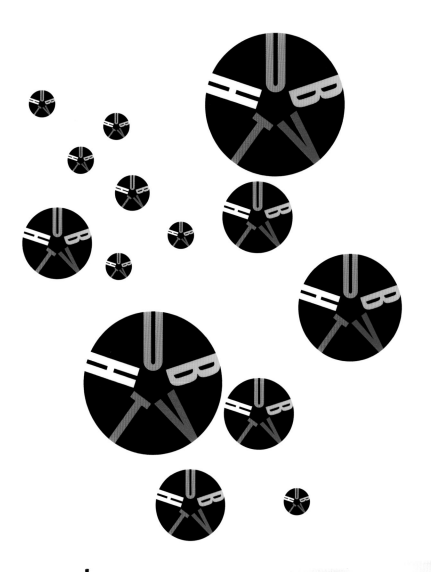

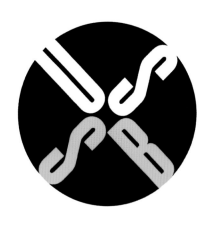

The star
configuration
is a persuasive
symbol.
It is universal,
memorable,
adaptable.
It says *the best*.

Here, it
evokes the image
of a *hub*
and a
satellite dish.

These
are happy
coincidences
and useful
memory aids.

142

143·

Other corporate design projects

As if the seventy-four year old Rand needed a professional boost, the NeXT logo earned considerable press and public attention, and many more commissions came his way. Among them, in 1991 he created the logo for Morningstar, a financial information company; the same year he developed the system for Okasan, a Japanese brokerage firm; in 1993 he designed the mark for EF (English First), a language school based in Stockholm; in 1995 he began work on USSB, a global television satellite company (which changed its initials half-way through the project); and shortly before his death in 1996 Rand unveiled the mark for Enron, a huge energy concern (both USSB and Enron were introduced to the public in television commercials only days after Rand's death). Finally, in pure Rand style, in 1996 he also designed a mark for the cancer centre of Norwalk Hospital, where he received treatment himself until his death.

While Rand claimed that he was proudest of his advertising and publishing output produced between 1941 and 1955, his corporate work had the greatest influence on both graphic design and popular culture. His logos are etched as much into the corporate landscape as they are on to popular perception. His visual identities for the corporations that have in many ways defined the twentieth century are as indelible, if not more so, than their specific products and services. And as if to provide a coda to this key aspect of his career, Rand said that 'a logo is more important in a certain sense than a painting because a zillion people see the logo and it affects what they do. It affects their taste, it affects the appearance of where they live, it affects everything.'[77]

Left to right by row: logos and trademarks

Wallace Puppets, 1938
Esquire, 1938
Coronet Brandy, 1941
Cresta Blanca, 1943

Alfred A. Knopf, 1945
Smith, Kline & French Laboratories, 1945
Hilbros Watch Company, 1944
Shur Edge, 1947

Left to right by row:
logos and trademarks

Theatrical Architectural Television, c.1949
Harcourt Brace and Company, 1957
IBM, 1956

Consolidated Cigar Company, 1959
Colorforms, 1959
Westinghouse, 1960
UPS, 1961
ABC, 1962
Atlas Crankshaft Corporation, 1964

IIT Research Institute, 1994
Ford (not used), 1966
U.S. Department of the Interior/Bureau of Indian Affairs, 1968

Left to right by row:
logos and trademarks

Cummins, 1962
Columbus Indiana
Visitors' Center, 1973
Tipton Lakes, 1980
AIGA (not used), 1982

Yale University Press, 1985
NeXT, 1986
PDR, 1987
Mossberg & Company,
Inc., 1987
The Limited (not used),
1988

Monell Chemical Senses
Center, 1989
Irwin Financial
Corporation, 1990
Okasan Securities Co.,
1991

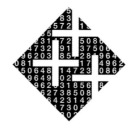

Left to right by row:
logos and trademarks

**Morningstar Investment
Advisers,** 1991

IDEO Design, 1991
Gentry Living Color,
1993
English First, 1993
Accent Software

International, 1994
Computer Impressions, 1995
USSB, 1995
Creative Media Center, 1994
Enron, 1996

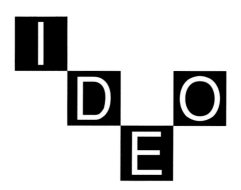

For Rand the poster was akin to a canvas. He created over fifty poster images, some enlargements of smaller designs, others designed to be posted; some were advertisements and announcements, others were components of larger corporate identities. The following is a sampling:

Left: **Interfaith Day**, poster, 1953
Rand produced a series of posters for this ecumenical celebration, each using personal symbols drawn with child-like abandon.

Below:
AIGA 50th Anniversary, poster, 1965
Not known as a slapstick artist, on occasion Rand succumbed to the urge to be silly. This is one of a series of images produced to celebrate the AIGA.

Sponsored by the Interfaith Movement, Inc.   Sidney O. Raphael, president   Mayor Robert F. Wagner, honorary chairman

Interfaith Day

Sunday September 26, 1 p. m.

Central Park Mall

All Star Program

Paul Rand

Tri Arts Press, poster,
1980
In the Cubist and Dada
tradition, Rand used
collage to introduce motifs
and design elements such
as arabesques, baroque
borders and novelty
letterforms that he would
not render by hand.

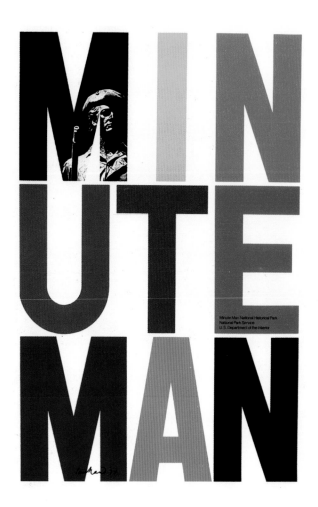

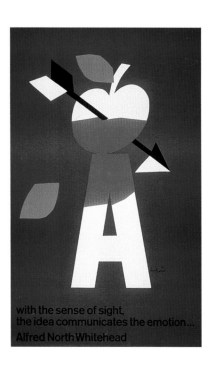

with the sense of sight,
the idea communicates the emotion...
Alfred North Whitehead

Left:
Minute Man, poster 1975
For the U.S. Department of the Interior, Rand reinterpreted the icon of the revolutionary Minute Man using collage and primary colours.

Below left:
A, poster, 1965
Collage was a noteworthy aspect of Modern art and a significant part of Rand's repertoire, as this poster for the Advertising Typography Association of America reveals.

Below:
Subway Posters Score,
poster, 1947
This lollypop/character/ toy – developed for the New York Subway Advertising Company, which commissioned various Modern designers to produce posters – transforms the cliché of the 'advertising bullseye'.

UCLA BC
DEFGHIJ
KLMN●P
QRSTUV
WXYZ 93

UCLA Summer Sessions 1993   University of California, Los Angeles   Session A: June 28–August 6
Los Angeles, California 90024   Session B: July 19–August 27
March 1993   Session C: August 9–September 17

Left:
UCLA Summer Sessions,
poster 1993

Below left:
UCLA 75, poster, 1994

Below:
**UCLA Extension Winter
Quarter,** poster, 1990

UCLA was one of Rand's best clients because, as he would say, 'I do the job, and they accept it.' These posters exhibit his interest in visual puns.

UCLA
Extension
Winter
Quarter
begins
January 6
1990

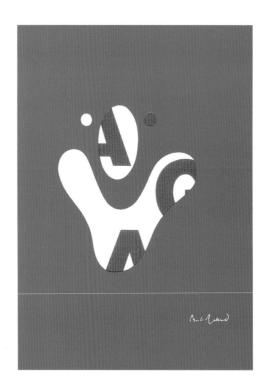

Left:
AIGA, cover/poster, 1968
Working gratis for the
pre-eminent design
organization in the United
States, Rand allowed
himself the licence to play
with pure form.

Below, far left:
'90, poster, 1990
A very restrained solution,
for Rand, for the bicen-
tennial of Benjamin
Franklin's birthday, which
incorporated image and
letterform.

'90
P. Franklin

1790–1990
Celebrating 200 years
of his Genius

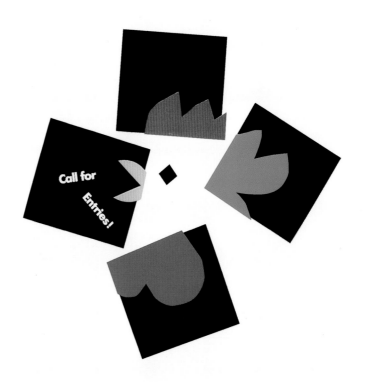

Call for
Entries!

The Art Directors Club, Inc.
3rd International Exhibition
New York, N.Y. U.S.A.
Deadline: 16 December 1988

Tokyo
Communication
Arts

Osaka
Communication
Arts

Paul Rand: Author

5

Paul Rand had an intuitive sense for the art of placement – whether juxtaposing a photograph with a word in type, relating a fragment of torn paper to a linear illustration or arranging a logo on a letterhead. One can't be taught such things; one can only hope to learn them.

Alan Fletcher, student at Yale, 1957

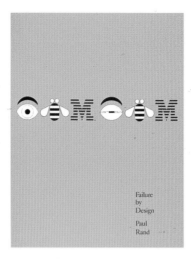

Failure
by
Design

Paul
Rand

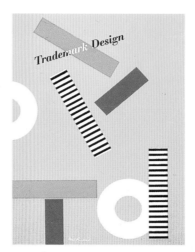

Trademark Design

Below:
Paul Rand, 1970
(photographer:
Milton Ackoff)
Rand did all his writing,
usually in long hand,
from his home in Weston,
Connecticut.

Paul Rand's presentation books balanced history and theory with common sense. They eschewed the dog-and-pony slide presentations that Rand detested, and elaborated complex ideas precisely through words and pictures. Rand often said that more time was spent writing, rewriting, designing, redesigning and overseeing the printing of these ersatz textbooks than it took to conceive a logo. His long-time typesetter Mario Rampone confirmed that for every book Rand marked-up, there were dozens of galleys with corrections ranging from changes in punctuation to recasting paragraphs and sentences. He was never satisfied until the text was flawless. And he was just as uncompromising on press; notorious for halting a run simply to correct an annoying line break. 'The art of presentation is part of our business,' Rand said, yet in the same breadth arguing that, 'it is also, paradoxically, the art of deception.' Rand complained that much bad design was sold through great presentations. So he turned his attention to writing, in part, to propagate further his doctrine of good design.

Rand was a born designer, but he had to teach himself writing. His early writing was somewhat formal and self-conscious. While he spoke articulately about design in his Brooklyn cadence, he was not comfortable using descriptive vernacular phrases in his writing. Taking as his mentors such modern writers and critics as John Dewey, Alfred North Whitehead and Roger Fry, he mimicked their methods and borrowed their vocabularies. Thus Rand experimented with words, writing the occasional article for trade magazines, yet resisted more ambitious authorship until 1945, when George Wittenborn suggested that it was time for Rand to chronicle his philosophy of advertising design.

In the early 1930s Rand practised what the European Moderns preached; by the early 1940s he preached what he himself practised. Published in 1946, *Thoughts on Design* was certainly not the first book to address the practice of advertising design, but it was the first to explain Rand's revolutionary ideas about the marriage of art and advertising. Comprised of what amounted to homilies on the role of humour, the function of symbols, and the application of collage and montage, among other themes, it quickly became the bible of modern graphic design.

Far left:
Design Quarterly 123,
cover, 1984
Rand was already working
on his second book in
three decades, *Paul Rand:
A Designer's Art* when he
was asked to develop an
issue of this esteemed
design journal.

Left, centre:
Failure By Design, leaflet
cover, Designers and Art
Directors' Association

Left: **Trademark Design,**
book jacket
(unpublished), Paul
Theobold and Company,
1951

Right:
Thoughts on Design,
book jacket, Wittenborn
Schultz, 1946
Rand's first book was a
monograph and manifesto.
Using his own work as
examples, his words
became authoritative for
the contemporary
advertising designer.

Thoughts on Design: Paul Rand

Rand continued writing sporadic articles for various trade magazines and annuals that addressed such issues as modern typography (*American Printer*, 1948), trademarks and symbols (*Type Talks*, 1949), the colour black (*Graphic Forms*, 1949) and art in advertising (*Art in Advertising*, 1954). With *Thoughts* Rand had developed something of a theoretical armature on which to hang his ideas, and was beginning to express himself through poetic structures and rhythms, but writing never came easily. Rand was not as sure-footed a writer as he was a designer, and almost forty years passed between the publication of *Thoughts* and his next major book.

Rand's presentation books served as a bridge between design and authorship, and enabled him to test his writing strengths and weaknesses in practical terms. From advertising he learned the virtues of focus and brevity and wrote what amounted to expanded captions for these books that provided rationales for the design decisions leading up to devising the specific logo. Employing various oratorical tropes, such as stringing together multiple adjectives building towards the dramatic climax of a sentence or phrase, he developed his own, distinctly sermonizing, style.

In 1960 Rand and his former wife, Ann, co-wrote and published 'Advertisement: Ad Vivum or Ad Hominem?', an essay for a special issue of *Daedalus* (*Journal of the American Academy of Arts and Sciences*) on 'The Visual Arts Today'

(guest edited by designer and writer Gyorgy Kepes). It was a didactic and opinionated fusion of Rand's practical, theoretical and philosophical sides. Critically targeted at advertising, it was nonetheless a manifesto that served as the foundation for Rand's later essays on design in general. The message was similar to earlier ones, but he had finally found his mature voice. Perhaps writing for such a prestigious intellectual journal made him more self-conscious of language and nuance; maybe he also realized that this was an opportunity to reach a broader audience. Needless to say, the piece went through even more than the usual number of rewrites to clarify the message and ultimately achieve Rand's particular cadence. The following excerpts evidence just how confident Rand had become in the rightness of his ideas:

'What has aesthetics to do with selling? The probable answer is: very little, directly; indirectly, perhaps a great deal. The commercial artist who wants to be more than a "stylist" must either become clear as to what his cultural contribution may be, or else be overwhelmed by the demands of clients, myths about public taste, consumer research surveys, etc.

'… Precariously perched between economics and aesthetics, his performance judged by the grimly impersonal yet arbitrary "Does it sell?", the commercial artist has great difficulty in finding his artistic personality, let alone asserting it.

'… I would say that an understanding of man's intrinsic needs, and of the necessity to search for a climate in which those needs could be realized is fundamental to the education of the designer … It is only when man (and the hordes of individuals that term stands for) is not accepted as the center of human concern that it becomes feasible to create a system of production which values profit out of proportion to responsible public service, or to design ads in which the only aesthetic criterion is "How sexy is the girl?"'

When the *Daedalus* essay was published, the forty-six-year-old Rand was at the peak of his form with three major consultancies and a thriving freelance business. Writing was so totally absorbing that he did it only sporadically. Despite the time put into each essay, he was a sprinter rather than a long-distance writer, preferring short essays to long narratives. Crafting a three- or four-page essay took weeks, possibly months of writing notes, preliminary drafts, and massaging text, which accounts for why it was not until 1984, around his seventieth birthday, that Rand decided to revisit the ideas put forth in his first book and started compiling essays for *Paul Rand: A Designer's Art*. Published in 1985, it combined revisions of essays that originally appeared in *Thoughts on Design* with several additional articles. For the generation of designers that had entered the profession long after *Thoughts* was out of print, the core essays were still relevant, indeed inspiring. Never mind that the new audience had no idea that Rand transformed advertising design in the 1940s and also the look of book jackets in the 1950s, here was the pioneer American Modernist, a legend in his time, explaining the essence of what makes good design.

Left:
Paul Rand, 1970
(photographer:
Milton Ackoff)
Rand at home with his cat.

Right:
**Paul Rand: A Designer's
Art,** book jacket, Yale
University Press, 1985
After three decades,
Rand decided to update
Thoughts on Design, add
new essays and claim
the role of modern
graphic design's leading
philosopher.

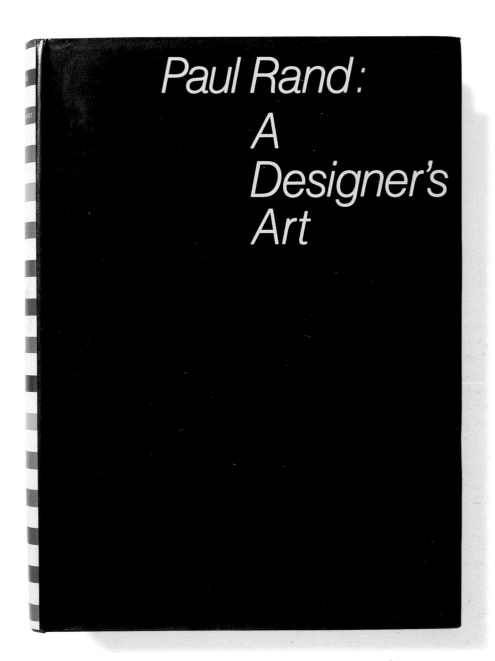

The new book was entirely recast, redesigned and newly illustrated both with Rand's vintage and more recent works. Rand also supervised the printing at Mossberg & Company in Indiana, and Charles Hillman, who headed the printing firm at that time, could not even estimate how often Rand stopped the presses to make alterations. Rand himself admitted to changing fifty per cent of the book on press because, 'that's part of the design process; being in complete control of production is essential for an artist.'[2]

Paul Rand: A Designer's Art was acclaimed on the front page of the *New York Times Book Review* (3 November 1985), an honour in itself, for its economy and precision. But the reviewer, Alan Fern, implied that it was the capstone of a long and influential practice. This, however, was no last will and testament. More than a summary of past achievements, *A Designer's Art* reiterated Rand's ideals and reaffirmed the standards – the rightness of form – that he had introduced to a moribund field fifty years earlier. Rather than an end, this book was the beginning of a new phase of his career. Over the next eleven years Rand became a prolific essayist and published two more books, *Design, Form, and Chaos* (1994) and *From Lascaux to Brooklyn* (1996).

In *A Designer's Art*, every essay was a commandment of sorts, not about what to design, but how to think of design as a unified activity based on analysis and governed by imagination. It began with Vasari's modest definition of design as 'the animating principle of all creative processes'.³ Rand then put to rest the common perception that design is simply applied as ornament on an otherwise functional object. He wrote that graphic design, 'is essentially about visual relationships – providing meaning to a mass of unrelated needs, ideas, words, and pictures. It is the designer's job to select and fit this material together – and make it interesting.'⁴

If Rand had not written another word after *A Designer's Art*, his eminent place would have been secured. There was no arguing with ideas that were aimed at enlivening the printed page through beauty and intelligence. It was applicable to every designer, regardless of aesthetic predilection. Even those who would never design like Rand could agree with his notions concerning the importance of repetition, symbol and humour. With the publication of this book and subsequent essays in periodicals, including the *AIGA Journal of Graphic Design* and the *STA Journal*, Rand was back in the spotlight as a pundit. But he also created a pulpit for himself that would ultimately place him at odds with a younger generation of graphic designers.

When he was working on *A Designer's Art*, Rand was hermetically sealed in a cocoon of his own ideas that dated back to his entry into the profession. After it was published, he opened himself up to the outside world, became more aware of the changes that had occurred in design practice during the 1970s and 1980s, and found them wanting. Perhaps it was inevitable that someone with such a fervent commitment to his own truths – underscored by his own doctrine of good design – would resist alternative truths. But Rand was not locked in the past for its own sake. Modernism was not merely a suit of clothes that could be taken off as styles or attitudes changed. He was devout to a fault and therefore intolerant to excess.

The first book in the Rand trilogy restated his principles, the second, *Design, Form, and Chaos*, published nine years later, was an exploration of aesthetics, the foundation of good design, which Rand believed was drowning in a torrent of supercilious fashions. *Design, Form, and Chaos* differed from *Paul Rand: A Designer's Art* in both its fundamental structure and critical stance. The book was designed with a deliberately more classical sensibility, and the essays were longer and more didactic. While the first book was Rand's Talmud, the next was his Talmudic commentaries on the nature of form and content. By the second book, Rand was both a more seasoned writer and world-weary commentator, as evidenced by this statement in the introduction to *Design, Form, and Chaos*: 'Design, as we shall see, is also an instrument of disorder and confusion. Design for deception is often more persuasive than design for good; seduction is one of its many masks.'⁵

Design, Form, and Chaos was divided into three sections loosely devoted to theory, practice and criticism. The first, 'Form and Content', included four essays, 'Form + Content', 'Good Design Is Goodwill', 'Intuition and Ideas' and 'Logos … Flags … Street Signs', which expanded on the fundamental principles that had driven

Rand's practice for fifty years. The second section, 'Presentation' included facsimiles of Rand's presentation booklets for NeXT, IBM, The Limited, Morningstar and others. The third section included four disparate essays on the state of design. It ended with 'From Cassandre to Chaos', which, originally published in the *AIGA Journal of Graphic Design* in 1991, was hardly a benign treatise on the verities of Modernism but rather a harsh critique of contemporary, especially 'deconstructive' or 'experimental', graphic design. Although Rand did not specify names, he provided a laundry list of mannerisms and conceits that were easily affixed to certain individuals and schools. The essay ignited a fiery dispute over aspects of form and style that cut to the very heart of how young designers practised. It polarized moderns and post-moderns – or rather those who adhered to the canon of economy and functionality versus those who believed that new theories and technologies demanded increasingly complex and expressive design. For this pre-emptive attack on indulgences that breached the tenets of modern design, young designers and a new breed of academic critic branded Rand a reactionary. Ironically, this former revolutionary was now the enemy.

Design, Form, and Chaos was criticized as a flawed sequel to *Paul Rand: A Designer's Art*. Writing in the *New York Times Book Review*, Victor Margolin acknowledged Rand was a great pioneer, but dismissed the pessimistic tone of his criticism as a disservice to his legacy. All of a sudden Rand became fair game for young critics, who argued against his views as defender of the modernist faith.

Design, Form, and Chaos, book jacket, Yale University Press, 1993 This was Rand's most critical commentary on contemporary design, and he himself was harshly criticized for it. But Rand was simply expressing the beliefs that guided him as a designer for over half a century.

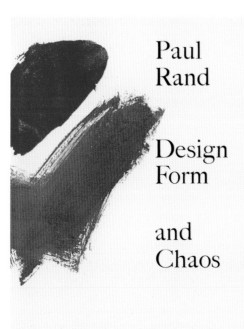

Paul Rand

Design Form

and Chaos

In *Graphis* (1993), J. Abbott Miller wrote: 'Rand positions himself outside of history and above the fray. What would have made a fascinating book would have been for Rand to exercise his magisterial and aggressively formalist sensibilities against the backdrop of contemporary design and media. Instead, Rand's wholesale condemnation of recent design becomes a blunt instrument for dismissing whatever comes in his path.'[6]

And in *Eye* (October 1993) Michael Bierut argued: 'Just when the forces of "deconstructivism" seemed about to overturn the verities of Modernism, Rand put his foot down. Much contemporary graphic design, he said, is degrading the world as we know it, "no less than drugs or pollution". No names, of course, but one could easily identify the culprits Rand had in mind from his litany of the *modi operandi*; "squiggles, pixels, doodles" (Greiman *et al.*), "corny woodcuts on moody browns and russets" (Duffy, Anderson, *et al.*), "indecipherable, zany typography" (Valicenti *et al.*), "peach, pea green, and lavender: (anyone from California named Michael, *et al.*), even "tiny colour photos surrounded by acres of white space" (which obviously only sounds harmless).'[7]

These critiques did in no way diminish Rand's achievements, but they challenged his relevance.

Of course, by 1993 Modernism was under heavy attack by academics and hothouse *habitués* as a cold, rigid and bankrupt style that had lost much of its relevance as corporate identity devolved into a litany of clichés. It is possible that they never really looked at the range of Rand's work or understood what differentiated the leader from the followers. But it is probable that many of the objections to Rand's position came from those designers and critics who felt it was their turn, and so demanded their right to generational ascendancy in the design community. Since Rand was one of the few of his generation who publicly spoke out, he unfortunately became a symbol of opposition.

'What colored the criticism and made their position almost untenable was the fact that his track record as a designer was unmatched,' affirmed Louis Danziger. 'Paul was the winningest racehorse talking about running races. Since none of his arguments could be refuted with equal or even reasonable authority the tactic was to treat him as being irrelevant. His very eminence contributed to the meanness of the generational schism and what I consider to be a non-debate.'8

This is not to say that his book was above criticism. *Design, Form, and Chaos* was more ambitious than Rand's previous book and, despite his matured writing, was in many ways not as cohesive as the first. The essays in the 'Form and Content' section were more laboured, and curiously suffered under the weight of quotations from Rand's esteemed philosophers, such as John Ruskin, Immanuel Kant and William James, as well as contemporary conservative critics such as William Safire and Christopher Lorenz. Rand sampled ideas from others as both justification and ratification of his own truths. But his reliance on other writers' words and thoughts somehow diminished his own authority. One only has to compare the 'Form and Content' essays to his 'Presentation' texts, where such quotations are not invoked, to read Rand at his most articulate and convincing.

Rand was surprisingly strengthened by the brouhaha surrounding *Design, Form, and Chaos*. So much so that by his eightieth birthday he contemplated writing yet another book. He considered a history of graphic design from a modern perspective, but put that aside and instead compiled a collection of new essays and presentation guides that were bound together through the overarching theme of aesthetics – the incontrovertible notions of form that governed his life. Humorously titled *From Lascaux to Brooklyn*, it was an attempt to combine autobiography with history and theory. 'It is naive to believe that one can explain in just a few words what others have considered it "a formidable task" to define: the complexities of the ineffable – of aesthetics – and the definitions of art, form, design, intuition, and expression, as well as the ramifications of communication,' he wrote in the introduction.

'My purpose in writing this book is to clarify problems that have always baffled me and to emphasize the importance of the idea as such, a unique thought and the very life of form. This book is not a comprehensive study of the philosophy of art. The ideas expressed here are based on empirical practices, laced with whatever wisdom I can claim or quote.'9

Rand was intuitively attempting a kind of closure or summation that would define his legacy. In fact, the book is dedicated 'To all my friends and enemies'. As it turned out, this *was* his final testament.

From Lascaux to Brooklyn also met with mixed reviews, which troubled Rand immensely. A few vocal critics in the design press opined that it was more sniping at contemporary practice, a response that was to be expected given the tenor of the times. But in the *New York Times Book Review*, Paul Shepheard, a post-modern British architect, dismissed the book as Modernist propaganda (prompting a flurry of dissenting letters to the editor). If this book had been the first of the Rand trilogy

rather than the last, it would probably have been praised as a revealing, albeit idiosyncratic, exegesis on graphic design practice by the pre-eminent American Modern. Actually, it is Rand's most eloquent book (for example, in just one concise, five-paragraph essay titled 'More about the Grid' he lays to rest the myth that 'the grid' is a repressive tool). Yet, given the prevailing 'culture of complaint', (as the critic John Hughes referred to academic thinking of the early 1990s) in certain quarters of the graphic design community, *From Lascaux to Brooklyn* was ultimately dissected by critics with a dull ideological knife.

In the final analysis, Rand's last book enlivened the debate on the role and ramifications of graphic design in contemporary culture. If not for this *provocateur* stance, the argument might not have had any passion or fury. His unparalleled devotion to design was indisputable and he had such acute insight that his books and essays as a whole are invaluable resources regardless of one's generational bias. Few designers, even those who are prolific authors, have written as eloquently and accessibly about theory and practice. Rand's design taught designers about the virtues of precision, economy and wit. Rand's writing continues to chart the routes of graphic design. In the preface to *Paul Rand: A Designer's Art* he wrote his own timeless epitaph: 'My interest has always been in restating the validity of those ideas which, by and large, have guided artists since the time of Polyclitus. I believe that it is only in the application of those timeless principles that one can even begin to achieve a semblance of quality in one's work. It is the continuing relevance of these ideals that I mean to emphasize, especially to those who have grown up in a world of punk and graffiti.'10

Left:
Paul Rand, 1985
(photographer:
Susan Ferguson)
This photograph was
taken to accompany the
cover review of *Paul
Rand: A Designer's Art* in
the *New York Times Book
Review.*

Right:
**From Lascaux to
Brooklyn,** book jacket,
Yale University Press,
1996
The witty title introduced
Rand's last testament on
design. In this book he
focused on understanding
and explaining aesthetics,
the most important issue
for him throughout
his career.

From Lascaux
to Brooklyn Paul Rand

Paul Rand: The modern professor *by Jessica Helfand*

Design is so simple, that's why it is so complicated.

Paul Rand in his last public lecture,
MIT Media Lab, Cambridge, Massachusetts,
14 November 1996

There is a story about the young Paul Rand (which is unlikely to be apocryphal since he used to tell it about himself) in which he recalled having had the opportunity to spend some time with his great mentor, Le Corbusier, on a European beach one sunny afternoon. The eager young Rand plied the older master with questions about form, system and design principles, prompting an impulsively honest, if exasperated reply. 'Young man,' said Le Corbusier, jumping into the ocean, 'you are simply too serious!'

In spite of the playfulness with which his work is so often remembered, Rand was indeed extremely serious about many things: about art, design, geometry, history, ethics, psychology, perception and form-giving. He never tired of certain fundamental questions, and never stopped questioning himself and those around him about the appropriateness, the applicability and the purpose of design. He hated trickery, decoration and trends, superfluous touches and cosmetic effect. He strove for purity, efficiency and durability, clarity and purpose, simplicity and practicality. Paul Rand – intellectually restless, creatively insatiable – was a wonderful teacher because he never stopped being a student. This also explains why he was loved by so many, feared by so many, and so utterly impossible to please.

He was, like many fascinating and fiercely intelligent people, a man of enormous complexity and great contradiction. Perhaps the greatest inconsistencies lay in the spaces between his writing and his teaching, both life-long passions that would seem, almost by necessity, to have been interconnected – and yet they were not. As a writer, Rand expressed his insights with an eloquence that was rarely, if ever, matched in the classroom: here he was impatient, easily distracted and often resistant to discourse. His writing, too, was peppered with references to a broad and interdisciplinary bibliography; yet this bibliography, though offered as a handout to those students who pursued him doggedly, was never truly integrated into the scope of his curricula. (It is worth noting, too, that Rand's bibliography changed and grew considerably over the years: while the 1965 version included a comprehensive section on gestalt psychology, later versions included more abundant literary references, more architectural sources and more periodicals.) Rand favoured certain key texts which he recycled again and again in his assignments: many former Yale students for example remember a classic publication design problem based on the seminal 1920 Le Corbusier/Ozenfant essay *On the Plastic in Art*.

Perhaps most puzzling of all, Rand's exhaustive knowledge of art history, which was perpetually well-documented in his books, seldom found its way into his classroom: here, he never showed slides, never lectured and never made conscious, explicit reference to the sources that lay at the very core of his own intellectual pursuits; his own self-made education. 'When I saw his library later in his life and all the other things that he studied and looked at I was stunned,' recalls Virginia Smith (Yale MFA 1958), now Chair of Design at Baruch College in New York. 'There was never a clue about that in class.' Netscape Design Director Hugh Dubberly (Yale MFA 1983) concurs: 'It surprised me that such an articulate writer could be so tongue-tied in person.'

Perhaps, in the end, Rand felt that it was up to the students to resolve these gaps, to find their own sources of inspiration, much as he had done, and indeed continued to do. While never articulated as such, it is likely that he presupposed in his students a certain degree of capability, independence and resourcefulness that inevitably would lead them to their own conclusions. His role was to guide them, to instill in them certain basic principles, and to encourage them to become demanding and objective editors of their own work. In this he was ruthless – and unparalleled. Consequently, the fact that he remains for so many students their most memorable professor is not at all surprising.

Rand's own education was uneven as he was essentially self-taught. 'When I went to school my education was lackadaisical. There was no system,' he once said. 'When I studied with George Grosz (at the New York Art Students' League) in the 1930s he had just come over from Europe, and he didn't speak a word of English. You can imagine what his classes were like. He walked around and looked at your work and made a few marks, and you wondered what he was driving at. I'm still wondering.' Rand later attended Pratt Institute, the Parsons School of Design and the Art Students League in New York. He taught briefly and sporadically at Pratt, Cooper Union and The New York Lab School before being invited to Yale as a visiting critic in 1956. Soon afterwards he was offered a formal appointment in the School of Art, a position he retained (with the exception of a brief hiatus in the early 1970s) until his retirement in 1993.

Looking back, given the breadth of his interests and the seriousness with which he pursued them, it seems somehow inevitable that Rand would come to a place like Yale University to teach. At that time – the mid-1950s – the schools of Art and Architecture included a number of European *émigrés* and Bauhaus disciples, among them Josef Albers who had been recruited by Louis Kahn several years earlier to head its art department. Albers had long advocated the benefits of interdisciplinary study in the arts, and from the beginning, graphic design students were required to study photography, printmaking, typography, print production, drawing and painting, as well as the famous Albers colour course – affectionately referred to by the students as 'spots and dots'. Soon after his arrival at Yale, Albers appointed Alvin Eisenman to direct the Department of Graphic Design, and together they extended the faculty to include a number of distinguished visiting critics, including among others, Lester Beall, Leo Lionni, Alexey Brodovich, Walker Evans, Bradbury Thompson, Herbert Matter and Rand, who came on the recommendation of Alvin Lustig.

Below:
Yale University, graduate school prospectus cover, 1982

Yale University School of Art
Graduate Program

If the combination of intellectual curiosity and street-wise scepticism caused Rand to question general design values, teaching provided him with the ideal opportunity to do so within the very specific context of a first-rate academic institution. Here, differences of opinion with his esteemed colleagues were rarely concealed; if anything, such conflicts helped to cement his growing convictions about the most effective ways to teach graphic design. Principal among these conflicts, in the early days, were his disagreements with Paul Rudolph, then Dean of Architecture at Yale.

To begin with, Rudolph was opposed to grades. 'Rudolph thought the idea of grading a work of art was too vulgar for words,' recalls Eisenman. Rand, on the other hand, completely objected to the idea of abandoning the grade system. His own challenging experience as a student at Pratt had led him to believe that there was enormous value in rewarding the deserving – and, by contrast, in punishing those who did poorly. Another bone of contention lay in the studio model itself. Rudolph favoured the notion of the open studio, where students could come and go somewhat freely during the class critique. This was a policy Rand objected to quite strongly, feeling that he couldn't possibly talk to students in an atmosphere where they were free to attend as they pleased. (He later confessed to Eisenman that one of the reasons he felt this way was that the Rabbi would never have stood for it!)

From the beginning, the Rand studios at Yale were framed within a certain prescribed set of rules. If at first these rules were functional, they later grew to include more formal and procedural limitations. Later, it was not uncommon for Rand to ordain which fonts could (and could not) be used, which techniques were objectionable, which presentation materials were acceptable, and so forth. In an effort to universalize and objectify these notions, Rand looked for confirmation outside the narrow confines of graphic design: here is where the doctrines of Modernism offered structure, discipline and a certain fundamental reasoning, which Rand believed to be enormously applicable to the practice of graphic design.

This discipline would remain central to Rand's teaching for the next thirty years. The fact that he would continue to examine and refine the rigours of such thinking reflected not only his dedication to teaching, but also the seriousness with which he approached art in general and design in particular. Ironically, however, while there is a certain clear trajectory in the evolution of his own professional career, Rand's teaching methodology would undergo significant developments between the mid-1950s and the mid-1980s. Most interestingly, the reasons and explanations for these changes reveal perhaps more about Rand as a Modernist than anything else.

There were personal influences from colleagues and mentors, among them Josef Albers, Le Corbusier and Josef Müller-Brockmann. There were professional influences, particularly in the corporate arena, as Rand would begin to develop design vocabularies and systems for such clients as Westinghouse and IBM. There were ideological influences, derived from his own reading and from observing the teaching methodologies of other members of the Yale faculty, including Alvin Eisenman, Armin Hofmann and Herbert Matter. And there were certainly practical influences which led Rand to adapt his problems to yield more successful results among his students. Ultimately, to trace the evolution of his pedagogical style over the course of more than thirty years illuminates the strength of Rand's ability to identify the most germane principles underlying the study of graphic design. This was undoubtedly his greatest strength as a teacher, and remains, for many former students, his most memorable and lasting gift.

In the beginning, Rand's assignments were typically product-specific, tending to mirror projects he might have taken on in his own studio: the design of an El Producto cigar box (1958) for example, or the redesign of a can label for Del Monte pineapple (1960). Former student Chris Pullman, (Yale MFA 1966) Director of Design at WGBH Television in Boston, recalls being asked to design the packaging for Duz soap flakes, and the real-world market analysis that followed. 'We made boxes and took them to the store,' he remembers, 'then we put them up on shelves and examined them.' Other Rand assignments during this period included childrens' books (nursery rhyme collections and vocabulary primers), calendars and posters, trademarks, stationery, record jackets, book jackets, as well as packaging for chocolate (Whitman's), coffee (Maxwell House) and wine (Château LaFitte Rothschild). While attention was always paid to clearly communicated solutions, these early assignments were articulated with perhaps less of an emphasis on formal issues *per se*. Indeed, many of the projects read like briefs from a client or specifications for a printer, the problems stated with no-nonsense brevity, and presented with staccato-like parameters outlining size, shape and printing limitations. 'Redesign the package for Spearmint-flavoured Diet sugarless gum using the existing size, copy, materials and printing process,' reads one of Rand's more prosaic project statements from this era. 'A memorandum from the manufacturer is posted in the drafting room.'

Duz, package design assignment. Student: Chris Pullman, 1965 One of Rand's earliest assignments to students at Yale was the practical/ theoretical packaging project. Initially these mirrored his own commissions, such as El Producto packaging, but later he broadened the scope. He stopped giving this assignment in the mid-1970s.

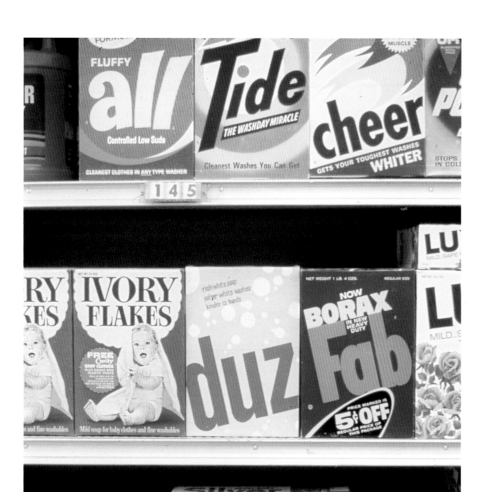

Design and the Play Instinct, publication project. Student: William Anton, 1985
For the publication project, Rand provided a text (in this case his own, but other art historical texts were also given), limited the students to a typeface, and supplied specific images (sometimes supplemented by the student's research).

However, over time, Rand began to back away from these more commercial projects, leaning instead toward a more principle-oriented, rational and increasingly formal approach to teaching design. This transition – some have even referred to it as a sea-change – occurred in the early 1960s, and marked what Chris Pullman has called 'Rand's transformation from a nuts-and-bolt guy to a true theorist'.

By the mid-1960s, Rand began to pay specific attention to the way a problem itself was expressed. Some ten years after he first began teaching at Yale, he expressed these views in the now-celebrated essay, 'Design and the Play Instinct'. 'I believe that if, in the statement of a problem, undue emphasis is placed on freedom and self-expression, the result is apt to be an indifferent student with a meaningless solution,' he writes. 'Conversely, a problem with defined limits, implied or stated disciplines which are, in turn, conducive to the instinct of play, will most likely yield an interested student and, very often, a meaningful and novel solution.'

Rand thus came to believe that the success of a given problem lay largely in the way it was articulated and the limitations within which it was given. In 'Arts and the University', a 1964 video documentary produced by WGBH-Boston, Rand explained: 'there are restrictions which are built in both by the student, by the client, and by the teacher, which tend to help the student solve the problem.' He would later further amend this thinking. 'If possible,' he wrote in a subsequent problem statement, 'teaching should alternate between theoretical and practical problems – between those with tightly stated "rules" imposed by the teacher and those with rules implied by the problem itself.'

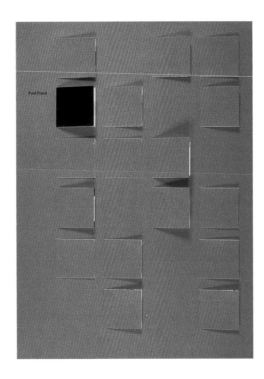

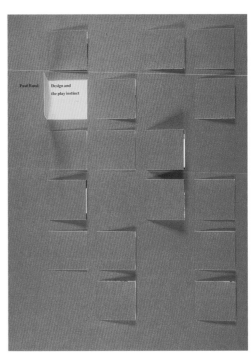

Mask: A Design Process,
Visual Semantics Project.
Student: William Anton,
1985
This was Rand's signature
assignment. Developing
skill in evolving words
into imagery embodied

most of the design issues
that Rand believed were
important. The mask
metaphor enabled the
student to trace the design
process from problem
through conception to
development.

Many of the projects Rand assigned during the 1960s reflect this yearning for, and struggle with, a practical-theoretical balance. A good, although unusual example (it was given only twice) is an assignment he gave to redesign the classic game of Parcheesi. Here, students were asked to abide by the strict rules of the game – a discipline that presaged the sorts of guidelines Rand would later impose upon other assignments. The Parcheesi project is significant for several reasons, not least of which lies in its dual appeal to qualities Rand would return to, in his own work as well as in his teaching, again and again: simplicity and playfulness. In retrospect, it was an early and comparatively radical exercise both in information design and interaction design as students were required to design both the game and its rule book. The results were playful, unusual and, in some cases, extraordinarily beautiful.

As Rand's emphasis shifted away from a product orientation, and towards exposing the underlying principles that collectively defined the practice of graphic design, the gap between teaching and writing began to grow narrower. While his bedside manner remained virtually unchanged, Rand's project statements came to be articulated with more exuberance, more specificity, and a great deal more thought. They grew longer, more detailed, more cross-disciplinary and, at the same time, more didactic. It was not uncommon for the text to be punctuated by declarations of the master's own non-negotiable design values: 'Literal interpretations should be avoided'; 'Initiation is more effective than imitation'; and the incontestable 'Originality is more a question of how than what' were among some of the manifesto-like statements Rand's students grew to know intimately. Most important for the professor, these assignments – given repeatedly – offered him the opportunity to fine-tune his ideas, his rationales and his principles. Consequently, the assignments themselves became much more focused. For the students, they became not only clearer, but more valuable and indeed, more widely applicable. 'Mr. Rand's class assignments were a marvel,' recalls Hugh Dubberly. 'His presentation of the problems was brief and clear. He constrained the assignments so well that it was difficult to do poor work.'

Rand's later assignments were, in a sense, intellectual explorations of the study of limited means – a pedagogical celebration of the Modernist ideal. Twenty years after his Diet gum assignment, Rand delivered the following project statement: 'The object of this problem is to sharpen your awareness of form and its relation to colour and content … It is the abstract, non-representational, two-dimensional quality of letters paired with content, that make the use of words so meaningful in modern painting and graphic design. The poetry of Mallarmé, the collages of Picasso, and the typographic antics of the Futurists have revealed the poetic side of familiar words.' Such language introduced a series of assignments that would soon become known as the Visual Semantics Projects.

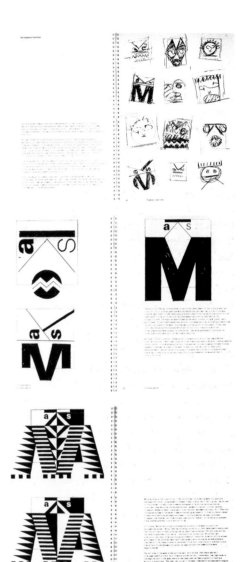

Clockwise from far left:
The Brissago workshop,
1982 (photographer:
Philip Burton)
Rand with student Kristen
Hughes; Rand going to
the school; Armin
Hofmann with students on
a boat trip; and student
Eri Ceputis working on a
class project.

'The term Visual Semantics refers to the meaning and manipulation of words (letters) to illustrate an idea, action or the evocation of an image,' Rand writes in his preface to the problem statement. 'The word serves a dual purpose, verbal and pictorial. This involves the arrangement of letters in such a way as to make a word visually self-explanatory – a kind of universal sign language.' In perfecting the assignment, Rand experimented with word choices: in the earlier years, for example, students worked with the words 'Mask', 'Banjo' and 'Circus'. It is likely that over time, Rand became more intrigued with the notion of asking students to explore the visual dynamics of the letterforms, particularly with regard to the work of certain artists: for example, 'Banjo' and Picasso, or 'Circus' and Calder. (Rand soon moved away from words–ideas and towards proper names themselves, later assigning 'Miró' and finally settling on 'Léger'.)

Students thus created visual compositions that reflected the supporting principles of a given artist's style rather than mimicking the artist's work itself. For Rand, this project effectively illustrated the value of principle-based teaching in a manner that was at once simple (students worked only with cut paper and glue) and succinct (students distilled their complex ideas into pure typography). 'It always had to do with the letters,' recalls Philip Burton, now Professor of Graphic Design at the University of Illinois/Chicago, who taught both at Yale and in Brissago, Switzerland, with Rand and Hofmann during these years. 'It always had to do with seeking to capture the essence of the artist – whatever the student perceived that to be.'

In effect, the Visual Semantics exercises would become Rand's signature projects. They formed the basis for the curriculum he would develop, with Armin Hofmann, at Yale's Summer Program in Brissago, which began in 1977 and continued until the early 1990s. Here, Rand typically spent an intensive week in the studio with approximately fifteen students and, unlike the Yale studios, absolutely no technology – no stat camera, and no computers. Nancy Mayer (Yale MFA 1984) now a principal of Mayer & Myers, Philadelphia, recalls: 'It was a big deal that there was nothing but pencil and paper. Plus we had a week with Rand all day every day: this in itself was a shockingly different experience. What Brissago offered was total immersion in a project. The total immersion over that period of time is a very different educational experience.' The intensity of the Brissago environment offered Rand a kind of concentrated laboratory within which to teach. Here he was in an ideal position to focus his students' attention on precisely the kinds of formal values he believed lay at the core of a serious, and lasting, design education. 'Paul was thrilled with the work that the students accomplished there,' recalls Burton. 'He was thrilled with every single aspect of it. He would tell me, "This is the way graphic design should be taught."'

Miró, Visual Semantics Project. Student: Catherine Waters, 1981 Rand did not vary his assignments often, but he did shift the theme of the Visual Semantics Project from time to time. Given the name of an admired artist, the problem was to design various iterations using colour, lettering and other forms that reflected the artist's work.

It is important to note that Rand was not alone in this thinking: indeed, many of his colleagues at Yale shared his concern for narrowing the focus, isolating the ideas and crafting assignments that would elicit a sharper understanding of the underlying principles of design – whereas the more product-specific problems seemed to allow students to bypass these principles. 'One of the things I found was that it was getting sort of boring to give yet another book jacket assignment,' recalls Alvin Eisenman. 'It didn't result easily in learning about the principles – and the only thing that made a real difference was learning about the principles. Rand wasn't alone in this, of course. Rand and Brad Thompson and Herbert Matter and myself – we all believed in the importance of design principles.' Looking beyond the parameters of the design department, the considerable influence which Josef Albers lent to students and faculty alike may also have been a significant factor in Rand's decision to move towards a more principle-based teaching strategy. As Rob Roy Kelly (Yale MFA 1955), former Chair of Graphic Design at Arizona State University in Tempe, writes in his *History of Graphic Design at Yale*, 'Albers had the ability to teach formal values in a manner which stimulated students to becomes more visually aware.'

Perhaps the member of the Yale design faculty who was most focused on the translation of formal values within the context of graphic design education was Armin Hofmann. His own classes centred on concentrated exercises in which students practised hand skills – working with brushes, mixing colour and drawing type – the intended result of which was to fine-tune their ability to see. It is likely that Rand's move away from practical and towards more formal coursework was significantly influenced by Hofmann, whose curricula at the Kunstgewerbe-schule in Basel were based on similar principles of rational, systems-oriented thinking. But once again it is likely that he disagreed with Hofmann as much as, if not more than, he agreed with him.

To begin with, there were disagreements about the way class problems were framed, and the amount of time within which they were expected to be completed – if they were to be completed at all. 'Rand very much believed that a project must have a very definite resolution within a specific time frame,' recalls Chris Myers (Yale MFA 1983) now a principal at Mayer & Myers, Philadelphia and Chair of Graphic Design at University of the Arts in Philadelphia 'whereas he referred to Armin's approach as "the endless problem" – in other words, that every solution generated more solutions. For Rand, understanding and coming to a conclusion was itself an enormously valuable lesson. And Rand believed that you had to make a decision.' Indeed, Rand felt that students should be given projects with a clear path of problem-solving – problems with a beginning, a middle and an end. Quoting Alfred North Whitehead on this topic, Rand once wrote: 'The pupils have got to be made to feel they are studying something, and not merely executing intellectual minuets.'

Yale
Summer Program
in
Graphic Design

Brissago,
Switzerland
15 June–22 July
1985

Yale Summer Program in Graphic Design, flyer, 1985 Rand alternated with other members of the faculty in designing the annual announcement for the Summer Program in Brissago. Here he combines harmoniously the slab-serifed Yale 'Y' with the Swiss cross. Rand was also enamoured with the Yale bulldog mascot, which makes frequent appearances in his designs.

Léger, Visual Semantics
Project. Student:
Edward Kensinger,
1983 (Brissago)
The student at Brissago
was required to begin the
iterations in black and
white and 'up the ante'
incrementally into a
colour piece, maintaining
the essence of Léger, in
this instance, while at the
same time interpreting the
subject with a modicum of
individuality.

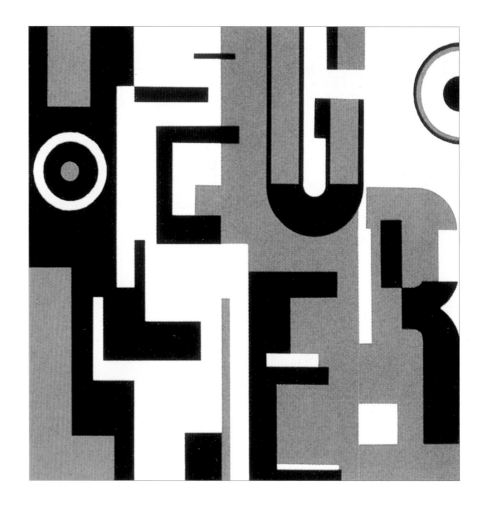

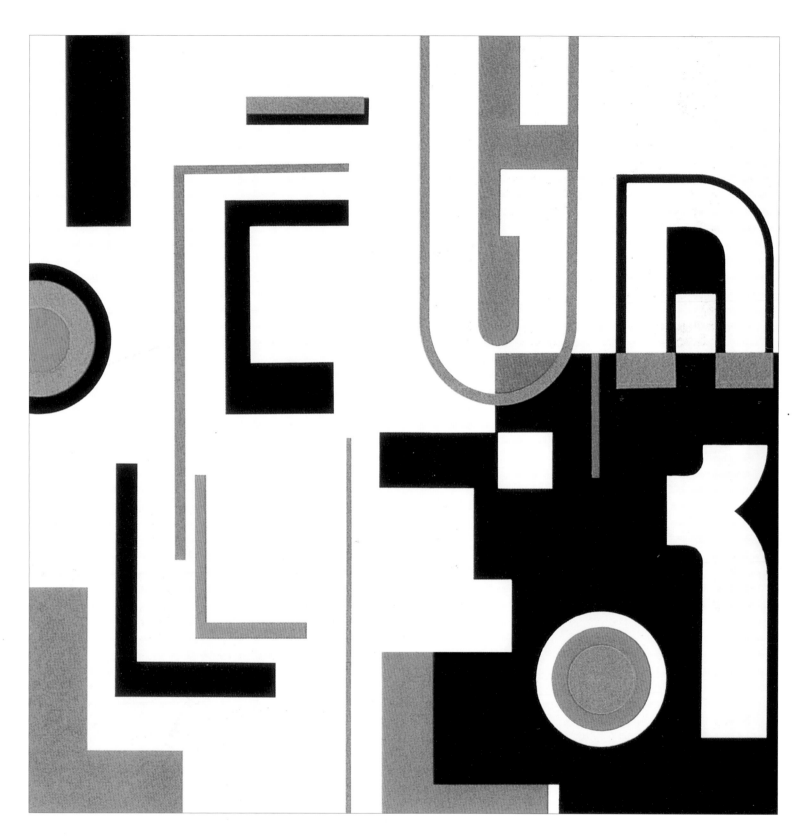

Rand was also a much tougher critic than Hofmann. This is well substantiated by more than thirty years of former students, many of whom share vivid memories of running from the studio in tears after a particularly gruelling Rand critique. ('I don't know of any other way of teaching Art except by criticizing,' Rand once remarked.) This harshness was especially apparent in Brissago: unlike at Yale, where he habitually met with only two or three students at a time, Rand met with the entire studio in one room, passing from desk to desk to critique students individually. 'He was blunt,' recalls Myers, 'and he would say something in an even tone but it would send a lot of people running from the room in tears. You'd hear him from the other side of the room, evaluate your own work in the context of what he was saying and then, all at once, you would start hearing the sound of sixteen people trying to crumple their sketches quietly and start over.'

Rand's growing interest in grid systems was also the source of some debate and consequent influence during these years. Rand was immediately taken in by the formal appeal to structure and system, the modularity, the harmony and balance which came from understanding the design, development and proper application of the typographic grid. His fascination was derived from conversations with Hofmann, from his reading of the seminal studies published by Josef Müller-Brockmann in the late 1960s and from his work with Ken Hiebert and others at Westinghouse during this same period. 'Rand's systems interests had been stimulated early on by Le Corbusier's Modulor and the Japanese Tatami Mat system,' recalls Ken Hiebert, former Chair of Graphic Design at the University of the Arts, 'but 1965 seemed to be a time of zeroing-in on typographic grid systems in his own work and teaching.' In the classroom in particular, the applications of the grid were of enormous consequence. 'The publications project was really about learning the value of a grid system,' notes Myers, adding that Rand's particular interest was in 'the idea of how much structure is necessary to carry an idea and to carry form.' Interestingly, Rand continued to be fuelled by his disagreements with others: for example, although he advised his students to read the book and judge for themselves, Rand openly opposed the orthodoxy with which Müller-Brockmann fundamentally approached this material. For many students, this controversy between a structural principle and its formal application made the grid problems especially challenging.

Yet ironically, in spite of his capacity for intellectual analysis, Rand's equally fervent need to simplify everything caused him to resist some of the more complex verbal and mathematical reasoning that the Europeans systematically brought to their grid evocations. Hiebert recalls: 'Rand was easily overwhelmed by brilliant Swiss and German grid manifestations, but his own language didn't fit the technical substrate. He kept it in very simple, humane, often childlike terms. There was something about Rand that resisted the technical as much as he admired it.'

While it is easy to assume Rand's technical resistance was generational, in fact it turns out to have had more to do with his Modernist tendencies than perhaps anything else. Ever the purist, he believed that all processes – mechanical, technical or otherwise – should be as neutral as possible: consequently, he viewed the celebration of modern technology, particularly in the studio and among his students, as enormously suspect. 'The quality issuing from any process, mechanical or otherwise, is a reflection of that particular process, and the visual effect (style) is closely related to it,' he once wrote. 'The more neutral the technique, the simpler the solution – unencumbered by eccentricities or confusing [he later changed this to 'sentimental'] associations.'

Finally, given the zeal with which Rand had long followed the pursuits of the European Modernists, and given the breadth of his own prolific (and constantly expanding) library, it is indeed possible that Rand's decision to move towards more formal instruction in the studio was considerably influenced by his own reading. As with everything else, he continued to question his findings, to filter them through his own understanding of what made for good design. In the end, the designer always won: 'Paul's eye was constantly prioritized for the aesthetic,' Hiebert remembers, 'and he allowed no distractions.' To this end, Rand willingly adopted certain tenets of formalism, even the 'gridism' espoused by his Swiss colleagues, but only as far as they serviced the emerging principles underlying his own design philosophies.

Of course, these philosophies radiated to an audience much wider than the privileged minority that attended Yale and Brissago, due in no small part to Rand's significant accomplishments as a writer. As in his teaching, Rand wrote to focus on what was important, to make sense of the complexity of the world – not to oversimplify, but to assess, to understand and, finally,

Léger, Visual Semantics
Project. Student: William
Anton, 1985 (Yale)
Rand continued to give
this project at Yale and
Brissago as a way of both
challenging the student's
design skills and imbuing
in them art and design
history.

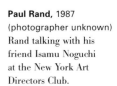

Clockwise from top left:
Paul Rand, 1962
(photographer unknown)
Rand flanked by Will
Burtin (right), Willhem
Sandberg (left) and Aaron
Burns (far left) at the
opening of an exhibition of
Sandberg's work.

Paul Rand, *c.*1985
(photographer unknown)
Rand with Lou Danziger
(centre) and James Miho
(right).

Paul Rand, 1987
(photographer unknown)
Rand talking with his
friend Isamu Noguchi
at the New York Art
Directors Club.

Paul Rand, 1960s
(photographer unknown)
Rand viewing the sights of
Switzerland with Josef
Müller Brockmann and
his wife, Shizuko
Yoshikawa.

to interpret. These focused observations lay at the core of much of his writing, and the lessons therein remain surprisingly applicable, despite the degree to which design has, in recent years, had to adapt to an increasingly complex and technologically sophisticated consumer society. Yet here too, the clarity of his thinking continues to astonish us and indeed, continues to prove invaluable. 'As I flipped through Rand's books I was humbled by the power with which he manipulated space and at the same time struck by the clarity of his accompanying prose,' recalls John Maeda, Professor of Aesthetics and Computation at MIT's prestigious Media Lab. 'I was immediately inspired to pursue the field of graphic design, not necessarily pertaining to the computer.' At Maeda's request, Rand was invited to lecture at the Media Lab exactly forty years after he was first invited to Yale; and in a pattern that

virtually duplicated his early days at Yale, a formal teaching appointment followed. In a triumphant, if poignant conclusion to his life as a teacher, Rand willingly accepted this position, but due to his failing health, was unable to fulfil his promise. He died less than two weeks later.

In the end, of course, Rand's strength of conviction about design principles was incontestable. It was apparent in his teaching and his writing, to his colleagues and his clients and to those who read and will continue to read his books for generations to come. 'That attitude was just hardwired in him,' recalls Chris Pullman. 'That complete conviction about issues formal and relational is, I think, one of the things that makes a memorable and great person. You know where a person stands. And Rand definitely stood for something.'

Paul Rand 1914 – 1996,
headstone.
Designed by Fred Troller,
1996

Chronology
by Georgette Ballance

1914–39

1914   Born August 15 in Brooklyn,
New York

1929–32   **Education:** Pratt Institute,
New York

1932   Parsons School of Design,
New York

1933   Art Students' League with
George Grosz

1934   **Illustrator:** Metro Associated
Services

1935   **Design Assistant:** George Switzer
Studio

1936–41   **Art Director:** *Apparel Arts* and
Esquire magazines

1938–45   **Cover Designs:** *Direction* magazine

1939   **Instructor:** New York Laboratory
School

1940s

1941   **Exhibition:** Katherine Kuh Gallery,
New York

1941–55   **Art Director:** William H. Weintraub
Advertising Agency

1942   **Instructor:** The Cooper Union,
New York

1944   **First Book Jacket:** *The Cubist
Painters* by Guillaume Apollinaire

1945   **First Book Design:** *The Tables of
the Law* by Thomas Mann

1946   **Instructor:** Pratt Institute,
New York

1946   **Advertising:** Ohrbach's

1947   **Author:** *Thoughts on Design*

1947   **Exhibitions:** Composing Room,
New York; National Museum,
Stockholm

1948   Philadelphia Museum of Art

1950s

1952–7   **Advertising:** El Producto, GHP
Cigar Company

1954   **Exhibition:** Contemporary Art
Museum, Boston

1954   **Award:** Voted one of the Ten Best
Art Directors by New York Art
Directors Club

1956–91   **Consultant:** International Business
Machines Corporation (IBM)

1956   **Illustrator:** *I Know a Lot
of Things*

1957   *Sparkle and Spin*

1956   **Trademarks:** IBM

1959   Colorforms

1956–69   **Professor:** Yale University,
New Haven, CT

1958   **Honorary Degree:** Tama
University, Tokyo

1958   **Exhibitions:** AIGA Gallery,
New York
Art Directors' Club of Tokyo

1959–81   **Consultant:** Westinghouse Electric
Corporation

1960s

1961–96   **Consultant:** Cummins Engine
Company

1960   **Trademarks:** Westinghouse

1961   United Parcel Service (UPS)

1962   American Broadcasting Company
(ABC)

1960   **Author:** *Trademarks of Paul Rand*

1960   **Exhibitions:** Pratt Institute,
New York

1964   Carnegie Institute, Pittsburgh;
School of Visual Arts, New York;
Carpenter Center, Harvard
University, Cambridge, MA

1962   **Illustrator:** *Little 1*

1962   **Citation:** Philadelphia College
of Art

1965   **Author:** *Design and the Play
Instinct*

1966   **Award:** AIGA Gold Medal

1968   **Exhibitions:** Temple University,
Philadelphia

1969   Louisiana Arts and Science Center,
Baton Rouge

1970s

1970   **Exhibitions:** IBM Gallery, New York; Virginia Museum of Fine Arts, Richmond

1974   107 Grafici dell AGI, Castello Sforzesco, Milan

1970   **Illustrator:** *Listen! Listen!*

1972   **Awards:** New York Art Directors Club Hall of Fame

1973   Royal Designer for Industry, Royal Society, London

1973   **Trademark:** Cummins Engine Company

1974–93   **Professor:** Yale University, New Haven, CT

1977   **Exhibitions:** Wichita State University, Wichita; Pratt Institute, New York

1979   Philadelphia College of Art

1977–96   **Professor:** Summer Design Program, Yale University, Brissago, Switzerland

1979   **Honorary Degree:** Philadelphia College of Art

1980s

1980   **Trademark:** Tipton Lakes Corporation

1982   **Exhibitions:** Reinhold Brown Gallery, New York

1984   International Typeface Corporation Gallery, New York

1984   **Author:** *A Paul Rand Miscellany,* Design Quarterly

1984   **Award:** Type Directors' Club Medal

1985   **Author:** *Paul Rand: A Designer's Art*

1985   **President's Fellow:** Rhode Island School of Design

1985   **Honorary Degrees:** Parsons School of Design; Yale University

1987   University of Hartford; Kutztown University

1988   School of Visual Arts, New York

1986   **Trademark:** NeXT

1986   **Exhibitions:** Pratt Institute, New York; Design Gallery 358, Tokyo

1987   Università Internazionale Dell'Arte, Florence, Italy

1988   School of Visual Arts, New York

1990s

1991   **Trademarks:** Morningstar; Okasan Securities Company

1993   English First

1992   **Exhibition:** Ginza Graphic Gallery, Tokyo

1993   **Author:** *Design, Form, and Chaos*

1993–6   **Professor Emeritus:** Yale University, New Haven, CT

1995   **Trademarks:** USSB

1996   Norwalk Cancer Center; Enron

1996   **Author:** *From Lascaux to Brooklyn*

1996   **Honorary Degree:** Pratt Institute, New York

1996   **Exhibition:** The Cooper Union, New York

1996   Died November 26 in Norwalk, CT

Notes

Chapter 1

1 Seitlin, Percy, 'Paul Rand', *PM*, October/November 1938, p2.
2 Interview with Paul Rand by author, 1987.
3 Ibid.
4 Seitlin, Percy, 'Paul Rand', *American Artist*, 1942.
5 Interview with Paul Rand by author, 1988.
6 Ibid.
7 Interview with Morris Wyszogrod by author, 1997.
8 Interview with Paul Rand by author, 1988.
9 Ibid.
10 Ibid.
11 Ibid.
12 Ibid.
13 Ibid.
14 Ibid.
15 Ibid.
16 Ibid.
17 Ibid.
18 Ibid.
19 Ibid.
20 Ibid.
21 Ibid.
22 'Modernism & Eclecticism', lecture at the School of Visual Arts, New York, 1992.
23 Ibid.
24 Ibid.
25 Interview with Paul Rand by author, 1988.
26 Ibid.
27 Interview with Paul Rand by author, 1987.
28 Ibid.
29 Ibid.
30 Interview with Morris Wyszogrod by author, 1997.
31 Interview with Paul Rand by author, 1987.
32 Ibid.
33 Ibid.
34 Ibid.
35 Interview with Frank Zachary, by author, 1997.
36 Interview with Paul Rand by author, 1987.
37 Ibid.
38 Cleland, T. M., 'Harsh Words', *A talk before the AIGA*, Carteret Book Club, 1940.
39 Interview with Paul Rand by author, 1987.
40 Ibid.
41 Interview with Paul Rand by author, 1990.
42 Ibid.

Chapter 2

1 Interview with Paul Rand by author, 1987.
2 Ibid.
3 Interview with Onofrio Paccione by author, 1997.
4 Interview with Paul Rand by George Lois, 1986.
5 Interview with Helen Federico by author, 1997.
6 Interview with Paul Rand by author, 1987.
7 Interview with Paul Rand by George Lois, 1986.
8 Ibid.
9 Ibid.
10 Interview with Paul Rand by author, 1987.
11 Interview with Morris Wyszogrod by author, 1997.
12 Ibid.
13 Ibid.
14 Interview with Bob Blend by author, 1997.
15 Interview with Helen Federico by author, 1997.
16 Interview with Morris Wyszogrod by author, 1997.
17 Ibid.
18 Interview with Paul Rand by author, 1987.
19 Ibid.
20 *Fashion Trades*, 22 November 1946.
21 Anger, Shana, *PM*, 20 April 1947, p23.
22 Interview with Frank Zachary by author, 1997.
23 Ibid.
24 Interview with Paul Rand by author, 1988.
25 Ibid.
26 Interview with Paul Rand by George Lois, 1986.
27 Interview with Frank Zachary by author, 1997.
28 Ibid.
29 Ibid.
30 Interview with Paul Rand by George Lois, 1986.
31 Interview with Paul Rand by author, 1988.
32 Interview with Paul Rand by George Lois, 1986.
33 Interview with Paul Rand by author, 1988.
34 Interview with Paul Rand by George Lois, 1986.
35 Ibid.
36 Ibid.
37 Interview with Onofrio Paccione by author, 1997.
38 Interview with Helen Federico by author, 1997.
39 Interview with Morris Wyszogrod by author, 1997.
40 Ibid.
41 Interview with Paul Rand by author, 1988.
42 Ibid.
43 Interview with Paul Rand by George Lois, 1986.
44 Interview with Frank Zachary by author, 1997.
45 Interview with Paul Rand by George Lois, 1986.
46 Interview with Naiad Einsel by author, 1997.
47 Interview with Paul Rand by author, 1988.
48 Ibid.
49 Interview with Betty Norgaard by author, 1997.
50 Rand, Paul, *Thoughts on Design*, Wittenborn Schultz, 1946, pV.
51 Rand, Paul, *Thoughts on Design*, Wittenborn Schultz, 1946, pp3–4.
52 Seitlin, Percy, 'Paul Rand' *American Artist*, 1942.
53 *Time* magazine, 23 December 1946.
54 Interview with Frank Zachary by author, 1997.
55 Interview with Bob Blend by author, 1997.
56 Interview with Gene Federico, by author, 1997.

Chapter 3

1 Interview with Paul Rand by George Lois, 1986.
2 Rand, Paul, 'The Politics of Design', *Graphis*, 1981.
3 Interview with Paul Rand by author, 1997.
4 Interview with Frank Zachary by author, 1997.
5 Ibid.
6 Ibid.
7 Ibid.
8 Interview with Paul Rand by author, 1997.
9 'Paul Rand: The Play Instinct', in: Anderson, Gail and Heller, Steven, *Graphic Wit: The Art of Humor in Graphic Design*, Watson Guptil, 1991.
10 Hurlburt, Allen, *CA*, January/February 1979.
11 Interview with Paul Rand by George Lois, 1986.
12 Dugald Stermer, 1989.
13 Heller, Steven, 'Paul Rand: The Play Instinct', op.cit.
14 Interview with Frank Zachary by author, 1997.
15 Ibid.
16 Interview with Harry Ford, by author, 1998.
17 Ibid.
18 Interview with Paul Rand by author, 1988.
19 Interview with Louis Danziger, by author, 1997.
20 Lee, Marshall, *Books For Our Time*, exhibition catalogue, Oxford University Press, 1951.

21 Rand, Paul, 'Critique of the Fifty Books', *Bookbinding and Book Production*, April 1948.
22 Rand, Paul, *Thoughts on Design*, Wittenborn Schultz, 1946, p107.
23 Ibid.
24 Dwiggins, W.A., *Post Scripts on Dwiggins*, Typophile Chap Books No. 36, 1960.
25 Ransom, Will, 'Problems in Book Design: No. 99', *Book Binding and Book Production*, October 1945.
26 Rand, Paul, 'Critique of the Fifty Books', *Bookbinding and Book Production*, April 1948.
27 Ibid.
28 Interview with Paul Rand by Myles Ludwig in *Art Direction Magazine*, 1971.
29 *The New York Herald Tribune Book Review*, 17 November 1957, p55.
30 *Library Journal*, 15 February 1963, p56.
31 Interview with Paul Rand by Joseph Giovanini in *The New York Times Book Review*, 1984.
32 Dreyfus, Patricia Allen, 'Paul Rand: Design in the American Context', *Print*, January/February 1969.

Chapter 4

1 Interview with Paul Rand by George Lois, 1986.
2 Rand, Paul, *Paul Rand: A Designer's Art*, Yale University Press, 1985, pXIII.
3 Watson, Thomas Jr., 'The Tiffany Wharton School Lecture', 1975.

4 Ibid.
5 Ibid.
6 Interview with Helen Federico by author, 1997.
7 Hurlburt, Allen, 'Paul Rand' *Communication Arts*, January/February, 1979.
8 Interview with Marion Swannie Rand by author, 1997.
9 Ibid.
10 Interview with Tom Hardy by author, 1998.
11 Interview with Paul Rand by author, 1988.
12 Ibid.
13 Interview with Marion Swannie Rand by author, 1997.
14 Interview with Paul Rand by author, 1988.
15 Watson, Thomas Jr., 'The Tiffany Wharton School Lecture', 1975.
16 Interview with Marion Swannie Rand by author, 1997.
17 Ibid.
18 Ibid.
19 Ibid.
20 'Trademarks by Paul Rand', *Portfolio 1*, 1950.
21 Interview with Marion Swannie Rand by author, 1997.
22 Ibid.
23 Interview with Paul Rand by author, 1988.
24 Ibid.
25 Notes by Paul Rand for a talk before an IBM design seminar in Washington, D.C., 1980.

26 Interview with Louis Danziger, 1997.
27 Interview with Paul Rand by author, 1988.
28 Interview with Tom Hardy, by author, 1998.
29 Interview with Paul Rand by author, 1988.
30 Ibid.
31 Interview with Tom Hardy, by author, 1988.
32 Paul Rand, *Design, Form, and Chaos*, Yale University Press, 1993.
33 Interview with Marion Swannie Rand, by author, 1997.
34 Ibid.
35 Interview with Tom Hardy, by author 1998.
36 Ibid.
37 Interview with Paul Rand by author, 1988.
38 Interview with Marion Swannie Rand, by author, 1997.
39 Ibid.
40 Interview with Dick Huppertz, by author, 1998.
41 Interview with Pete Seay, by author, 1998.
42 Interview with Dick Huppertz, by author, 1998.
43 Interview with Pete Seay, by author, 1998.
44 Ibid.
45 Interview with Dick Huppertz, by author, 1998.
46 Ibid.
47 Interview with Grant Smith, by author, 1998.
48 Letter from Kenneth Heibert, to Jessica Helfand, 1997.
49 Ibid.
50 Ibid.

51 Interview with Grant Smith by author, 1998.

52 Interview with Reid Agnew by author, 1998.

53 Interview with Randy Tucker by author, 1998.

54 Ibid.

55 Ibid.

56 Ibid.

57 Ibid.

58 Interview with Paul Rand by author, 1988.

59 Ibid.

60 Ibid.

61 Ibid.

62 Ibid.

63 Interview with Paul Rand by author, 1990.

64 Interview with Paul Rand by author, 1988.

65 Ibid.

66 Ibid.

67 Letter from Steven Jobs, 1997.

68 Interview with Paul Rand by author, 1988.

69 Excerpted from Paul Rand's NeXT presentation booklet, 1988.

70 Ibid.

71 Ibid.

72 Ibid.

73 Ibid.

74 Ibid.

75 Ibid.

76 Interview with Steven Jobs by author, 1988.

77 Interview with Paul Rand by author, 1988.

Chapter 5

1 Interview with Paul Rand by George Lois, 1986.

2 Interview with Paul Rand by author, 1990.

3 Rand, Paul, *Paul Rand: A Designer's Art*, Yale University Press, 1985, pxiii.

4 Ibid.

5 Rand, Paul, *Design, Form, and Chaos*, Yale University Press, 1993, p3.

6 Miller, J. Abbott, book review of *Design, Form, and Chaos*, *Graphis*, 1993.

7 Bierut, Michael, book review of *Design, Form, and Chaos:* 'Playing the Game by Rand's Rules', *Eye*, October 1993, p100.

8 Interview with Louis Danziger by author, 1998.

9 Rand, Paul, *From Lascaux to Brooklyn*, Yale University Press, 1996, px.

10 Rand, Paul, *Paul Rand: A Designer's Art*, pxi.

Bibliography

Books by Paul Rand

Rand, Paul, *Thoughts on Design* (New York: Wittenborn Schultz, 1946)

Rand, Paul, *Thoughts on Design* (London: Studio Vista/New York: Van Nostrand Reinhold Art Paperback, 1970)

Rand, Paul, *The Trademarks of Paul Rand* (New York: George Wittenborn, Inc., 1960)

Rand, Paul, *Paul Rand: A Designer's Art* (New Haven: Yale University Press, 1985)

Rand, Paul: *Design, Form, and Chaos* (New Haven: Yale University Press, 1993)

Rand, Paul: *From Lascaux to Brooklyn* (New Haven: Yale University Press, 1996)

Children's books illustrated by Paul Rand

Rand, Ann and Rand, Paul, *I Know a Lot of Things* (New York: Harcourt, Brace & World, Inc., 1956)

Rand, Ann and Rand, Paul, *Sparkle and Spin* (New York: Harcourt, Brace & World, Inc., 1957)

Rand, Ann and Rand, Paul, *Little 1* (New York: Harcourt, Brace & World, Inc., 1962)

Rand, Ann and Rand, Paul: *Listen! Listen!* (New York: Harcourt, Brace & World, Inc., 1970)

Articles by Paul Rand

Rand, Paul, 'Critique of the Fifty Books' in: *Bookbinding and Book Production*, April 1948

Rand, Paul, 'Too Many Cooks' in: *Art and Industry*, 1948

Rand, Paul, 'What is Modern Typography?' in: *American Printer*, 1948

Rand, Paul, 'The Story of a Symbol' in: *Type Talks*, May 1949

Rand, Paul, 'Black in the Visual Arts' in: *Graphic Forms* (Cambridge, MA: Harvard University Press, 1949)

Rand, Paul, 'Modern Typography in the Modern World' in: *Typographica #5*, 1952

Rand, Paul, 'The Trademark as an Illustrative Device' (Chicago: Paul Theobald and Company, 1952)

Rand, Paul, 'Guest Editor: Paul Rand' in: *Art in Advertising*, August 1954

Rand, Paul, 'Paul Rand: Ideas about Ideas' in: *Industrial Design*, 1955

Rand, Paul, 'The Good Old "Neue Typografie"' paper published in proceedings of: *Typography USA* (The Type Directors Club, 1959)

Rand, Ann and Rand, Paul, 'Advertisement: Ad Vivum or Ad Hominem?', Kepes, Gyorgy, guest ed., *Daedalus*: 'The Visual Arts Today', Winter 1960

Rand, Paul, 'The Art of the Package, Tomorrow and Yesterday' in: *Print*, January/February 1960

Rand, Paul, 'Our Biggest Threat is Conformity' in: *Printer's Ink*, 2 December 1960

Rand, Paul, 'Modern Typography in the Modern World' in: *Print*, January/February 1964

Rand, Paul, 'A Mentor (Jan Tschichold: The New Typography)' in: *Print*, January/February 1969

Rand, Paul, 'Integrity and Invention' in: *Graphis Annual*, 1971

Rand, Paul, 'Politics of Design' in: *Graphis Annual*, 1981

Rand, Paul, 'A Paul Rand Miscellany' in: *Design Quarterly*, 1984

Rand, Paul, 'Good Design is Good Will' in: *AIGA Journal of Graphic Design*, 1987

Rand, Paul, 'Intuition and Ideas' in: *American Center for Design Journal*, 1987

Rand, Paul, 'The Case for the Ampersand' in: *New York Times Book Review*, 10 September 1989

Rand, Paul, 'Logos, Flags and Escutcheons' in: *AIGA Journal of Graphic Design*, 1991

Rand, Paul, 'Computers, Pencils, and Brushes' IBM, 1992

Rand, Paul, 'Confusion and Chaos: The Seduction of Graphic Design' in: *AIGA Journal of Graphic Design*, 1992

Rand, Paul, 'Object Lessons' in: *The New Criterion*, 1992

Rand, Paul, 'Typography: Style Is Not Substance' in: *AIGA Journal of Graphic Design*, 1993

Rand, Paul, 'Failure By Design' in: *New York Times*, Op-Ed Page, 5 April 1993

Rand, Paul, Preface for: *The 100 Best Posters from Europe and the United States 1945–1990* (Toppan, 1995)

Rand, Paul, 'Wolfgang Weingart: from Mainz to Basel' in: *AIGA Journal of Graphic Design*, 1996

Articles and books on Paul Rand

Seitlin, Percy, 'Paul Rand' in: *PM*, October 1938

'Paul Rand' in: *The Insider*, March 1939

'Paul Rand' in: *The Insider*, September 1939

Moholy-Nagy, L, 'Paul Rand' in: *AD*, February/March 1941

Weisenborn, Fritzi, 'Adventure in Art' in: *Chicago Sunday Times*, September 1941

Seitlin, Percy, 'Paul Rand' in: *American Artist*, 1942

Kraus, H. Felix, 'Dubo-Dubon-Dubonnet' in: *Art and Industry*, October 1942

'About the Designers' in: *Advertising and Selling*, September 1945

Ransom, Will, 'Problems in Book Design: No. 99' in: *Book Binding and Book Production*, October 1945

'Ads With a Punch By Ohrbach's'
  in: *Fashion Trades*, 22 November 1946
'Esthetic Ads'
  in: *Time*, 23 December 1946
'Paul Rand, Industrial Designer'
  in: *Interiors*, February 1947
'A Designer Thinks'
  in: *Interiors*, February 1947
Seitlin, Percy, 'Paul Rand, Advertising Artist'
  in: *Magazine of Art*, March 1947
'Paul Rand, Advertising Artist'
  in: *Magazine of Art*, March 1947
Ager, Shana, 'Art is Like Digging Ditches'
  in: *PM*, April 1947
Oeri, Georgine, 'Paul Rand'
  in: *Graphis*, June 1947
'Rand: Thoughts on Design'
  in: *AIGA Journal*, June 1947
Ettenberg, Eugene M., 'Variations on the Theme
  of Garamond Oldstyle'
  in: *American Printer*, August 1948
Henrion, F.H.K., 'Paul Rand'
  in: *Printed Advertising*, November 1948
Ettenberg, Eugene M., 'What is "Modern"
  Typography?'
  in: *American Printer*, 1948
'Effect of Advertising on Commercial Design'
  in: *Journal of the Royal Society of Arts*,
  30 January 1948
Devree, Howard, 'Art and Formulas'
  in: *New York Times*, 6 June 1948
'Stafford's Stallion: A Case Study'
  in: *Tide*, 24 December 1948
'Modern and Traditional Typography in America'
  in: *Penrose Annual*, 1949
'Workshop School'
  in: *Interiors*, February 1949
'Exhibition of Advertising and Editorial Art'
  in: *Advertising and Selling*, April 1949
Miller, Arthur, 'Art in Advertising Shown at Its
  Best' in: *Los Angeles Times*, 24 June 1949
Campbell, Heyworth, 'Trends'
  in: *Art Director & Studio News*, December
  1949

'Trademarks by Paul Rand'
  in: *Portfolio #1*, 1950
'N.S.A.D. Nominates Twelve for 3rd Annual
  Award' in: *Art Director & Studio News*,
  March 1950
'Impression of an "Abacus" by Paul Rand'
  in: *New York Times Magazine*, 28 May 1950
'Current Art and Typographic Examples Worthy
  of Note' in: *Art Director & Studio News*,
  December 1951
'Paul Rand's Designs Exhibited At A-D Gallery'
  in: *Publishers' Weekly*, February 1952
'Contemporary Trends in the Evolution of
  Advertising Art' in: *Art Director & Studio
  News*, October 1952
'Cigar Box – New and Improved'
  in: *Printers' Ink*, 19 December 1952
'Paul Rand Designs Cigar Album'
  in: *Art Director & Studio News*,
  December 1952
Ettenberg, Eugene M., 'The Paul Rand Legend'
  in: *American Artist*, October 1953
Louchheim, Aline B., 'Art Directors Show
  Their Work' in: *New York Times*, 1953
Margolis, Sanford, H. and Silverstein, Morton,
  'This Week is Really Going to be Something'
  in: *Printers' Ink*, 2 January 1953
'It's Colorful, Its Partitioned, It's a Cigar Box'
  in: *Packaging Parade*, February 1953
'The Year's Work: Residence'
  in: *Interiors*, August 1953
'Weintraub Bids for RCA Account in *Times* Ad'
  in: *Advertising Age*, 1 February 1954
'Code Followed Direct Mail'
  in: *Art Director & Studio News*, March 1954
'Five Designers for Under Five Dollars'
  in: *Industrial Design*, December 1954
'Marketing Hot Spots for 1955'
  in: *Printers' Ink*, 31 December 1955
'Ten Best Illustrated Books of the Year'
  in: *New York Times Book Review*,
  17 November 1957
'Sparkle and Spin'
  in: *N.Y. Herald Tribune Book Review*,
  17 November 1957

'America Who's Who Taps Whopping 42
  Area Dwellers'
  in: *Town Crier*, 5 August 1958
'Paul Rand's Work, The AIGA's Show of
  the Month'
  in: *Publishers' Weekly*, 3 March 1958
'Paul Rand'
  in: *AIGA* Newsletter, March 1958
'Art and Creative Thinking: Paul Rand'
  in: *Advertising Review*,
  November/December 1958
'Borzoi Books: Alfred A. Knopf'
  in: *Borzoi Quarterly*, vol. 7, no. 4, 1958
Grossman, Robert S., 'The Work of Paul Rand'
  in: *Productionwise*, October 1959
Kamekura, Yusaku, ed., *Paul Rand: His Work
  from 1946 to 1958* (Tokyo: Zokeisha
  Publications Ltd, 1959)
'Tribute to a Designer'
  in: *Esquire*, December 1959
Kaltenborn, Howard S., 'New Seal –
  New Signature'
  in: *Sales Record*, June/July 1960
'Westinghouse Redesign'
  in: *Printers' Ink*, 1 July 1960
'Westinghouse Design Program'
  in: *Industrial Design*, August 1960
'IBM's New Look'
  in: *Print*, November 1960
'IBM Annual Report Wins for Design/
  Typography'
  in: *Art Direction*, January 1961
'More Upgrading in the Field of Light-bulb
  Packaging'
  in: *Modern Packaging*, March 1961
'Pros and Cons: Some Views of AIGA's
  Paperback Cover Show'
  in: *Publishers' Weekly*, 4 December 1961
'Print That Matters'
  in: *Communication Arts*, June 1962
'Fine Art in Industrial Ads?'
  in: *Industrial Marketing*, July 1962
'Little 1'
  in: *N.Y. Herald Tribune Book Review*,
  11 November 1962

'Little 1'
in: *Library Journal*, 15 February 1963
'The Story Behind: W'
in: *The Kiplinger Magazine*, September 1963
'Two New Logos'
in: *Industrial Design*, June 1964
'IBM Image-maker Paul Rand: "Design is a forever job"'
in: *Modern Packaging*, October 1965
'AIGA Medal Will Be Given to Paul Rand At "50 Books" Fete'
in: *Printing News*, 16 April 1966
'Paul Rand, AIGA Medalist'
in: *Journal of the American Institute of Graphic Arts*, 1966
Dreyfus, Patricia Allen, 'Paul Rand: Design in the American Context'
in: *Print*, January/February 1969
Seitlin, Percy, 'Paul Rand, Commercial Artist: His Fantasy is Boundless'
in: *American Artist*, October 1970
'An interview with William Bernbach'
in: *Communication Arts*, vol. 13 no. 1, 1971
Dougherty, Philip H., 'Advertising: Graphics Awards Handed Out'
in: *New York Times*, 8 September 1972
'Paul Rand',
in: *New York Art Directors' Hall of Fame*, programme 1972
Ludwig, Myles Eric, 'Document Rand' Art
in: *Direction*, October 1972
'Graphic Design: You've Come a Long Way'
in: *Pratt Reports*, August 1975
Snyder, Gertrude, 'Profiles: The Great Graphic Innovators'
in: *U&LC*, March 1977
'Rand is Design Pioneer'
in: *Pratt Campus*, vol. 4, no. 7, 8 December 1977
Fletcher, Alan, 'Getting Going'
in: *Design*, 1978
Hurlburt, Allen, 'Paul Rand'
in: *Communication Arts*, January/February 1979

Poe, Randall, 'The Old Gray Annual Report Ain't What It Used To Be'
in: *Across the Board*, December 1979
Meggs, Philip B., *A History of Graphic Design* (New York: Van Nostrand Reinhold Co., 1983)
'Design 84: On Beauty and Utility'
in: *Adweek*, October 1984
'Design '84: George Lois Talks with Rand'
in: *Adweek*, October 1984
'Paul Rand Awarded 1984 TDC Medal'
in: *Gutenberg and Family*, vol. 1, no. 1, January 1985
'President's Fellows Awards: Rhode Island School of Design'
programme, June 1985
'Honorary Degree Citations: Paul Rand'
in: *New School Observer*, June/July 1985
Fern, Alan, 'In the Beginning Was the Logo'
in: *New York Times Book Review*, 3 November 1985
'Steve Jobs Turns to Big Blue'
in: *Newsweek*, 23 June 1986
'Spotlight on Airwick Advertising: Putting Our Products in the Eye of the Consumer'
in: *Interface*, February 1987
'Rand Wins Florence Prize for Visual Communication'
Yale Weekly Bulletin and Calendar, 6–13 April 1987
Weiss, Eric, 'Orchestrating Corporate Identity: Playing the Symbols'
in: *M magazine*, October 1987
Smith, Virginia, 'Paul Rand' interview
in: *Artograph No. 6*, 1988
Heller, Steven, 'Paul Rand' interview
in: *ID*, November/December 1988
Heller, Steven, 'Interview with Paul Rand',
in: ed. Friedman, Mildred, *Graphic Design America*, (Walker Art Center/Harry N. Abrams, 1989)
Woudhuysen, James, 'Hand Stand'
in: *Designweek*, 16 August 1991

Heller, Steven, 'Paul Rand: The Play Instinct'
in: Anderson, Gail and Heller, Steven, *Graphic Wit: The Art of Humor in Graphic Design* (Watson Guptil, 1991)
'Paul Rand'
in: *HQ*, November 1992
Margolin, Victor, 'More Than Meets The Eye'
in: *New York Times Book Review*, 2 May 1993
Kemper, Steve, 'Conversations: Logos To Go, Paul Rand'
in: *Hartford Courant Northeast*, 4 July 1993
Miller, J. Abbott, book review of *Design, Form, and Chaos*
in: *Graphis*, June 1993
Abrams, Jan, 'Paul Rand'
in: *ID*, September/October 1993
Bierut, Michael, book review: 'Design, Form, and Chaos: Playing the Game by Rand's Rules'
in: *Eye*, October 1993
Poynor, Rick, 'Rereading Rand'
in: *AIGA Journal of Graphic Design*, 1993
Heller, Steven, 'In Defense of Rand'
in: *AIGA Journal of Graphic Design*, 1993
'Leading Graphic Designer Speaks About Design and Then Some'
in: *FIT Network*, Spring 1994
Ferris, Byron, book review: 'From Lascaux to Brooklyn'
in: *Communication Arts Design Annual*, 1994
Shepheard, Paul, 'Grand Designs'
in: *New York Times Book Review*, 24 March 1996
'Pratt Institute Honorary Degrees'
Commencement Program, May 1996
Heller, Steven, 'Thoughts on Rand'
in: *Print*, March/April 1997
Helfand, Jessica, 'Paul Rand: American Modernist'
in: *The New Republic*, September 1997
Esplund, Lance, 'Rand the Magician'
in: *Modern Painters*, 1997

Index

Page numbers in *italic* denote illustrations.

A

'A' *210*

ABC (American Broadcasting Co.) 12, 174, *190*, 190, 205

Accent Software International 207

AD magazine *see PM*

Advertising Typography Assn of America 210

AEG corpn 147

Agha, M. F. 88

Agnew, Reid 179

AIGA *see* American Institute of Graphic Arts

Air-Wick air freshener 38, 39, 48, *49*

Albers, Josef 227, 228, 234

American Advertising Guild 77

'Americana' page *24*

American Artist magazine 13, 80, 85

American Institute of Graphic Arts (AIGA) 112, 206, 208, 212; Books of Our Time [Fifty Books of the Year] (1951) 122, 124, *125*; *Journal of Graphic Design* 125, 220

American Printer magazine 16, 69, 124, 218

Anchor Books *114*

Anger, Shana 66

Anton, William *230-1*, 239

Apparel Arts magazine 20-2, *22-5*, 26, 31, 88, 89, 91

Architectural Forum, The magazine 78-9, 90, *90*

Art in Advertising magazine 218

Art Deco movement 19

Art Directors Club 212, *240*

Art Director and Studio News magazine 82

Art and Illusion (Gombrich) 112, *113*

Art & Industry magazine 79

Art Nouveau movement 147

Arts & Métiers Graphiques magazine 89

Art Students' League 17, 40, 227

Atheneum publishers 112, *114*

Atlas Crankshaft Corpn 205

Autocar Corpn 35, 69, *69*

Ayer, N. W., agency 35, 38

B

Babbitt, B. T., 39

Bab-O cleanser *35, 38*

Bauhaus movement 12, 15, 17, 26, 77, 147, 227; *and* corporate identity 147-8, 150; New Bauhaus 31; *and* publishing 31, 69, 89, 92, 124

Bayer, Herbert 88, 89, 122, 147, 148

Beall, Lester 26, 88, 89, 188, 227

Behrens, Peter 147

Bel Geddes, Norman 18, 20, 34

Bell for Adano, A (Hersey) 104, *105*

Bemelmans, Ludwig 40

Benton, Thomas Hart 69

Bernbach, William [Bill] 66-72, *67*, *69-71*, 79

Bernhard, Lucian 18, *19*, 226

Bierut, Michael 221

'Big Families' *73*

Bill, Max 150

Binder, Joseph *46*, 77

Blend, Bob 40, *43*, 44, 82

Bollingen Series (books) 106, 112, *112-13*, *116-21*

Book Binding and Book Production magazine 122

Book Jacket Designers' Guild 91

books/book jackets 13, 65, 87-8, 91-143, *93-103*, *105-21*, *123*, 174, 217, 218, 219, 221, 223; children's 126-41, *127*, *129-42*, 174, 228

Books of Our Time exhibition/catalogue 122

Borzoi Books 96, *96*, *98-9*, 204

Boston Evening Transcript 86

Brancusi, Constantin 92

Brandy Distillers Inc. *39*

Braque, Georges 36

Breuer, Marcel 146, 152

Brinkley, Mel 14

Brissago (Switzerland) *232*, 232, *234-6*, *238*, *239-40*

brochures 69, *69-71*, *88*, 90

Brodovitch, Alexey 89-90, 227

Broom magazine 26

Burchartz, Max 22

Burnham, Donald 178, 179

Burns, Aaron *240*

Burtin, Will 89, *240*

Burton, Philip 232

C

Calder, Alexander 232

calendars 37, 228

Calkins & Holden agency 35

Camel cigarettes 20

Capital Cities 190

Captive Mind (Milosz) 108

Cassandre, A. M. 16, *44*, 46, 89, 220

'Cathy' (drawing) *126*

CBS (Columbia Broadcasting System) 148

CCA *see* Container Corpn

Century Theatrical Lighting 205

Ceputis, Eri 232

Cézanne, Paul 36

Chappell, Warren 96

Charles of the Ritz cosmetics 19

'Christmas' page *24*

Cleland, T. M. 89, 124; *Harsh Words 26*

Colorforms 205

Columbus, Ind., Visitors Center 206

Commercial Art magazine 15, 17, 22

Compton agency 126

Computer Impressions 207

Condé Nast publications 88

Consolidated Cigar Co. 149, 205

Consolidated Edison Co. 18

Constructivism 12, 26, 29, 48, 88, 103, 122, 151

Container Corpn of America (CCA) 38, 147-8

Cooper, F. G. 18

Cooper Union 227

Coronet Brandy 40, *40-3*, 56, 62, 86, 204

corporate design 12, 38, *113*, 126, 134, 135, 141, *142*, 145-204, 221, 228

Cotton, William 88

Coty Cosmetic Co. 69

counter cards *60*

Country Club Ice Cream Co. *39*

Craw, Freeman 152

Creative Media Center 207

Creative Revolution 66, 72, 83

Cresap, Mark 174, *175*

Cresta Blanca *204*

Cross, Gerald 128

Cubism 16, 26, 36, 92, *92*, 158

Cubist Painters (Apollinaire) 92, *93*

Cummins Engine Co. 126, *182-6*, *182-7*

D

Dada (Motherwell) *94*

Dada movement 17, 26, *29*, 48, 88, 151

Daedalus: Journal of AAAS 56-7, 218

Danziger, Louis 106, 145, 156, 188, 222, *240*

Davis, Stuart 90

Deberney & Peignot 89

Defke, Wilhelm 22, 147

DeHarak, Rudolf 188

Del Monte canned goods 228

Designers and Art Directors' Assn 217

design manuals 164, *164-5*, 176

Design Quarterly Magazine 219

De Stijl movement 12, 29, 48, 88, 147

Dewey, John 216; *Art and Experience* 77

Dexel, Walter 22

Direction magazine 26-31, *26-31*, 38, 86, 88, 89, 90, 91

Disney Hats 35, 38, 48, *50-1*

'Documents of Modern Art' series 92, *92*

Doubleday publishers 112, *114*

Doyle Dane Bernbach agency 66

Dreyfus, Patricia Allen 142

Dreyfuss, Henry 20, 34

Dubberly, Hugh 227, 231

Dubonnet apéritif 35, *44-7*, *45-8*, *56*
Dunhill Clothiers *72*
'Duz soap flakes' 228, *229*
Dwiggins, William Addison 77, 86, 91, 96, 124, *216*

E

Eames, Charles *and* Ray 152, 172, 174, *219*
Einsel, Naiad 77
Eisenman, Alvin 153, *226*, 227, 228, 234
El Producto cigars 56-7, *56-61*, 66, 67, 125, 149, 154-6, 228, *229*
Emerson Radios 35, *37*
English First (EF) school *200-1*, 204, 207
Enron energy 204, 207
Esquire magazine/Esquire/Coronet co. 20-6, *20-1*, 31, 34, 35, 36, 90, 204
Ettenberg, Eugene M. 124
Evans, Walker 227
Eye magazine 221

F

Fashion Trades magazine 66
'Father Knickerbocker' 18
Federico, Gene 82
Federico, Helen 36, 44, 73, 149
Feininger, Andreas 69
Fern, Alan *219*
Fletcher, Alan 215
flyers *73*
Ford, Harry 104
Ford, Henry, III *190*, *191*
Ford Motor Co. 34, 191, *191*, 205
Fortune magazine 20, 89
Franklin, Benjamin *213*
Fry, Roger *216*
Futurism 92, 103, 139, 231

G

Garretto, Paolo *44*, *46*, 88
GDK agency 158
Gebrauchsgrafik magazine 15-16
Geismar, Brownjohn Chermayeff 188
Gentry Living Color 207

Gerstner, Karl 158
G.H.P. Cigar Co. *56*
Glaser, Milton 152
Glass Packer magazine 18, *18*
Golden Blossom honey 19
Goodbye, Columbus ... (Roth) *123*
Goodman & Theise co. *62*
Goudy, Frederic 124, *216*
Graphic Forms magazine 218
Graphis magazine 221
Gray Advertising agency 69
Gris, Juan 15
Gross, Flora 112
Grosz, George 17, 69, 126, 227

H

Hadank, F. W. O. 147
Hamburg American Line 19
'Happy Hooligan' 14
Harcourt, Brace & Co./& World publishers 126, 128, *128*, 133, 135, *138*, 140, *142*, 205
Hardy, Tom 149, 150, 158
Harper's Bazaar magazine 89
Harren High School, New York 14-15
Harris, Marguerite Tjader 26
Harvard University Press 112, *114*
Harvest Books 112, *114*
Heibert, Ken 178-9, 238
Herriman, George 14
Hilbros Watch Co. 35, *204*
Hillman, Charles 219
Hofmann, Armin 228, 232, *232*, 234-8
Hormell meats 20
house design 87, *124-5*
Hub TV *202*
Hughes, Kristen *232*
Huppertz, Dick 174, *175*, *176-8*
Hurd, Peter 69
Hurlburt, Allen 40, 82, 92, 149

I

IBM (International Business Machines) corpn 12, *113*, 126, *148*, 149-72, *150-2*, *154-7*, *159-72*, 194, *195*, 205, 220, 228; Gallery 102, 172, *172-3*; 'Think' motto 150
IDEO Design 207
IIT Research Institute 205
I Know a Lot of Things 126, 127, 128, *129-31*, 132, *133*
Industrial Arts Exposition 16
Insider magazine 11
Interfaith Day (1953) *208*
interior design 31, 87, 159-64, *162-3*
International Paper co. 188
International Style 147
Irwin Financial Corpn *198-9*, 206
Isaac Goldman Printers 37

J

Jacobs, Sidney A. 124
Jacqueline Cochran cosmetics 48, *54-5*
James, Henry *American Essays 108*
Jazzways magazine 90-1, *90*
Jensen, Gustav 19, *19*
Jobs, Steven 194, *195*, 196, *196*
Jugendstil movement 147
Jung, Carl Gustav 77, 112

K

Kahn, Louis 227
Kaiser-Frazer Corpn 35, 48, *52-3*
Kauffer, E. McKnight 16, 88, 89
Kaufmann, Edgar, Jnr 152
Kaufmann's store *74-5*
Kelly, Rob Roy *History of Graphic Design at Yale* 234
Ken magazine 21, 90
Kepes, Gyorgy 218
Klee, Paul 12, 73, 90, 91, 97, 122
Knopf, Alfred A., Inc. 96, *97-102*, 102, *104*, 104, *106-7*, 112, *121*, 122, 124, *204*
'Krazy Kat' 14
Krone, Helmut 82

L

Laboratory School of Industrial Design 77, 227
Landor 188
Leave Cancelled (Monsarrat) 102, *102*
Le Corbusier 12, 26, 124, 179, 226, 228, 238; 'On the Plastic in Art' 226
Lee, [Frank H.] Hats 35, 77
Lee, Marshall 122
Léger, Fernand 15, 31, 232, *236-7*, *239*
Levy's Jewish Rye 66
Life magazine 22
Limited, The, stores 192, *192-3*, 206, 220
Lindner, Richard 16, 40
Lionni, Leo 227
Lippincott and Marguiles 188
Lissitzky, El 12, 22, 122, 126; *Story of Two Squares* 139
Listen! Listen! 126, *138-41*, *139-41*
Little 1 126, *134-9*, *134-7*, 143
Little Review magazine 26
Loewy, Raymond 20, 34
Look magazine 82
Luce, Henry 89
Lustig, Alvin 26, 122, 227
Lyendecker, J. C. 14

M

McEldery, Margaret 126, 128
McKay, Dean 153, 156
McMurtrie, Douglas *Modern Typography and Layout* 25
Macy, R. H., agency 20
Macy's store 15
Madelois store 89
Maeda, John 240
magazines 16, 18, 21-2, 22, 24-5, 26-31, *26-31*, 38, 87-91, *89-90*
Maidenform lingerie 82
Mallarmé, Stéphane 231
Margolin, Victor 220
Marguiles, Landor design agency 188

'Mask' assignment *231, 232*

matchbook covers 150

Matisse, Henri 15, 88

Matter, Herbert 227, 228, 232, 234

'MAYA' ('Most Advanced Yet Acceptable') 34

Mayer, Nancy 232, *236*

'Mechanized Mules ...' brochure *68, 69, 69-71*

Meier, Richard 182

Mellon, Andrew W. 112

Mencken, H. L. *Prejudices ...* [ed. Farrell] 102, 103, *103,* 104

Meridian Books 122

Metro Associated Services 18

Metzl, Ervin 20, 77

Michelangelo 16; 'Moses' *96, 97*

Mies van der Rohe, Ludwig 124, 149

Miho, James *240*

Miller, Irwin 182, 186

Minotaure magazine 31, 88

'Minute Man' *210*

Miró, Joan 88, 122, 232, *233*

MIT (Mass. Institute of Technology), Media Lab 225, 240

Moholy-Nagy, László 15, 22, 31, 77, 147, 148, 216; *New Vision, The* 77

Monell Chemical Senses Center *206*

Morningstar Investment Advisers 204, *207*, 220

'Morse Code' 82, *83*, 149

Mosberg & Co. *206*, 219

Müller-Brockmann, Josef 158, 228, 238, *240*

Myers, Chris 234, *237*, 238

N

Nabisco 20

Neue Grafik 147, 158

New Directions publishers 122

New York Herald Tribune 33; *Book Review 132-4*

New York Subway Advertising Co. 210

New York Times 33, 82, 83, 149; *Book Review* 219, 220, 222; 'Ten Best Illustrated Books' 132

New York World magazine 14

New York World's Fair (1939) 34, 69, *88*, 147; (1964) *151, 152*

NeXT computers 194-6, *194-7*, 204, *206*, 220

'90' *213*

Nitsche, Erik 69

Noguchi, Isamu *240*

Noonday Books 122

Norgaard, Betty 77

Norman, Norman B. 82, 146; agency 82

Norwalk Hospital 204

'No Way Out' (film) 35

Noyes, Eliot *148*, 149, 150, 152, 156, 172, 182; at Westinghouse 174, *175-6*, 178

'N. S.' page 25

Nutri Bottling Co. *39*

O

Ohrbach, Jerry 69

Ohrbach's store 66, *66-7*, 69, 71

Okasan Securities Co. 204, *206*

Olivetti, Adriano 149

Olivetti corpn *76, 148, 148,* 149

Opper, Frederick 14

Origins of Modern Sculpture 92, 95

Ozenfant, Amédée 'On the Plastic in Art' 226

P

Paepcke, Walter P. 148

Paccione, Onofrio 36, 73, 82; agency 82

packaging 34, *38-9*, 41, 56, *60-1*, 72, 87, 96, *158-9, 159-61, 168, 178, 178,* 179, *183*; student assignments 228, *229*

Packaging Parade magazine 56

Palmolive soap 14

Pantheon Books 112, *112-13, 116-21,* 122

Parcheesi game 231

Park & Telford *13*

Parsons School of Design 17, 227

PDR *206*

Pei, I. M. 182

Penn, Irving 71

Pensyl, William 83

Picasso, Pablo 13, 15, 31, 36, 88, 90, *108,* 231, 232; *Three Musicians* 91

Pintori, Giovanni 148

Playtex lingerie 34

PM magazine; (formerly *AD*) 12, 26, 31, 66, 88, *88-9*

Portfolio magazine 21, 44, 90

posters 35, 89, *166-9, 172-3, 176,* 179, *208-13,* 228

post-modernism 220-21

PR *see* Rand, Paul

Pratt Institute 14-15, 16, 227, 228

presentation books 182, *192-3, 194-6, 195-6, 200-1, 204-5,* 216, 218, 222

Priester Match co. 18

Procter & Gamble 82

publishing 72, 86-143, *see also* books; magazines *etc.*

Pullman, Chris 228, *229,* 230, 240

R

Rampone, Mario 216

Rand, Ann (2nd wife of PR) 86, 128, 132, *134, 135,* 149, 150, 218; 'Advertisement ...?' 218; *I Know a Lot of Things* 126, 127, 128, *129-31,* 132, *133; Listen! Listen!* 126, *138-41, 139-41; Little 1* 126, *134-9, 134-7, 143; Sparkle and Spin* 126, 132, *132*

Rand, Catherine (daughter of PR) 86, *125, 188, 189*

Rand, Marion (*née* Swannie; 3rd wife of PR) 149, 150, *151,* 152, *153, 153,* 154, 158, 172, 182

Rand, Paul (*né* Peretz Rosenbaum) (PR) appearance/portraits *15, 21* 1930s/40s *20, 21, 35,* 77; 1950s *34-6, 86-7, 146-9, 153,* 228; 1960s/70s *103, 172,* 216, 240; 1980s/90s *189,* 222, 232, 240;
Art Directors' Medals 48; childhood/youth 12, 14-31, *15*; daughter *see* Rand, Catherine; death 12, 182, *186, 204, 204,* 240, *241*; *with Esquire 20-35*; exhibitions *102, 172-3*; homes *87, 124,* 179; Brooklyn 14-15, *15*; Harrison, N.Y. 146, 153; Manhattan 72; Weston, Conn. *124-5,* 179, *189,* 216, 219; honorary degree 215; *as lecturer/teacher* 73-4, 77, 216, 225, 226-40; marriages 86, 134, 149, 172, *see also* Rand, Ann; Rand, Marion; name changed 20; paintings/illustrations 88, *126-8, 126-43, 132-9, 141-2,* 146; publications 77-82, 216-22, 226, 238-40; 'Advertisement ...?' 218; in *Book Binding ...* 122; 'Designer's Role, The' 80; *Design, Form, and Chaos* 158, 219, 220-22, *221*; 'Design and the Play Instinct' *230, 230*; 'Failure by Design' 217; *From Lascaux to Brooklyn* 219, 222, *223*; *Graphic Wit ... 91, 96, 103*; 'IBM Logo, The' *156, 166*; 'IBM Logo Use and Abuse' *156, 156*; in *Journal of AIGA 125*; *Paul Rand: A Designer's Art 141-2,* 146, 217, *218-19, 219,* 220, 222, *223*; 'Paul Rand Miscellany' *216*; *Thoughts on Design* 12, 72, 77, 80, 124, *141-2,* 216, 217, 218, *219*; 'Too Many Cooks' 79; *Trademark as an Illustrative Device* 57, 62; 'Trademark Design' (not pub.) 217; 'What Is "Modern" Typography?' 124; *as scholar* 226-28; video film *230*; *with Weintraub 35-83*

Random House publishers *103, 108-11*

Ransom, Will 124
RCA (Radio Corpn of America) 19, 82, *83*, 149
Reichl, Ernest 96
Revlon cosmetics/Charles Revlon 35, 36, 82
Rivera, Diego 89
Robeson Cutlery Co. *39*
Roche, Kevin 182
Rockwell, Norman 14, 31
Rodchenko, Alexander 122
Rogers, Bruce 124
Rosenbaum family 14, 20; Fishel (Philip; brother of PR)) 14, *15*; Peretz *see* Rand, Paul
Rothko, Mark 122
Rudolph, Paul 228
Ruzicka, Rudolf 96

S

Saarinen, Eero *and* Eliel 152, 182
Sachplakat concept 18
St Patrick's Cathedral 104
Saks Fifth Avenue store 89
Salter, George 106
Sandberg, Wilhelm *240*
Sapper, Richard 172
Sarnoff, General 82, *83*
Sauerlander, Wolfgang 112
Saybrook fabrics 20
Schenley Liquors 35, 38, *39*, 86, 96
Schifrin, Jacques 112
Schwitters, Kurt 22, 126
Scope magazine 89
Seay, Pete 175, *176*
Secessionism 19
Seeman Brothers *39*
Seitlin, Percy 'Paul Rand ...' 13, 80, 85
'Self-Portrait' (painting) 126
'serial stories' 57, *59*, 66, *67*
Shepheard, Paul 222
Shur Edge *204*
signage *174*, *176*, *179*, *180-1*, *190*
Smart, David 35

Smith, Gordon 150
Smith, Grant 178, *179*
Smith, Virginia 227
Smith, Kline & French Laboratories 49, 149, 204
Sparkle and Spin 126, 132-4, *132-3*, 139, *151*, *173*
Spinnell, Abe 34
Squibb pharmaceuticals 20
Stafford Fabrics 35, *39*, 62, *62-5*
Stanton, Frank 148
STA (Soc. of Typographic Arts) 220
Steig, William 40
Stillwell, C. W. D. 18
Stork Club Bar Book (Beebe) 126, *128*
Stravinsky, Igor *108*
'Subway Posters Score' 210
'Summer' pages *23*, *25*
Surrealism 26, 31, 48, 88
Sutnar, Ladislav 22
Swannie, Marion *see* Rand, Marion
Switzer, George 20, 89

T

Tables of the Law, The (Mann) 96, 97, 122, 124
Teague, Walter Dorwin 20, 34
textile designs 31, 87, 142
Theobald, Paul, & Co. publishers *219*
Thompson, Bradbury *226*, 227, 234
Thompson, J. Walter, agency 82
Tiffany 149, 152
Time magazine 80-2
Tipton Lakes *206*
Tokyo Communications Arts *213*
Tomectin (pharmaceutical) *73*
Transition magazine 88
Tri Arts Press *209*
Troller, Fred *241*
Trump, Georg 151
Tschichold, Jan *Neue Typographie, Die* [*The New Typography*] 16, 22, 25, 77, 124

Tucker, Randy 183, 186
Twentieth Century Fox *35*
Type Talks magazine 218
typography 72, *81*, 124-5, 147, 231; 'appropriateness' 72; book design 92, *92*, 96, *97-8*, *109*, 139; children's books 139; corporate 150-1, 154, *154-5*, *159*; *and* graphic design 86; International Style 147; logos 194-6; magazines 88; minimalist 38, 55, *98*; New 16, 22, 25-6, 34, 72, 124; 'perfume scripts' 34; script *39*, *159*; *and* space 124, 125; 'stencilled' 57; type 'furniture' 122; 'typewriter' 48, 49, 69, *69-71*, *see also* lettering

U

UCLA (Univ. of California at Los Angeles) *211*
Ulm Hochschule für Gestaltung 150, 164
Unimark design agency 188
United Airlines 40
United Cigar Co. 35
United Parcel Service (UPS) 12, 174, 188-90, 205
United States, Dept of Interior 205, 210
'Untitled' (drawings/painting) 126, *128*
Upjohn Co. 89
USSB *202-3*, 204, *207*

V

Van Doesburg, Theo 31
Vanity Fair magazine 88, 89
Vasari, Giorgio 220
Verve magazine 31, 88
Vichy water 17
View magazine 26
Vignelli, Massimo 188
Vintage Books 103, *108-11*, 112
Visual Semantics 231-4, *231*, *233*, *236-7*, *239*
Vogue magazine 88-9
Volkswagen cars 66

W

Wallace puppets *204*
Waters, Catherine *233*
Watson, Thomas, Snr 150
Watson, Thomas J., Jnr *148*, 149, 150, 152, 156, 172
Weintraub, William H./agency 35-46, *36*, 62, 66, *74-5*, 77, 82, *83*, 87, 92, 149; *and* Bernbach 69; PR works half-time 72, 146; Norman takes over 82; PR leaves 82-3, 126, 146
Westinghouse Electric corpn 12, 34, *80-1*, 126, 174-9, *174-81*, 205, 228, 238; 'Image by Design' 174
Westinghouse, George 174
WGBH-Boston channel 230
Wharton School 149, 152
Whelan, Grover 69
Whitehead, Alfred North 216, 234
Wittenborn, George/Wittenborn & Co./Wittenborn, Schultz 77, 92, *92*, *94*, 216, *217*
Wolf, Helen and Kurt 112
Wyszogrod, Morris 14, 20, 40, 44, 73

Y

Yale University 226, 227-40, *227*, *229-37*, *239*; Press 206, *219-20*, *223*
Yoshikawa, Shizuko *240*
Young & Rubicam agency 20
Young, Dick *159*, 164
Young, Frank *Technique of Advertising Layout* 25

Z

Zachary, Frank 21, 66, 69, 71-2, 74, 104; *and Jazzways* 90-1; *and Portfolio* 21, 44, 90
Ziatara, Valentin 16
Zwart, Piet 22

Author's note and acknowledgements

I never studied with or worked for Paul Rand. He just was my friend. We met when I did a telephone interview with him for an essay I was writing about Herbert Matter, who was awarded the 1983 AIGA medal, the first designer profile that I had ever written (prior to that my beat was the history of satiric art and illustration). During the course of the interview our conversation turned to mutual interests about art and design and we decided to meet the following week at the Yale Club in New York for lunch. At that time I knew of Rand's eminence, but I was not completely familiar with Rand's work *per se*. Of course, I understood that he was responsible for IBM, Westinghouse, UPS and ABC logos, and he was the leading influence on corporate identity in the United States, but I was ignorant of how important he was to advertising during the 1940s and 1950s and the extent of his contributions to book and book cover design. I hadn't read his first book *Thoughts on Design*, although I had been given a dog-eared copy.

So why was he the least bit interested in me? I think that contrary to his gruff persona, Rand was genuinely interested in meeting new, especially young, people and sharing ideas with them. Our mutual interests in German art and design seemed to be a good starting point for discussing a wide variety of topics. After our first meeting he invited me to his home in Connecticut, an offer which I gladly accepted. From that visit on I was embraced not just as an acquaintance but as a friend. We spoke often on the telephone (I wish I had taped those conversations), exchanging both professional and personal confidences. We recommended books and articles to each other, and argued about their merits. But, equally important, since I was beginning to write more about the history of graphic design, I used him as a resource; in turn he offered me his remarkable insights.

Rand was indeed a wellspring of historical information, not the least of which was his own history, which *is* arguably the history of Modern American design. As our relationship developed I became a kind of Boswell to Rand's Johnson, starting when I was invited to speak at a day-long design history symposium about the 1940s sponsored by Yale University's design graduate programme and organized by its then chair Alvin Eisenman. Rand had requested that I present a paper about his early career – so began the first of many hours of taped interviews that I conducted with him over the ensuing years, many of which serve as the background for this book.

Rand did not enjoy making public appearances and was deliberately absent from this event. But a few months later in 1985 he was invited to speak before an audience at the School of Visual Arts' Masters Lecture Series to coincide with the publication of his book, *Paul Rand: A Designer's Art*. In this instance, he agreed on the condition that I interview him. As honoured as I was, I was also quite timid and suggested that we have a rehearsal. He agreed to a visit to my home, but insisted that a rehearsal would destroy the spontaneity. Nevertheless, the morning of the event he called in sick (probably from nerves) and cancelled the show. I must say, I was somewhat relieved, too. Shortly afterwards, however, we were scheduled to try it again before the first AIGA National Conference in Boston, which this time coincided with a major hurricane causing Rand to cancel once again.

Despite his eminence, during the better part of Rand's long career he felt vulnerable in front of large audiences and so avoided them – even when he taught at Yale he limited the size of his classes to a few students at a time. A year later, however, we attempted our ill-fated event once more at the first *Modernism & Eclecticism* symposium at the School of Visual Arts. This time he actually appeared on stage (conditional on the assurance of a dark auditorium, with only

a small desk lamp for illumination) and answered questions for over an hour. I'm sure that I was much more nervous than he was, and in the end he did a superb job. Over the subsequent nine years he requested that I act as his interlocutor (or whipping boy, as the case may be) at over a dozen of the many frequent speaking engagements that he accepted from design schools and organizations around the country.

On 3 October 1996, a month and a half before he died, we appeared together at the Cooper Union Great Hall in New York, where 130 years earlier Abraham Lincoln and Stephen Douglas held their historic Presidential debates. On that evening there was no debating that Rand was a powerful draw. Over one thousand attendees, at least half of them young students (many more, boasted the school's Dean, than attended David Carson's lecture the previous spring) packed the hall for Rand's penultimate public appearance (he appeared at MIT a week before entering the hospital for the last time). The 'conversation' between the two of us inaugurated Rand's successful retrospective at Cooper Union's Houghton Gallery and Herb Lubalin Center (curated by Georgette Ballance). It was the best of many such conversations that we had together.

All I did was turn on the switch and Rand waxed on about his favourite subject, graphic design. 'Design is a disease', he kibitzed. 'There's no other way to explain why I've stuck with it, or it has stuck with me, this long.' And with infectious enthusiasm he spoke of his life as inextricably wedded to design. Those who came expecting to hear diatribes against declining standards were in for a surprise. Although Rand practised design over three generations, various epochs and numerous styles, he did not pine aloud for the good old days. Rather, he talked matter-of-factly about the inviolable truths inherent in the principles that he had embraced sixty years earlier about form, content and, of course, humour. Dispelling prevailing rumours, he asserted that Modernism was alive and well as long as *he* was alive. For Rand, Modernism was not merely a historical relic, fleeting style or nostalgic conceit. It was a foundation on which he built Randism, a practical philosophy that combined concerns of aesthetics, economy and functionality with wit and commercial savvy.

This book is a celebration of the man who has taught me the meaning of uncompromised dedication. I am privileged to have known Paul Rand; to be considered one of his confidants; and to have helped chronicle a life and work that have in turn made such an indelible impression on my own life.

In the course of working on this volume many people have provided encouragement, help and assistance. I am in their debt. But no one has been more supportive and generous than Marion Swannie Rand, Paul's companion, friend and wife, who opened up his archives, shared her memories, and has always been available to me when I needed her advice and friendship. This book would have been very difficult to do without her and I extend my sincere thanks.

The following people at Phaidon Press have proved invaluable, as well: Vivian Constantinopoulos, Commissioning Editor; Paul Harron, Project Editor; Erica Rosen, Production Controller; David Jenkins, former Editorial Director; and Alan Fletcher who recommended the book be done in the first place. Thanks also to Hans Dieter Reichert, designer, for creating a format of which I am most proud.

My collaborators in the USA were indispensable and I cannot imagine having done this book without them. They include: Elinor Pettit, researcher, who scoured Rand's personal and professional archives, catalogued all the material and databases, acted as guardian of the flame and was otherwise a rock of support; Georgette Ballance, who created the chronology, read the manuscript and helped with the captions (and co-directed the April 1998 Paul Rand Symposium with me); Bob Burns who helped me navigate through Rand's archive; George Lois, a master of advertising in his own right, whose admiration for Rand is revealed in the first sentence of his wonderful introduction to this volume; Armin Hofmann for his devotional foreword; and Jessica Helfand for her insightful analysis of Rand as a teacher which serves as the book's concluding essay.

I am especially grateful to two of Paul's friends for their critical eyes and ears: Louis Danziger for generously reading the manuscript and offering thoughtful suggestions; and Nathan Garland for allowing me to read portions of the book to him over the phone.

In addition to Marion Swannie Rand, many of Rand's friends and colleagues were interviewed. The following, from various stages and epochs of Rand's life, provided me with many of the biographical details and rare insights – from the William H. Weintraub Agency era: Helen Federico, Morris Wyszogrod, Frank Zachary, Naiad Giblin Einsel, Robert Blend, Betty Norgaard, Gene Federico, Onofrio Paccione and Carl Fisher; from the book and book jacket/cover era: Gerald Gross and Harry Ford; from the IBM years: Tom Hardy and Mario Rampone; from the Westinghouse period: Dick Huppertz, Pete Seay, Reid Agnew, Grant Smith, and Ken Heibert; and from the Cummins Engine period: Randy Tucker. Thanks to Philip Burton, Clarence Lee, Margaret McEldery and Steven Jobs for their additional contributions.

Finally, I must thank two people who have put up with my obsessive behaviour for well over a year: Louise Fili, my wife, and Nicolas Heller, my son, who supported my devotion to this project, sometimes at the expense of my devotion to them.

Illustration acknowledgements

Illustrations in Jessica Helfand's essay have been provided courtesy of William Anton, Edward Kensinger, Chris Pullman and Catherine Waters; thanks are extended to Nancy Mayer and Chris Myers for their supply of material. All other illustrations and photographs have been provided courtesy of Marion Swannie Rand / Paul Rand Archives.

WITHDRAWN